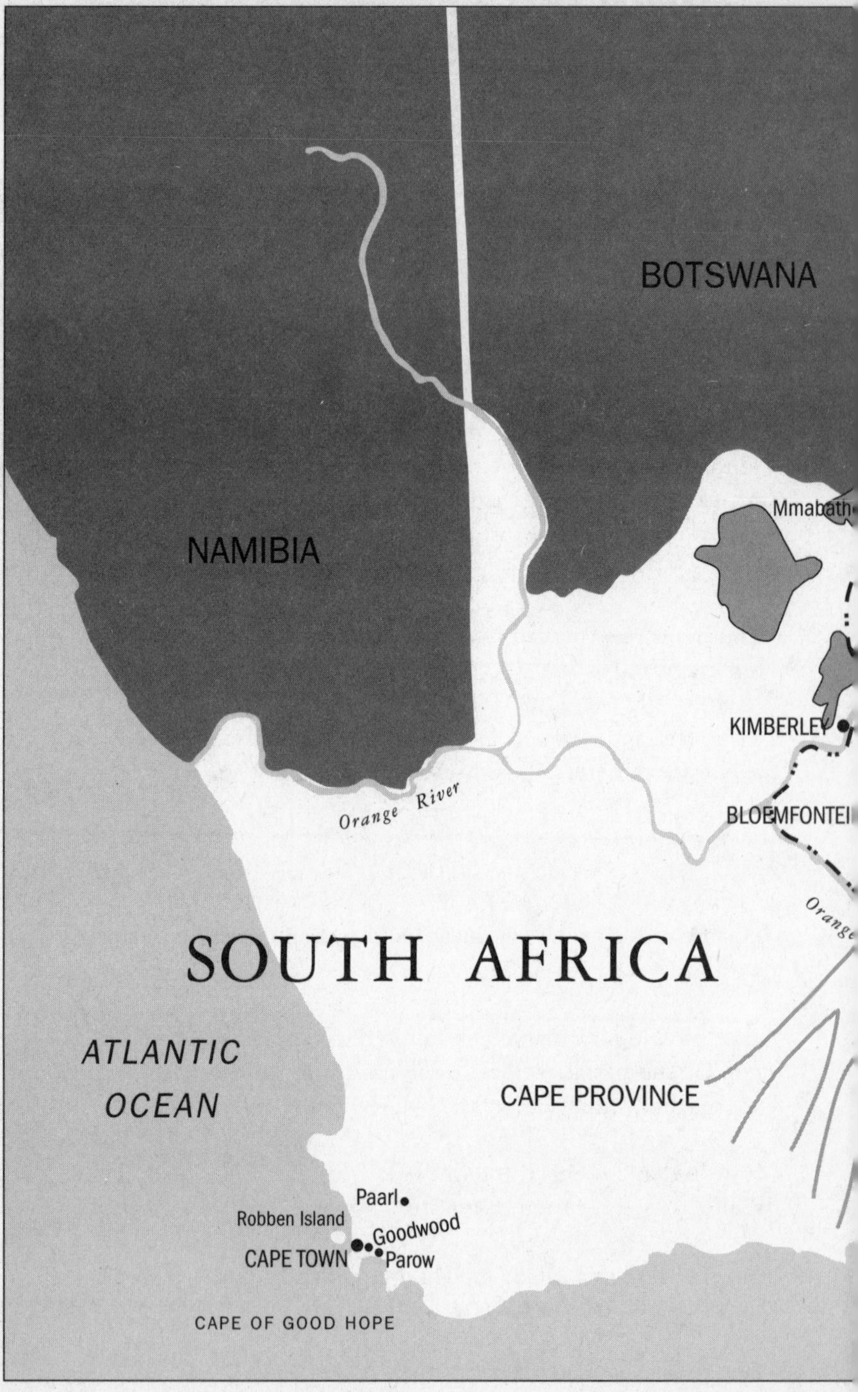

BOTSWANA
NAMIBIA
Mmabath
KIMBERLEY
Orange River
BLOEMFONTEI
Orange
SOUTH AFRICA
ATLANTIC OCEAN
CAPE PROVINCE
Paarl
Robben Island
Goodwood
CAPE TOWN
Parow
CAPE OF GOOD HOPE

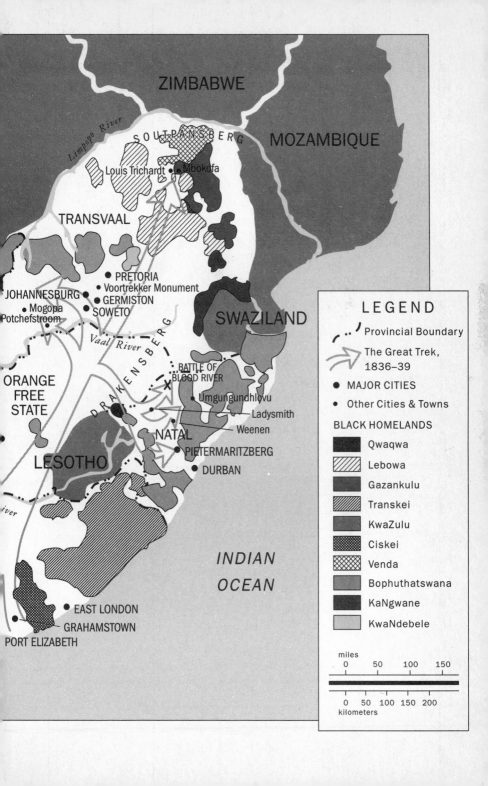

BOOKS BY
ADAM HOCHSCHILD

*Half the Way Home:*
*A Memoir of Father and Son*

*The Mirror at Midnight:*
*A South African Journey*

*The Unquiet Ghost:*
*Russians Remember Stalin*

*Finding the Trapdoor:*
*Essays, Portraits, Travels*

*King Leopold's Ghost:*
*A Story of Greed, Terror, and*
*Heroism in Colonial Africa*

*Bury the Chains: Prophets*
*and Rebels in the Fight*
*to Free an Empire's Slaves*

# The MIRROR
# at MIDNIGHT

## *A South African Journey*

Adam Hochschild

A MARINER BOOK
*Houghton Mifflin Company*
BOSTON • NEW YORK

First Mariner Books edition 2007

Visit our Web site: www.houghtonmifflinbooks.com.

*Library of Congress Cataloging-in-Publication Data*
Hochschild, Adam.
    The mirror at midnight : a South African journey / Adam Hochschild.
—1st Mariner Books ed.
        p. cm.
    Originally published: New York : Viking, 1990. With new preface
and epilogue.
    Includes bibliographical references and index.
    ISBN-13: 978-0-618-75825-8
    ISBN-10: 0-618-75825-9
    1. Blood River, Battle of, South Africa, 1838—Anniversaries, etc.
2. Afrikaners—Race identity. 3. South Africa—Race relations—History—20th century. 4. Hochschild, Adam—Travel—South Africa.
5. South Africa—Description and travel. 6. South Africa—Social conditions—1961–1994. 7. South Africa—Politics and government—
1989–1994. I. Title.
    DT2247.B56H63 2007
    305.800968—dc22        2006103110

Printed in the United States of America

MP 10 9 8 7 6 5 4 3 2 1

Portions of this book first appeared, in somewhat different form, in *Mother Jones,
Harper's,* and the *Boston Review.*

Grateful acknowledgment is made for permission to reprint the following copy-
righted material: Lines from the poem "The Contraction and Enclosure of the
Land" by St. J. Page Yako. Reprinted by permission of the publisher, Perskor,
from *The Making of a Servant* (Johannesburg, 1972), an anthology translated by
P. Kavanaugh and Z. Qangule. The poem "In Detention" by Christopher Van
Wyk. Reprinted by permission of the author. Lines from the poem "The Price
of Freedom" by Mathews Phosa, as translated by William Mervin Gumede. Reprinted by permission of Struik Publishers, from *Thabo Mbeki and the Battle for
the Soul of the ANC* (Cape Town, 2005).

FOR

DAVID AND GABRIEL

"Looking into South Africa is like looking into the mirror
at midnight . . . A horrible face, but one's own."

BREYTEN BREYTENBACH

# Contents

# Preface to the Mariner Edition

Few countries on earth have ever undergone as dramatic and hopeful a political sea change as South Africa did at the end of the twentieth century. At the close of the 1980s, it was one of the world's most notorious police states, for decades the object of protest marches and demonstrations around the globe. Thousands of black political dissidents were in jail, torture was routine, and only the small percentage of the population that was white could, in any meaningful way, vote. Nelson Mandela and other top African National Congress leaders had been in prison for more than a quarter of a century. And to all who cared about this beautiful and long-suffering country, it looked as if they would be serving out their life sentences.

But a mere few years later, in 1994, every adult South African could vote in the nation's first democratic election. Mandela was elected President, and his coalition-government cabinet included people who had spent decades in prison or exile—and the former head of the government that had once kept him behind bars.

Not only was the startling turnaround a peacefully negotiated one, it was one of history's most unexpected. In 1988, when I made the journey described in these pages, there was not a single journalist or commentator anywhere—nor, so far as we know, an intelligence agency of any government—predicting a democratic South Africa at any time soon. Every South African politician, activist, or academic I talked to believed that any real change was at least twenty or thirty years off, if then.

The changes that astonished the world, the first free election campaign—which I witnessed—and some of the bumps in the road South Africa has encountered since then, I have described in a new Epilogue. However, I have left the rest of this book entirely unchanged; its present tense refers to 1988, not to today. This, then, is a portrait of the country at the very peak of the state violence and repression that preceded one of the most remarkable transformations of our time. And, along the way, it is also a glance back at a crucial early episode of South African history.

A. H.

# *Beginnings*

From a distance, Johannesburg's Alexandra township looks as if wisps of fog had collected above it, despite the sun-scorched day. Coming closer, I see that it is not fog but dust, for most streets here, unlike those in the white suburbs that surround Alexandra, are unpaved. This morning some fifty thousand pairs of feet are kicking the dust aloft as they make a pilgrimage over the hills, in long streams that converge on one spot. Seventeen Alexandra youths, from age twelve up, will be buried here today. They are victims of police bullets during six days of recent fighting in this township, one of the bloodier battles in South Africa's long civil war.

It is March 5, 1986. I am heading toward the funeral with some white friends. They assure me we will be safe, but it is hard not to worry: our skin is the same color as those whose government shot the young men who are to be buried today. As white people on this emotion-laden day, won't we be targets for community rage? Adding to my uneasiness is the fact that South Africa's division is one of class as well as race: the people I'm with are in a larger convoy of white supporters of the resistance movement, all of whom are in cars, some of them new Audis and Peugeots. This line of cars is entering an overcrowded township whose black citizens mostly must travel by foot, van, or bus. As we drive into

Alexandra, we pass its ramshackle bus station: cracked and battered open-air concrete platforms with destination signs whose very names—Rosebank, Ferndale, Parktown—speak of the leisured white suburbs of swimming pools, tree-shaded streets, and well-sprinkled lawns. These are the places Alexandra residents commute to each day, to work as cooks, maids, and gardeners.

Through the open window of the car, I can smell the sewage ditches at the side of the road and hear the sound of dozens of small gasoline generators: in most of "Alex," if you want electricity, you have to make your own. Goats, chickens, and an occasional cow wander the streets. Small, tin-roofed homes are cramped together. Desperate for housing, some families have even moved into a row of abandoned buses. Their wheels, stripped of tires, have sunk into the soil. Scattered about are reminders of recent street fighting: smashed windows, a few burnt-out cars.

Astoundingly, as our white caravan jounces slowly over the rutted road toward the funeral, we are cheered. Older people clap from the roadside. Children smile and wave from doorways. Young men give the clenched-fist salute—right arm extended, thumb outside fist. I see the same spirit a few moments later, when we walk into the overflowing soccer stadium where the funeral is to take place. Just outside the stadium is a large warehouse under construction, a skeleton of bright yellow steel girders. Several dozen young black men have climbed high up and are sitting precariously astride this framework. Despite a police order forbidding them, they hold banners with slogans like FORWARD TO PEOPLE'S POWER! Two white university students approach the structure, carrying their own banner of support. It takes them ten minutes to clamber up the steel beams while holding their sign; at every level, black hands reach down to help them up. Finally two Alexandra youths reach down from the topmost girder, take the students' banner, and hold it aloft.

The ceremony begins. Mourners have filled every seat in the stadium and the entire dirt soccer field. The crowd rises and begins to sing, in spontaneous harmony, the stirring hymn that for three quarters of a century has been the freedom anthem of southern Africa:

> *Nkosi sikelel' iAfrika*
> *Maliphakamis'we 'pondolwayo. . .*
> (God bless Africa,
> Let our nation rise. . . )

I feel humbled at the majesty of the singing and the solemnity of the crowd, many of whom are weeping. Near a speaker's platform at one end of the field, the seventeen coffins lie in a row; each is covered with banners in the black, green, and gold colors of the African National Congress. Mothers and other relatives sit next to each coffin. An honor guard of teenage boys in brown berets and red armbands stands at attention next to them. For four hours under a broiling sun, speaker after speaker comes to the rostrum.

One is Albertina Sisulu, sixty-eight, whose husband, ANC leader Walter Sisulu, spent more than twenty-five years in prison. She and her children have been in and out of jail too many times to count. In 1956 she was one of the leaders of twenty thousand women who made a famous protest march to government buildings in Pretoria. She is introduced, to much cheering, as "our mother, Comrade Mrs. Sisulu."

"This country is governed by frightened cockroaches!" she shouts.

The crowd responds with a distinctive cheer: *"OOOOahhh!"* There are more *OOOOahhhs* as she mentions Nelson Mandela and the other African National Congress leaders.

But in her talk, as in those of several other speakers, there is an undertone of anxiety. Since South Africa's latest wave of uprisings began in 1984, several hundred black collaborators, usually police informers, have been "necklaced"—burned to death with old gasoline-filled tires around their necks. Some of these revenge killings have been done by volatile, angry crowds of mourners at mass funerals just like this one. "Enough now!" Albertina Sisulu warns the young people. "There is no need for you to be fighting like dogs, man! The youth must be strong enough to say NO when something is wrong."

Addressing the informers, she adds, "We will deal with you when we are free."

The speakers talk mostly in English, sometimes in one of the African languages. The organizers are clearly edgy. "Comrades!" a minister urges the crowd, "Please be *disciplined*." And disciplined they are. Almost everyone on the soccer field is sitting cross-legged in the dirt. If more than four or five people in the same place get up, a half-dozen marshals in blue T-shirts that say ALEXANDRA MASSACRE rush to the spot to make sure no one is about to be necklaced. Wary marshals watch a small group of children, some not even teenagers, who are parading through the crowd single-file, holding up a hand-lettered sign: AWAY WITH MOTHIBE AND YOUR WIFE THERESA WE DON'T NEED YOU. Is this a threat to an informer? I can't tell.

Hidden deep in the mass of people, someone tosses a bunch of leaflets into the air; they are blown across the crowd by the wind. The leaflet is from an underground cell of the African National Congress: it lists the times and shortwave frequencies where you can hear Radio Freedom, the ANC program broadcast from outside South Africa. And it appeals to blacks in the police and army: "Brother soldier, policeman! Refuse to shoot your own people; point your guns at the enemies of freedom."

At the rostrum now is Mzwakhe Mbuli, a tall man with a powerful voice who is South Africa's most popular composer of oral poetry, an ancient art form recently reborn and politicized. Arrested and tortured several times, Mbuli has also been the target of assassination attempts. In ringing tones, he recites verses beginning, "I have been to the mountaintop, and I have seen the dreams of Africa to come ... "

Using handkerchiefs or folded newspapers, mourners try to shade their faces against the ferociously hot sun. Between speakers, or when the sound system breaks down, the crowd bursts into song, fists going up and down in rhythm, feet stamping and shuffling in the dance step known as the *toyi-toyi*. One song is translated for me as "We'll kill the Boers ... " But the crowd politely applauds Rev. Beyers Naude, an anti-apartheid white churchman, who speaks with the rolling *r*'s and clipped speech of someone whose native language is Afrikaans.

More children march through the crowd with signs. One addresses the Minister of Law and Order: LE GRANGE, HOW ARE YOU GOING TO FEEL IF WE GO TO WHITE SUBURBS AND KILL THEIR CHILDREN AS YOUR POLICE DO IN OUR HOMES!

Again and again speakers and crowd trade chants, like a litany:
"Viva Mandela viva!"
"*Viva!*"
"Viva Sisulu viva!"
"*Viva!*"
"Long Live ANC long live!"
"*Long Live!*"

Mike Beea, chair of the Alexandra Civic Association, gestures at the coffins and speaks with his voice almost breaking: "Here are our brothers lying in front of me and you! I am standing here with tears rolling to the bottom of my heart. When is this barbarism going to end?"

When the prayers and speeches are over, scores of young men hoist the coffins onto their shoulders and slowly bear them out of the stadium. As our convoy of cars leaves, we are stopped by a roadblock. A dozen blue-uniformed police are wearing boots and riot gear. Some carry shotguns; long bandoliers of buckshot crisscross their chests, as in old photos of Boer War guerrilla fighters. One holds a *sjambok,* the frightening-looking heavy whip of elephant or hippo hide, embedded with bits of lead or steel. This one is mounted on a long handle that stands higher than a policeman's head. My palms begin to sweat. The police open the car trunks and glove compartments and the women's purses, searching for cameras and tape recorders, which have been banned today. They find nothing, and wave us on.

The crowd accompanies the coffins, all seventeen in a row, down a hill and across a streambed toward the cemetery, a mile in all through Alexandra's streets. Singing, keening, they pass tiny patches of bare dirt, on almost every block, where people have made miniparks, some in spaces no more than fifteen feet square. They have arranged rocks or half-buried tires in a semicircle, added a small bench, painted everything green or white, and labeled it with a hand-lettered sign: LOVERS' PARK, WILLOW TREE PARK, or, where a wheel is set into the ground, WAGON WHEEL PARK. Those miniparks with names like MANDELA PARK or STEVE BIKO PARK have all been crushed by police bulldozers and only rubble remains. The crowd chants, the pallbearers now begin to run under their burdens, in step, in a slow, shuffling jog-trot. Around them the dust rises in clouds.

It is at moments like that funeral that a visitor feels most strongly that the conflict in South Africa is about something much larger than the fate of a single nation at the other end of the world. South Africa seems a moral battleground as well as a physical one, and a battleground that poses choices for other nations as well, as did events like the rise of Hitler or the Spanish Civil War.

Certainly that is a major reason I have been drawn back to South Africa again and again. But it is not the only reason. Never believe a writer who claims to have chosen a subject purely for its intrinsic importance. There is always something more.

The beginning of my own involvement with South Africa, which has lasted through half a dozen visits over nearly thirty years, had to do with growing up in an American family that made its living largely through the mining business in southern Africa. The mines owned by the U.S. company where my father was an executive were mostly not in South Africa itself. But South Africa was then, as it still is today, the commercial heart of the subcontinent, the archetype of the economic system in which the low-paid labor of large numbers of black people, working in hot, damp, and dangerous mine corridors far under the earth, pays for the comfortable suburban life of a much smaller number of white people, both in Africa and overseas. Ever since my father took me along with him on a business trip to Africa when I was a teenager, I always felt that I was *complicit* with what went on there, and that so many of the good things I enjoyed in life—travel, a private education, my parents' summer home—could be traced back, in the end, to the red earth of southern Africa and to the mineral wealth that had been taken from it.

Partly in reaction to that feeling, when I was a college student I spent a summer working for an anti-apartheid newspaper in South Africa, in 1962. It was an extraordinary time. Nations throughout the continent were jubilantly celebrating their newly won inde-

pendence. Blacks in South Africa followed this news with great
hope; jolted out of decades of complacency, South African whites
began to feel that they had their backs to the wall. Alarmed South
African newspapers reported hundreds of thousands of whites
fleeing Algeria; white mercenary "freedom fighters," fresh from
battling United Nations troops in the Congo, were welcomed as
heroes by cheering white crowds that lined the streets of Johannesburg. And one day that summer, after a nationwide manhunt,
shouting newsboys on street corners waved banner headlines announcing that at last police had captured Nelson Mandela. Parliament rushed through new, draconian security legislation which
allowed the death penalty for such vaguely defined offenses as
"endangering law and order." A wave of house arrests and im-
prisonments began. Hundreds of opponents of the government,
mostly black but a few white, decided to continue their battle from
underground or exile. That summer was the first time I had been
around men and women for whom political activism was not
merely a matter of what opinions you expressed at a meeting or
in arguing with friends. Instead, it could, and often did, lead directly to prison, torture, or death.

For an American college student, seeing all this was a momentous, life-changing experience. In all of life, but especially when
young, we are looking for heroes, for people whose lives suggest
an answer to the question of how to live. In South Africa, it was
as if I had stepped, for a brief few months, into moral territory
that previously I had only read about, in accounts of events like
the resistance to the Nazis. Suddenly I was among people who
lived in such a situation every day, and who would continue to
face it after I went home. One man I knew fairly well later died
on the gallows. A friend fled the country one step ahead of the
police and later died in exile. Others ended up spending years in
prison. A warm, strappingly handsome black activist with a fine
singing voice, with whom I used to have wonderful long talks over
*samosa* meat pastries at an Indian café in Johannesburg, later was
driven out of his mind by police torture. Would I be willing to
take such risks for my beliefs? I did not know. But the dilemmas
of those who did face those choices became a kind of moral touch-
stone that I carry with me still.

There was another reason, I think, that being in South Africa as a nineteen-year-old had such an effect on me. It had to do with being an American, and a relatively privileged one. We live in a country where, according to our ruling mythology, social class is not that important, and, in principle, everybody is equal. We all vote; we call each other by first names; we dress informally; and far less than the British do we show class origin in our accents. In South Africa, by contrast, the differences of class and power that exist in every society—although there they are far greater—are also, almost completely, differences of skin color. And so, in a way, something usually hidden becomes naked.

I think I was particularly struck by this when I went to South Africa for the first time, because I had grown up in a home where, as is common in well-to-do families in the United States, discussion of differences of wealth and power was generally taboo. Oh, of course some people were a little more "fortunate" than others, but one didn't talk about such discrepancies in too much detail. To do so might suggest that the United States was not the land of equality that 1950s school textbooks said it was. It is strange how deep that taboo went in our household, for, in many other ways, my parents were remarkably liberal for their time. But the fact that we had a larger house and more money than our neighbors or my schoolmates, and that they might be envious about this, and I uncomfortable about it, was never something we discussed around the dinner table.

Then, going to South Africa, I found myself fascinated by the country's whites: for here were *an entire people,* several million strong, living, relative to the miserably poor blacks around them, in a caricature of the privileged position I felt myself to be in at home. Some South African whites were unaware that they lived in a state of such privilege at all—or, if threatened with glimmerings of that awareness, they worked hard to deny it. Some were aware, but felt their position to be God-given and normal. Some felt badly about it. A few felt determined to change the society that allowed such inequalities. It was as if this spectrum of attitudes represented the different stages of denial, guilt, and awareness I was groping my way through in my own life. I could not have articulated all this at the time, of course. But looking

back on it now, I think that's why South Africa intrigued me so
deeply.

That summer in South Africa was a watershed in my life; the
world has not looked the same since. I have written about that
time in my book, *Half the Way Home: A Memoir of Father and Son.*
I mention the subject again now only because those months were
for me a prologue, emotionally, to the much more recent journey
described in this book.

After that memorable summer, I did not go back to South Africa
again for nearly twenty years. Finally I returned in 1980, and again
in 1986, to write some magazine articles. Then I made a longer,
different kind of journey in November and December of 1988,
on which this book is largely based. Almost all the present-tense
reporting in the pages that follow is from this last trip, although
a few conversations and episodes in that voice are from earlier in
the decade. But whenever the fact that an interview or event took
place on an earlier visit is relevant, I've dated it. For example,
large mass funerals, like the one for victims of the Alexandra
massacre in 1986, were not permitted for several years after that.

When I went back to South Africa in 1988, more than a quarter
century after my first visit there, it was with several thoughts in
mind. I went not to make a case, for surely no one needs yet
another book whose only purpose is to prove apartheid evil. Instead, I wanted to go back to this scene of a turning point in my
own life and to see what thoughts and feelings a visit there today
would evoke in me now. Why, when I cumulatively had spent less
than six months of my life in South Africa, was it so often the
landscape of my dreams?

As I prepared to set off on this new trip, I also had a set of
more down-to-earth questions about South Africa. They had to
do with the unexpected lasting power of tyranny. Visiting the
country as a nineteen-year-old, I had been overwhelmed by what
I had seen around me: the white bus driver kicking a black pas-
senger, the stony-faced security police watching every political
meeting, the white farmers pouring truckloads of milk into the
sea near Cape Town to keep prices up, while black children went
hungry. I was certain: this *can't* go on. With the entire world against
them, how could the tiny minority of South Africans who are

white keep control for so long? But, despite promises of change, they have. And so now, on this new trip, I wanted to look more deeply at just what those control mechanisms have been.

To do so would mean, among other things, looking into the country's past. Visiting South Africa as as a young student, I had not sufficiently understood that apartheid did not come instantly into being when the National Party took power in 1948, but was rooted in three hundred years of history of which I knew little. It is that three hundred years that makes achieving real change in South Africa far more difficult than it first appears. To peel off this layer of the onion, then, and to really understand the enduring power of white domination, I wanted to look at white South Africans and their history, at the myths by which they justified their long rule, and at the ways that this mythologized past bolsters their power. Certainly nowhere outside of Russia have I ever been in a country where the past is as much celebrated, cursed, and argued over as it is in South Africa. It was for this reason that I chose the time I did to revisit South Africa. December 16, 1988, would be the 150th anniversary of a pivotal event in South African history.

The background to this event lies far earlier. When the Pilgrims landed at Plymouth Rock, ships on their way from Europe to the Far East were already regularly stopping at the southern tip of Africa for fresh meat and water. Three decades later, in 1652, Dutch traders established their first permanent outpost at the Cape of Good Hope. For the following 180 years, white settlement in what is today's South Africa seldom stretched more than a few hundred miles inland from its southern coast. Within this fairly narrow strip of land, immigrants from Europe squabbled with each other, settled their differences, killed or enslaved much of the native population, and for nearly two centuries built almost all their farms and forts and towns within a few days' horseback ride of the sea. Except for an occasional report brought back by an adventurous hunter or explorer, the interior of what is now South Africa—where its vast mineral wealth and most of its population lies today—remained, to the whites, unknown.

In the Napoleonic wars, Britain gained control of this strip of coast. Some years later, in the mid-1830s, several thousand white farmers living in the colony became restive under English rule. They were men and women of Dutch, French, and German background who spoke a language then evolving from seventeenth-century Dutch into what is today called Afrikaans. They loaded their belongings into ox wagons, herded their sheep, horses, and cattle alongside, and began migrating inland in search of new land. During the next few years these thin streams of migrants in their ox wagons fanned out across thousands of miles of unmapped territory. Collectively known as the Great Trek, this was one of the epic migrations of history: within several years, these Voortrekkers, as they were called, with muskets, ox whips, and Bibles in hand, in effect staked out the borders of today's South Africa and placed it on the road to white rule. It is almost as if the half century's expansion of the American frontier from the Louisiana Purchase to the Mexican-American War had all been compressed into a mere half decade.

As we look back today at those ox wagons creeping across the African plains, a certain twilight of foreboding covers the scene. I think it is this that, for me, gives the story of the Great Trek its ominous fascination. It was a migration that could only end in battle with the peoples who lived in its path, and in the bitter conflict over South Africa's land that, in one way or another, has raged ever since. At least one person at the time of the Trek seemed to foresee something of the sort. "Thus far their course has been marked with blood," the English explorer Cornwallis Harris wrote of the Voortrekkers he observed in 1837, "and with blood it will be traced to its termination."

In few nations has a single historical event so energetically been turned into myth. No South African is ever allowed to forget the Great Trek. Dozens of South African towns have a Voortrekker Street or Voortrekker High School, and the Voortrekkers' grievances against the British are studied by every schoolchild, including blacks—who couldn't care less. A Voortrekker powder horn is part of the emblem of the ruling National Party; paintings of ox wagons adorn stamps and placemats and notecards; and, at the start of World War II, South Africa's many Nazi sympathizers (several of whom later became Prime Ministers) belonged to the

*Ossewabrandwag,* or Ox-wagon Fire Guard. Half a dozen South African cities, including the capital, Pretoria, are named after individual Voortrekkers.

The word *Voortrekker* means pioneer, and like the westward trek of the American pioneers with their powder horns and ox wagons that was taking place at the same time, the Great Trek was studded with battles against the indigenous people who were there first. In the Trek's first two or three years, thousands of them fell before the Voortrekkers' guns, but ambushes and surprise attacks killed hundreds of white Trekkers as well. Indecisive skirmishes left unclear whether the Trekkers could seize most of the land they wanted, particularly the fertile, rolling hills dotted with the villages of the Zulus, southern Africa's most successful black warrior people. In this coveted green land, on a wide plain rimmed by distant mountains, the turning-point battle of the Great Trek took place on December 16, 1838. The Ncome River, which runs past the spot, turned red with the blood of the dead, and forever after has been known as *Bloedrivier,* or Blood River.

The Battle of Blood River is more than a historical event, however; it is a foreshadowing of the battle that goes on in South Africa today. Today the whites' fortified *laager* is not made of linked ox wagons but of high brick walls and razor-wire fences; the weapons are not muzzle-loading muskets, but helicopters, the midnight explosion that leaves a church office in ruins, the death squad, and, sometimes, the press conference announcing vague sweet promises of reform.

I will come back to Blood River in the following pages—to what actually happened, and to the way the event has been transformed into myth. Over the years the legend of Blood River has gathered extraordinary strength. December 16th has long been the South African national holiday, and for the most fervent of the country's Afrikaans-speaking whites it is Columbus Day, Memorial Day, and the Fourth of July rolled into one. On December 16th each year an estimated five hundred commemorative ceremonies or pageants reenacting the battle take place across the country.

Once, even the commemoration of the battle had immense political impact of its own. In 1938, as the one hundredth anniversary of Blood River approached, thousands of Afrikaners, some dressed in period costumes, set out for the capital. On December 16th itself, a huge crowd gathered on a hillside outside Pretoria. One hundred thousand people were there, one in ten of all Afrikaners then alive. It is believed to have been the largest crowd ever assembled in South Africa up to that time, and, indeed, has been surpassed only a few times since, most notably by the huge throngs that welcomed Nelson Mandela's release from prison more than half a century later. The size of the 1938 gathering startled the country, as did what it revealed of the depth of Afrikaner nationalist feeling, which was then directed as much against the wealthier English-speaking whites as against blacks. This outpouring of emotion triggered the rapid rise of the National Party, which won victory in the whites-only parliamentary elections only ten years later. Prime Minister Jan Smuts, who was then voted out of power, reportedly said, "I really lost on that day in 1938."

For black South Africans, December 16th has been a day of anger and fear. On that date each year, writes the author Vusamazulu Mutwa, "our parents locked us up inside our huts near Potchefstroom, where we had to sit all day, for fear that the White 'baases' would beat us up." Bob Leshoai, a black writer who grew up in Bloemfontein, remembers the same thing: "Every year on December 16th, I had to make sure not to go into the town."

Blacks have often picked this symbolic day to fight back. On December 16, 1930, four thousand Africans in Durban gathered to burn their passes; police attacked the crowd, beating four of the protesters to death. And when, banned after many decades of non-violent but unavailing protests, the African National Congress started its underground guerrilla campaign, it chose December 16, 1961, to launch its first attacks: bomb blasts at government offices and electric pylons in Johannesburg, Port Elizabeth, and Durban.

Long before December 16, 1988, the South African government began planning celebrations to mark the 150th anniversary of the Battle of Blood River. The day itself, and the weeks leading up to it, seemed a good time for me to return to South Africa—with some history books in my suitcase. Capturing a clear image of any country is always a matter of sketching in sand: things change, and for no nation does one wish greater changes than South Africa. But that anniversary seemed a particularly revealing moment at which to draw South Africa's portrait, as the country marked a major event in its past and was poised for what seemed certain to be a tumultuous period to come. I wanted to make a journey both in geography and time: to look back at the Great Trek and at Blood River, to see how people were celebrating or mourning those events now, and, above all, to look at the different, more drawn-out battle between the descendants of those who fought on both sides at Blood River, a battle that continues throughout the country today.

*Part One*

---

# PROMISED LAND

# Summer Folk

The most unexpected thing about going to South Africa is that the plane is full. I had hoped that a half decade of well-publicized bloodshed would discourage enough travelers so that I could stretch out across a few empty seats and get a good night's sleep. But every seat on my 747 from Europe to South Africa is occupied. One of my seatmates is a cheerful German who visits the country twice a year on business, but whose real enthusiasm is for its hunting:

"Springbok, antelope, an incredible variety! The professional hunter takes along his boy; they're out in the bush together all day; they've been working together for years. No race problems there. . . . Politics? Oh, South Africa just needs *time* to solve its problems."

Judging from the tennis racquets they carry, many other passengers are tourists, among the several hundred thousand, I later learn, who visit South Africa each year, heading for the country's beaches and game parks. And judging from other statistics, some of my fellow passengers must be immigrants. Years of upheaval have reduced that number, but some ten thousand newcomers still arrive in the country each year, lured by skilled jobs and good pay, and black house servants at $30 a week or less.

After my plane lands at Cape Town, the pilot announces, "The safest part of your journey is now over. On leaving the airport, *please* drive carefully." There is a burst of nervous laughter from the passengers: the road between Cape Town and its airport runs past a number of black townships, and at times in the last few years when tensions have been high, black youths have stoned vehicles driving past. At the airport, an armored car with the bright yellow paint of the South African Police is parked on the tarmac; its hull, high and V-shaped to deflect the blast of land mines, gives it the look of a steel sailboat on wheels. On the freeway into the city, some buses have wire mesh over the drivers' windows, against the stones. How do builders overcome a brick shortage? runs one South African joke. Answer: They send a couple of buses through a township. But today things are quiet, and from the freeway I can see black teenagers playing soccer on gravelly patches of dirt.

Cape Town is heartbreakingly lovely, its setting, as the intrepid traveler Anthony Trollope observed in 1877, "one of the most picturesque things to be seen on the face of the earth." The flat-topped Table Mountain looms above the city, its famous "table-cloth" of fog rolling off the top and dissolving into the air. The mountain throws a protective, tree-covered spur around Table Bay, a beckoning arm of land which welcomed ashore the first Dutch settlers more than three centuries ago. To the south stretches the rocky, surf-fringed Cape Peninsula, pointing downward like a finger toward the junction of the Atlantic and Indian Oceans. Surely it was not only the Cape's strategic location that made those sailors stop here, but also its uncanny beauty.

This hillside sea-city's charm haunted me when I lived here for part of that summer twenty-six years ago, and it still does so today. Perhaps because it is in such contrast to what goes on here. For the full panoply of apartheid has been legislated into being in a setting of transcendent loveliness. By night the lights of the Alpine cable-car station on the summit of Table Mountain twinkle like an earthbound star. By day a wash of brilliant sunlight covers arcaded nineteenth-century streets, stately public buildings, statues of white statesmen and generals, and a Botanical Gardens with palm trees and aviaries full of chirping birds.

At the edge of all this greenery stands the majestic Parliament

building. One afternoon I sit in the press gallery and listen to a
"reading" (a formality; almost anything the President wants is
passed) of a bill asking for some $100 million worth of extra funds
for the police, army, and prisons. All the members rise in silence
as a white-gloved functionary carries in a huge gold mace, preceded
by other officials in black tailcoats. The Speaker wears a black
gown, and the building's walls are filled with gilt-framed paintings
of other white men in wigs or old high-collared uniforms. Pages
in green jackets with gold braid carry messages. Later, Honorable
Members from here or there rise to ask questions of the Minister
of this or that: is such-and-such an item covered by the supple-
mentary appropriation or the general appropriation? So solemn is
the sense of ceremony, so dark and cathedral-like is the wood
paneling of the chamber's walls, so respectfully hushed are the
white schoolchildren in shorts and blazers who watch from the
visitor's balcony, that for a moment you can almost believe that
the whole thing is legitimate.

Outside Parliament, trees shade the streets from the summer sun;
a few blocks away, the air is filled with fresh smells from open-
air flower stalls near the cobblestones of Greenmarket Square.
Immaculate parks are laced with walking paths. At first glance
there is little to remind you that the scene is not some exceptionally
unspoiled city in southern Europe.

For most whites, it *is* Europe. "Read Gorky's *Summer Folk*," a
friend here tells me. "It's the best thing written about white South
Africa today." When I read this play about turn-of-the-century
Russian gentry, I see what he means. Maxim Gorky's characters
are families on vacation in the country. They read poetry aloud,
play the piano, and prepare endlessly for some amateur theatricals
which never come off. The characters talk of flamelike love and
prisonlike marriage; everyone is having an affair with someone
else's mate. From time to time they argue about the country's
dreadful poverty, which they vaguely know exists somewhere off
in the distance; then they go back to their piano playing and love
affairs. All the while, watchmen patrol the woods around the summer houses, cleaning up picnic debris, chasing away beggars, blow-

ing their whistles to scare off thieves. We rarely see the watchmen, but the sound of their whistles recurs; it is the last sound in the play.

I'm reminded of these summer folk when I look at the South African newspapers. By now I would have expected, no matter how much distortion or censorship, that their pages would be dominated by the ongoing violence and political upheaval: the country has been in non-stop turmoil for the better part of a decade, after all, and thousands of army conscripts have been patrolling the black townships during most of that time. But most newspapers are filled with the same kind of stories that I remember from being here many years ago, stories that evoke that nation of dreams that most white South Africans imagine they live in. It is the country the tourist brochures call Sunny South Africa.

Sunny South Africa's inhabitants, judging by the newspaper photos, are almost all white, although a sprinkling of them are unthreatening blacks—Zulu dancers, cute children, an Indian cricket champion, an African businessman in a three-piece suit gratefully receiving an award. In clothing advertisements, only one model in three or four is black, a proportion doubtless calculated to catch the eye of black buyers without scaring off white ones.

Above all, the Sunny South Africa of the newspapers is relentlessly *normal*. There are ads for computer matchmaking, advice-to-the-lovelorn columns, articles about beauty tips, lost cats, high school reunions, tennis matches, and even one piece on an all-white bank robbery, long and lavishly illustrated, as if the editors were relieved at finding some violence that was not racial. A personals column: "White male professional, 35; likes wine, sports; seeks female companionship." "Selective top quality Jewish only introductions. Miriam, 783-5892." Human interest features: a water-skiing dog; a story, WOMAN MARRIES HER FATHER; and another, URBAN MAN IN A CAGE: "With grunting rhinos and roaring lions for neighbors, Bernard Rich quietly goes about his business of living in a cage in the Johannesburg Zoo. The 27-year-old salesman is being exhibited as Homo Sapiens Urbanus. . . . 'The hardest part will be having to ignore the public,' says Bernard."

Why has the Sunny South Africa of the newspapers always so fascinated me? As a cocky nineteen-year-old, I think, it was because I, with my superior knowledge, knew this country was about to have a violent revolution, and the insensitive, carefree whites who lived here didn't. Reading their newspapers was like having a window onto the last days of Louis XVI. Now, of course, the revolution hasn't happened, but few whites are unaware that big changes are inevitable. So the fascination lies in something else: in how they choose to push aside that awareness. And in how the whole society is arranged to make that an easy thing to do.

For white South Africans, as for Gorky's summer folk, the simmering violence is out of sight. Of the more than five thousand people who have died in the upheavals since 1984, less than half a dozen have been white. Only now and then can Sunny South Africa hear the watchmen's whistles. In the post office, for example, a poster shows a picture of a limpet mine and warns in the two official languages, Afrikaans and English: SO LYK DIE DOOD!/ THE LOOK OF DEATH! But the actual warfare is almost entirely confined to the black townships. And to the summer folk, the townships are almost invisible.

Indeed, many whites go through the average day encountering no blacks at all—except those who are maids, waiters, or the nannies that I can see accompanying almost every white child on the grass of those downtown parks. There is a moving song about the nannies, by Thembi Mtshali and Barney Simon:

> *My sister breast-fed my baby*
> *While I took care of you*
> *We met when you were three months old*
> *and I a woman of forty-two. . . .*
> *Your first word was my name*
> *Your first song was in Zulu. . . .*
>
> *My children watched Soweto burn*
> *while I took care of you*
> *My children breathed tear-gas smoke*
> *while I took care of you*
>
> *Your eyes are bright and clever now*
> *Your legs are straight and strong. . . .*
> *my children sing at funerals*

*while I take care of you . . .*
*child of my flesh*
*May God protect my children from you.*

One morning I leave the land of the summer folk and visit the
African squatter settlement of Crossroads. It is surprising how
swift is the passage from one South Africa to another. Twenty
minutes drive from downtown Cape Town, with its elegant sea-
food restaurants and well-stocked delicatessens displaying half a
dozen varieties of ham, are the sand streets of Crossroads, where
women are going door to door selling sheep's and pigs' heads,
the very cheapest type of meat. At an intersection on the edge
of Crossroads, several dozen men are sitting on rocks, waiting,
in the hope that pickup trucks will come by and collect crews
for temporary labor, paying 10 or 12 rand (less than $5) for a
day's work.

The African huts I walk past here are made of corrugated zinc,
tarpaulins, plastic sheeting, or pieces of the walls of demolished
buildings, with painted advertisements still on them. Cocks are
crowing. The sand streets and shack floors are dry today, but in
the rainy season they will be mud.

In one two-room hut I visit, the ceiling is black from the smoke
of a tiny kerosene stove and the room smells of its fumes. There
is no room for a closet: clothes, in plastic bags, are hung high up
near the ceiling. Twelve adults and children share four beds in
these two rooms. But what strikes me most is the walls. They are
wallpapered with the shiny paper from Sunday newspaper ad sup-
plements. And so lining this pair of cramped rooms are hundreds
upon hundreds of color photos of dishwashers, remodeled kitch-
ens, dining table-and-chairs sets, sofas, stereos, deck chairs, and
Jacuzzi tubs.

On the street outside this house, I see a giant Casspir armored
car following a small white truck. "That's the post office truck,"
explains a woman who lives in these rooms. "Without the Casspir
the comrades would burn it." The war is still on.

These days, however, the "comrades"—the young militants—
are in retreat here; in most of the Cape Town African townships

a conservative black vigilante group is in control, backed up by
the armored cars of the army and the police. That police force
itself is now more than half black. An unemployment rate of more
than 50 percent in places like Crossroads means the police have
little trouble recruiting. But at the height of the current wave of
violence a number of black policemen were "necklaced" by angry
crowds; nationwide, more than nine hundred others had their
homes burned. In some parts of the country, black police and their
families had to be evacuated from townships in the middle of the
night and moved to special tent villages behind barbed wire, next
to police stations. As they now take revenge for homes destroyed
and companions burned alive, they become as feared as the white
police.

Standing outside a clinic in Crossroads, I see some of that history
in the grim face of a black policeman, as he looks down from an
open-topped armored car that suddenly roars into view along a
winding sand path—in search of someone? Or just on patrol? His
eyes are narrowed; he is holding a submachine gun. Children
shrink away from the vehicle's path.

Inside the clinic this morning, a white pediatrician is seeing
patients. She is instructing some medical students as she does so.
She explains to them that the swollen cheeks on some of these
children are not due to infection, as medical textbooks might have
them believe, but to kwashiorkor, a disease of malnutrition. Bot-
tle-baby syndrome is a major problem here, the doctor tells me:
this is the tragic near-starvation that occurs when a mother does
not breast-feed, then can't afford enough baby formula or the fuel
to boil water for it. "Mothers have so little confidence they can't
believe that something they produce *themselves* is what's best for
their baby." The doctor examines each child carefully, hands out
packets of protein powder, explains the importance of vegetables,
then fishes into a big box of old clothing and gives each mother
a wool blanket or sweater. Incongruously, a shelf behind the
packed benches of waiting mothers and babies holds some children's books donated from some household in Sunny South Africa:
*Walt Disney's Wonderful World of Knowledge, Black Beauty,* and *The
Young Ballet Dancer.*

□

Back in Sunny South Africa myself one afternoon, I am jogging through the beautiful pine and eucalyptus forest on the slopes of Table Mountain. I round a bend and come upon some stone ruins. A plaque explains that this was the house of a local dignitary, built in 1797. Everywhere around Cape Town I constantly stumble onto vine-covered houses, museums, three-hundred-year-old farms, all with brass plaques celebrating the longevity of white settlement in this corner of the country. Hundreds of monuments and oil portraits show the early Dutch *burgers* of this city, stern-looking men with ruffled lace collars and a somber, righteous gaze. Scores of history books record the conflicts between the English and the Dutch and the activities of the Dutch East India Company, to whom the colony for its first 150 years actually belonged. But, until recently, nobody paid much attention to the fact that this was a society built not only on conquest but on slavery. When I was here in 1962, I lived in a rented room off cobblestoned Greenmarket Square, unaware that it had once been the city's slave market.

The threat of punishment kept the slaves in line, and those who revolted or escaped were dealt with harshly. A major instrument of control, then as it is now, was Robben Island, one of the oldest penal colonies on earth. You can see it from the hill above Cape Town harbor, a low smudge on the horizon. Even before Dutch settlers arrived at the Cape, both British and Dutch ships left mutinous sailors on Robben Island to die. The Dutch later used the island as a prison for rebellious slaves, and for members of the Cape's native population who resisted Dutch rule. Two prisoners stole a leaky boat and escaped to shore in 1659.

No prisoner has successfully escaped since. For a time the island was put to other uses—a lunatic asylum, a leper colony, a military base. But when South African jails began filling with long-term political prisoners in the early 1960s, Robben Island, a blacks-only prison, was where most of them went.

One evening, I talk to one of them, Neville Alexander. He spent ten years on Robben Island. For four years after that he was under house arrest. His large, alert eyes are touched with humor and intelligence as they take in everything around him; his brown face is gentle, scholarly, easily forming into a quizzical smile. Classified as "Coloured," or of mixed race, he works today as an author and teacher. With the cachet of being a veteran of "the Island," he is an influential strategist of the resistance movement in the Cape Town region. When a wave of preventive detentions began a few years ago, the police came looking for him and he lived in other people's houses for some months. But for the moment things seem to have cooled off, and, wearing sandals and a tan windbreaker, he is willing to spend a few hours at a friend's house talking. After a decade of confinement in a notoriously harsh prison, I would have expected an angry or bitter man. But instead, Alexander talks of the experience almost as a privilege, and one that he was able to learn much from:

"Of course that time on the Island was a bit long. But it was never boring, never uninteresting. To come to one's maturity under those circumstances was an important experience. I found myself among older people who had thought deeply." Though Alexander has degrees from universities in both South Africa and Germany, he says, "Robben Island was certainly the best university I could have gone to."

Alexander describes the psychological effect of prison as a closed space: things you say rebound back to you; you cannot run away from anyone or from any opinion you've voiced. "The impetuosity of a young person runs up against those you are in close contact with. You realize the seriousness of words. For instance, if out of a sense of pride, vanity, immaturity, you push a particular polemic too far, it leads to strained relations. That affects the unity of the whole group. And you are responsible to the whole group; you have to stand together against the authorities.

"Through exchanging hints and opinions we were able to teach one another how to learn, the best way of making notes, the best way of writing an essay, and so on. We were able to have seminars and tutorials even while we were working. Although most talk has to take place while you are working in the lime quarry. People would make sure that they worked together. Everyone was picking and shoveling, but we'd use lunchtimes or weekends to do diagrams and things like that.

"The other thing about maturing was to be with people like

Mandela, Sisulu, and Mbeki, who have had decades of experience. Amidst the petty quarrels you find in all prisons, they were people who ennobled their environment. Mandela even the warders treated with great deference.

"In prison you have a lot of time. I had a two-year discussion with Mandela about what a 'nation' means in South Africa—is there an African 'nation'? A Coloured 'nation'? And so on. He is a man with a judicial temperament and an abiding interest in people. Even when you disagree with him, you never feel offended. I learned a hell of a lot from him, even though I disagree with some ANC policies. I admired particularly his lack of sectarianism. You can always reopen a question. It is an event in one's life to meet someone like that.

"On an emotional level, I discovered things about myself. I think the thing I missed most was children, not women. I remember the first time all of us heard children's voices in the quarry. They were from the warders' village there; they're normally kept well out of sight of prisoners. It was as though we'd been struck by lightning. All of us. We all stood dead still. The warder quickly went and made sure we didn't actually see the kids. But that reminded me, those lone voices, that that was the one occasion in ten years when I actually heard the voice of a child."

In downtown Cape Town, however, the fog rolls off Table Mountain like a silent waterfall, and Crossroads and Robben Island are out of sight. The newspaper announces public events: Captain Steven Banks, chairman of the SA Antique Collectors' Society, will speak on miniature paintings. The Kennel Association will hold its all-breed championship dog show at the Cape Hunt and Polo Grounds. Swami Yatiishvarananda will lecture on meditation and self-realization. Charlie Parker's Fully Licensed Restaurant and Disco will present the Miss SA Wet T-Shirt Contest. In the center of the city, a few blocks from Parliament, inside a gate guarded by plaster lions, white schoolboys are playing cricket: red knee socks, white shorts, and a satisfying *thock* as bat hits ball. For the moment, the watchmen's whistles are still in the distance, and the summer folk are still at play.

# "Laugh Like We've Been Laughing"

In the century and a half after the Dutch East India Company established its trading post at Cape Town in 1652, thousands more European immigrants arrived. During that time, the area covered by their farms and towns gradually expanded farther and farther eastward along the continent's beautiful southern coast, a crescent of fertile land and abundant rainfall. As the settlers moved east, they clashed repeatedly with the original inhabitants of this coastline, the Khoisan people. The Khoisan had been living at the southern end of Africa for many centuries before the Dutch came, possibly for millennia. They were yellow-skinned, and some of what we know about them comes from the detailed cave paintings they left behind. They painted up until the last, desperate days of their existence, when, on the cave walls, pictures of white invaders with guns replaced those of natural predators like lions.

Some Khoisan were herders of cattle and sheep; others were hunters who lived off eland (a kind of antelope), other game, roots and berries, wild honey, and fish they caught with harpoons made of sharpened bone. They believed in a god named !Kaang (the "!" represents a clicking sound) who made all things. To an early white traveler who asked, "Where is !Kaang?" a Khoisan hunter replied: "We don't know, but the eland do. Have you not hunted and heard his cry, when the eland suddenly started and ran to his call? Where he is the eland are in droves like cattle."

Living in small clans and not given to organized warfare, the Khoisan crumbled before the onslaught of a civilization that possessed the musket, the wheel, and the smallpox bacillus. In South Africa today, they are virtually extinct. Their features, however, survive in the faces of most of the people now living along that southern coastline. Many Khoisan women were raped or taken as common-law wives by the early white settlers, who were almost all male. The descendants of those unions today make up the great majority of the more than 3 million brown-skinned South Africans of mixed racial ancestry, who are officially designated as "Coloured."

The Coloureds, together with approximately a million people of Indian descent and some 28 million people whom we now speak of as Africans, make up the roughly 87 percent of South Africa's population that is usually referred to as "black." But word definitions, like everything else in South Africa, are battlefields. The government and its supporters use "black" only to refer to Africans, in order to stress the differences between them and the Coloureds and Indians. But democratically-minded South Africans increasingly use "black" to refer to anyone not white, and I have done so in this book. When it needs a word of its own for that purpose, the government uses "non-white"; formerly, it used "non-European." (When I was in South Africa in the early 1960s, language politics had not caught up with street politics, and in Cape Town militant young leftists were getting arrested under the banner of the Non-European Unity Movement.)

By the early 1700s, migrating white settlers had come some four hundred miles east from Cape Town. At this point, they encountered the black-skinned Africans for the first time. These were the first Iron Age people in southern Africa, and, unlike the lightly armed Khoisan, they were warriors. They wielded metal spears and were often organized into regiments of hundreds of men, who could put up a stiff fight. After English rule replaced Dutch along this coast in the early 1800s, British troops fought a series of bloody frontier wars against the Xhosa-speaking Africans at its eastern end. Slowly, the British pushed the Xhosa back; some Xhosa were captured and made slaves.

To further consolidate their hold over this threatened frontier of their colony, a territory known as the Eastern Cape, in 1820 the British brought in some five thousand settlers from England. They came ashore from their long voyage near a stone fort on the Indian Ocean shore, and the town which grew up there, soon the largest in the region, became known as Port Elizabeth.

Inland from Port Elizabeth, however, the farms of the Eastern Cape were still mainly owned by whites who spoke a language rooted in seventeenth-century Dutch. Often several days' horse-back ride from the nearest British Army post or tax collector, these farmers only reluctantly considered themselves British subjects. By the end of the nineteenth century they would be calling themselves Afrikaners; now, in the early 1800s, they thought of themselves as *Boers*. The word meant "farmer" in Dutch, but had a few added echoes here: it usually meant someone who raised cattle or sheep; it also implied a farmer who might sell stock once or twice a year in order to buy gunpowder and a few metal tools, but who otherwise grew or made almost everything he and his family consumed. Finally, it meant a farmer who measured his wealth not by his land and the rudimentary house he built on it, but by the size of his herd. A Boer also was likely to have anywhere from a handful to several dozen African or Coloured slaves, who tended and herded the huge droves of animals.

Land, once the natives were pushed off it, was the one thing the Boers thought there was plenty of. A proper Boer had enough of it, it was said, so that he need never see the smoke from another man's chimney. You needed several thousand acres for summer pasture and several thousand more for winter; you staked out this land by trotting to the four corners on horseback. When your sons grew up, one of them inherited this land and the others found new places to farm on nearby land that stretched endlessly back into the continent's interior.

At times, as I delve into the books I've brought along on my trip, I feel a grudging admiration for these ornery and fiercely self-sufficient people, slaveholders though they were. "They were almost paranoically independent," writes James Morris in his history of the British Empire.

> They wanted to be alone. They asked nothing of government, and offered nothing in return. Bold, bloody-minded, sanctimonious outdoor people, they wanted only freedom to wander where they liked, establish their farms as they pleased, worship their own God and mind their own business. With their great creaking ox-wagons and their herds of long-horned cattle, their plump wives in poke bonnets and their rangy dogs behind, they had long ago become indigenous to Africa, and adopted some of its values. The local Hottentots [Khoisan cattleherders] they enslaved, the local bushmen [Khoisan hunters] they virtually exterminated, the fierce and magnificent tribes of the African interior they kept at bay by force of arms.

Most Boers had as little as possible to do with the growing British colonial towns like Port Elizabeth. Some farmers were even known as *trekboers;* they did not even bother to build houses. They lived like gypsies in their ox wagons, each pulled by a "span" or team of sixteen oxen, and they moved on to new grazing land as they needed it. Growing up with the idea that Africa's spaces were infinite, the Boers romanticized their almost nomadic existence. They were filled with what they called *trekgees,* or wanderlust. As one Boer of that time put it: "A drifting spirit was in our hearts."

The coastline between Cape Town and Port Elizabeth is still fertile and beautiful. Known as the Garden Route to today's tourist industry, it is dotted with green vineyards, orchids, and beach resorts for wealthy whites. By train, it is a two-day trip from one city to the other: part of the route offers a spectacular vista as the rail line winds along clifftops from which you can look far down to the surf.

Now, in 1988, some of the towns along this route have just been playing host to caravans of Afrikaners rumbling across the country in ox wagons, part of the celebrations scheduled to come to a climax on December 16th, the 150th anniversary of the Battle of Blood River. South African newspapers and TV screens are filled with pictures of costumed people commemorating the Great Trek; I make plans to rendezvous with some of them later on. But before doing so, I have decided, I will spend the first half of my time in South Africa visiting spots around the country that were the scene of some of those events of the 1830s. I've not been to the Eastern Cape before and am curious to see it, because of its place both in history and in the country's more recent upheavals.

On the day I arrive in Port Elizabeth, however, few people are thinking about the Great Trek commemoration. Instead, the main event in town is something else. Beneath a frieze of brightly colored children's paintings, in the concrete and cinderblock auditorium of a technical training center for African and Coloured workers, several hundred people are attending a conference. It is marking the fortieth anniversary of the United Nations' Universal Declaration of Human Rights.

The most unusual thing about this Human Rights Festival, the people attending it seem to agree, is that it's happening here in Port Elizabeth. As I sit in the auditorium, the people in the audience look around gingerly, rather surprised the event hasn't been shut down, which it well might have been at various points in the past. For the Eastern Cape, home to a long tradition of black resistance and a militantly unionized workforce, is known for having the harshest police in the country. It was in the Port Elizabeth jail that Steve Biko was given the beating he died from. The office here of the Black Sash, an anti-apartheid women's group, largely white and upper middle class, was recently burned down. The office of the Human Rights Trust, the local organization putting on this festival, was broken into this very week. A recent study of torture and detention in South Africa, financed by the Ford Foundation, compared the experience of political prisoners in different parts of the country. It found that 93 percent of those imprisoned here in the Eastern Cape (the highest score of five regions) reported "beatings," 34.9 percent "electric shocks," and 30.2 percent "bag over head"; 52.4 percent of Eastern Cape prisoners said they had been "threatened with execution of self or family." Only 4.7 percent (the lowest score of five regions) reported "no physical torture." With these statistics of municipal achievement in mind, I look around the auditorium and wonder which people in the multiracial crowd are the undercover cops. A local activist tells me he recognizes at least five, which means there are probably a dozen or more. Who are they? The blond fellow on my left? The crew-cut man with a disapproving frown, chewing a pencil? Or this studious-looking black man filling a steno pad with notes?

One speaker at the conference is Archbishop Desmond Tutu. He tells a story: he dies, and two weeks later the Devil himself knocks on the pearly gates. St. Peter says, "What do *you* want here?" The Devil says: "Well, you sent Bishop Tutu down there and he's causing so much trouble I've come to ask for political asylum."

Everyone laughs. Or almost everyone. Then I realize one way you can tell the plainclothesmen. They don't laugh.

Fikele Bam, an eloquent African human rights lawyer and former political prisoner, talks about how the white Afrikaans-speaking warders on Robben Island referred to labor gangs of prisoners as "spans," as if they were Voortrekkers speaking of oxen. The commands to the gangs were the same, too: *"Vorentoe!"* ("Forward") and *"Staan vas!"* ("Stop").

Sakhumzi Macozoma, a church official, describes growing up here in Port Elizabeth and foraging for food at the garbage dump. And he talks about how police vans prowled through the city's black townships at night, but keeping no records of who was arrested where or for what. The next morning at the station, police would look at a list of what crimes had been committed during the night, and arbitrarily pick which prisoners to charge with which.

What surprises me most about this Human Rights Festival is its extreme civility. One speaker, a white woman from the Black Sash, describes a past activity of her organization, a "dinner party subgroup," that discussed ways Sash members could deal, in a "skillful but still gracious" way, with touchy race relations questions when they came up at all-white dinner parties. How must the many black veterans of prison and torture in the audience feel about this? *Dinner parties?* But they clap politely when she is finished.

The real guest of honor at the conference doesn't sit in the auditorium, but everyone knows he's here. He is Govan Mbeki, seventy-eight: scholar, editor, organizer, and the first Secretary of the armed wing of the African National Congress. For some twenty-five years, along with Nelson Mandela and Walter Sisulu, Mbeki was one of the three senior ANC leaders in prison. Much of his book *South Africa: The Peasants' Revolt* was written in solitary confinement, on toilet paper. He was released to his home here in Port Elizabeth in 1987, the first of the top-ranking ANC leaders to be let out of jail. Smiling, peaceful, and with a magisterial presence, he talks knowledgeably about world affairs as he receives visitors two or three at a time. At the time of this conference, Mbeki is still under restriction orders: he is not allowed to speak for quotation, and is not allowed to be in a room with more than ten people. Sticking to the letter of the law, he follows the proceedings of the Human Rights Festival from a separate room: the auditorium's movie projection booth.

In the countryside around Port Elizabeth, the 1830s saw the Boers grow increasingly unhappy under British colonial rule.

The British had gradually come to realize that the rich belt of land they possessed at Africa's southern tip was more than just a convenient resupply point for ships en route to India. And so they grew more rigorous about collecting taxes from the Boer farmers and asserting their control over the Boers. The British also preferred to settle their fights with the Xhosa over land and livestock by means of proper, businesslike wars that ended in fixed boundary lines, rather than by allowing the Boers to stage informal commando raids into Xhosa territory to seize Xhosa cattle.

Another problem for the Boers was that they were running out of land. Many Boer families had a dozen or more children. When each son took several thousand new acres, it pushed settlement farther and farther inland. But the British disapproved: eager to stabilize the eastern and northern borders of their colony, they did not want to be drawn into new frontier wars.

Finally, there was the uncomfortable issue of slavery. Boer farms, then as now, depended heavily on black labor. When blacks captured locally couldn't fill this need, others were shipped in chains to the Cape from East and West Africa. But religious anti-slavery feeling was growing in Britain; the slave trade was ended in 1807, and slavery itself was abolished throughout the British Empire in 1833. The reasons were not only humanitarian; one British motive was to bring slaveowning groups like the Boers more firmly under the Empire's thumb. Much to the Boers' outrage, their slaves were not only set free, but the compensation paid for them—a mere £50 a head in some cases—was far less than what a slave's lifetime of labor was worth. And, most humiliating, rubbing in the fact that the Boers were really British subjects after all, this compensation could only be collected *in London*—more than six thousand sea miles away. This meant selling your claim to a London agent for a fraction of its value.

Furthermore, the Boers fumed, you could barely even flog your own farmhands anymore. For the British colonial government, under the influence, as the Boers saw it, of do-gooder missionaries fresh off the boat, granted all sorts of rights to the newly freed slaves. These even included the right to swear out complaints against their masters—who could then be compelled to ride several days to the nearest magistrate to defend themselves. Furious at these various limits on their previously unfettered existence, the Boers had had enough. It was time to leave.

". . . it is not so much [the slaves'] freedom that drove us to such lengths," later wrote Anna Steenkamp, a member of a leading Boer family, "as their being placed on an equal footing with Christians, contrary to the laws of God and the natural distinction of race and religion, so that it was intolerable for any decent Christian to bow down beneath such a yoke; wherefore we rather withdrew in order thus to preserve our doctrines in purity."

The Boers' sense of outrage also shows in a play written later in the century by a Dutch Reformed clergyman:

> *These English courts proclaim*
> *The white and black in law have equal rights! . . .*
> *Shall I yield unto rule so tyrannous,*

*That taketh from us our most sacred rights,*
*That giveth unto Hottentots and slaves*
*The honours which their present ignorance*
*Cannot appreciate, but doth abuse?*
*No, never, never!*

And so the Great Trek began. The Boers turned their eyes to the endless expanse of land to the north, which, whatever dangers or mysteries might lie in it, at least was beyond British reach. The Great Trek was not a single organized caravan under a single leader, nor did it leave on one date for one destination. It was, instead, a mass migration of groups of Boers ranging from a half dozen to a few hundred families. It was preceded by several *commissie treks,* or scouting expeditions, and followed by several thousand latecomers. Coming mainly from the Eastern Cape, the Boers loaded their ox wagons with pots, pans, furniture, seeds, plows, hens, and Bibles. Riding their small, shaggy horses alongside, the Boers headed north, into new territory and into a new role in myth, as the heroic vanguard of an oppressed people seeking independence. "They were escaping in fact," writes Morris, "from the modern world, with all its new notions of equality and reason."

Between 1836 and 1839, in the first wave of the Great Trek, some six thousand Boers from the Eastern Cape moved north. They were accompanied by black servants, who were now called "apprentices" rather than slaves. They also brought with them their religion. The Boers practiced a fundamentalist Old Testament Calvinism that was unsoftened by the previous century's Enlightenment—which had occurred after their ancestors left Europe. For them the Bible was literal truth, ordaining the hierarchies of patriarch and wife, of believers and heathen, of Chosen People and hewers of wood and drawers of water. There was no doubt who were the Chosen People.

Piet Retief, a Trek leader who was later to play a fateful part in this exodus, published a manifesto in the *Grahamstown Journal,* the newspaper of a British colonial town inland from Port Elizabeth. Writing on the eve of his departure, Retief boldly declared the Trekkers' independence from British rule, listed their hopes and grievances, and—a point today's Afrikaners tend to gloss

over—acknowledged that he and his fellow Trekkers knew that
the land they were heading into was not empty:

> . . . we are induced to record . . . our intentions respecting
> our proceedings towards the Native Tribes which we may
> meet with beyond the boundary.
>     . . . We are resolved, wherever we go, that we will uphold
> the just principles of liberty; but, whilst we will take care that
> no one shall be held in a state of slavery, it is our determination
> to maintain such regulations as may suppress crime and pre-
> serve proper relations between master and servant. . . .
>     We are now quitting the fruitful land of our birth, in which
> we have suffered enormous losses and continued vexation,
> and are entering a wild and dangerous territory. . . .

The Trekkers knew they would be able to feed themselves and
their large livestock herds off the land they would pass through
on their journey, but of other supplies they were not so certain.
As the Boers headed north from the country around Port Elizabeth, they carried with them in their wagons an average of 300
pounds of gunpowder apiece.

Seated in a back row at the Human Rights Festival, and looking
restless and impatient with all the speechmaking, are several big,
broad-shouldered white men who look as if they are part of the
defensive line of the San Francisco 49ers. But the game at which
they have earned their fame is not football but rugby. They are
the Watson brothers, and for years I have been wanting to meet
them. It is one reason I've come to Port Elizabeth. I leave the
conference early with them one evening, and in the apartment
where two of them live, we spend several hours talking.

White Americans or Europeans often tend to search for a particular kind of white South African hero. Sometimes our desire
to find such white heroes is so strong that it obscures from sight
the black ones—who are far more numerous and in the long run
will be far more important. The most appalling example of this is
Richard Attenborough's film *Cry Freedom,* in which the figure of
Steve Biko—indisputably one of the great South Africans of his

time—was largely eclipsed on the screen by the adventures of his white friend, newspaper editor Donald Woods. The white anti-apartheid heroes Americans and Europeans like to identify with tend to be high-minded, articulate intellectuals, like Donald Woods, or, in works of art with far more integrity, the character of Arthur Jarvis in Alan Paton's *Cry, the Beloved Country,* or the schoolteacher Ben du Toit in the film (and André Brink novel) *A Dry White Season.* Usually a period of guilt, or an eye-opening experience of some kind, or the tragic death of a black friend, precedes this character's decision to nobly switch sides, after which he becomes a social outcast. We like such heroes partly because they are our idealized selves, projected onto the South African scene. But what has long intrigued me about the Watsons is that they don't fit this pattern at all.

To fully appreciate these four cheerful, husky brothers, you must first understand that South Africans in general, and the leisured white South Africans in particular, are possibly the most sports-mad people on earth. Sports stories are not in a back section of the newspaper; they are spread across the front page. In a single TV newscast one night—the evening news, not a sports show— I see clips of auto racing, kayaking, surfing, rugby, golf, and cross-country motorcycle racing. Soccer players are great idols in Soweto, and virtually all male Afrikaners can name you the leading players of the Springboks, the national rugby team. Few South Africans of any color can tell you exactly which of their products are boycotted by what countries, but they all know which foreign teams won't play here. If an Australian provincial badminton team breaks the international sports boycott and comes, it's a major news event.

Three burly Watsons are crowded around a coffee table: Valence, thirty-six; Ronnie, thirty-eight; and Gavin, forty, whose apartment this is. A fourth brother, Cheeky, thirty-four, isn't here this evening. I estimate that I am in the presence of some 800 pounds of muscle. The Watsons interrupt each other constantly but smoothly, one carrying along the thread of a story another has begun, as if they are passing a rugby ball back and forth as they run down a field. They all share a square-jawed, open-faced look. Gavin and Valence have black hair, and Ronnie curly blond, but except for that, after a while it begins to feel as if you are talking to one person in triplicate.

The Watsons grew up on a farm not far from Port Elizabeth; their father was a Pentecostal preacher. All four boys played with black children from infancy and are fluent in Xhosa. It never occurred to them that there was anything unusual about this until they went to school. That was "the first time we really experienced racism," says Gavin, the oldest, "when our black friends couldn't come to the same school we went to."

By high school, it was obvious that the brothers were national-caliber rugby players. After they graduated, Valence became vice captain of the all-white provincial team for the Eastern Cape; Cheeky was about to win a position on the Springboks, the national team. Then it gradually became clear that the Watsons were not going to fit the usual white South African mold. While doing his compulsory military service in the Namibia-Angola war, Ronnie, assigned to an ambush, took all the bullets out of his rifle and threw them to the ground. Back at home in Port Elizabeth, all four Watsons decided they would no longer play rugby on all-white teams.

Instead, they went to play and coach on the rugby fields of the city's black townships. The police banned them from these areas, but the Watsons stowed away in car trunks and delivery trucks, and went anyway. "It was lovely," says Valence. "Really, the warmth of the welcome was unbelievable." At first, several of the brothers played for the same black club, but then "they asked us please to spread ourselves out across the clubs."

Conditions were radically different from what the Watsons had been used to at white schools and rugby clubs: grass fields floodlit by night and watered by sprinklers. Most black rugby is played on stony vacant lots. Black school fields are little better: a study in Pietermaritzburg showed that government spending per pupil on school sports facilities was twenty-four times as much for white schools as for black schools. The first black township game the Watsons played in was at night, illuminated by the headlights of four parked cars.

"But you had to get used to it," says Valence, "[you] had to forget that you're used to grass. You know, on nice turf you don't mind falling, but here you've got to be careful how you fall. You could bust a knee on a rock or something. But the players were phenomenal players. And still are. But they're hidden from white eyes."

While playing rugby evenings and weekends in the townships, the Watson brothers made their living running several retail clothing stores. When the 1984–86 black revolts hit South Africa, the Eastern Cape was a major battleground. Port Elizabeth and other cities were the scene of a series of consumer boycotts. Blacks refused to shop in white-owned stores until streets, lights, and schools in the townships were improved. White merchants were hard hit; in Port Elizabeth, almost all stores lost 30 percent or more of their business. These shopowners and the government were furious when the Watsons' stores were exempted from the boycott.

Not only did blacks still shop in the Watsons' stores, but boycott organizers asked them to stock extra goods black shoppers needed. "We used to only sell men's clothing," explains Gavin. "They wanted us to diversify into ladies' and kiddies'. You can imagine what a threat that was to our white colleagues." The local police colonel, who had been the manager of a white rugby team Cheeky Watson had once played on, sent rifle-carrying officers to patrol the Watsons' stores, to try to frighten customers away.

Over the years, the Watsons have been the target of an extraordinary series of attacks. Only luck, boxers' physiques, and, according to them, the hand of God have allowed them to survive. Between the late 1970s and today, the Watsons' enemies have repeatedly tried to injure or kill them:

- While working in one of their stores, Gavin was stabbed with a knife an assailant had hidden in a handkerchief. Valence tackled the man before he could escape. Gavin almost died from shock and loss of blood: his heart stopped twice on the operating table. But today he and his brothers roar with gleeful laughter when they describe the beating given to the attacker by Archie Mkele, a black man who worked in their store.

  "Archie proceeded to kick him half to death!" says Valence. "Gavin is standing there saying, 'Stop, Archie! Stop, Archie!

You'll kill him!' Meanwhile Gavin is dying himself, mind you! He's turning white and the perspiration is streaming off him."

"Now when you imagine this guy Archie," Gavin interrupts, "it's important to realize he wears *a size twelve and a half shoe.* And at the time he was wearing a Florsheim Brogue. Those are *heavy* shoes."

Gavin's attacker "escaped" from police custody. Eventually, after much pressure from the Watsons' lawyers and the press, he was rearrested and given a long jail sentence.

· On another occasion, on the eve of the Blood River battle anniversary one year, Ronnie and Valence Watson and Archie Mkele were jumped by five white men in army uniforms and four in plain clothes—with knives. The two Watsons and Mkele defended themselves with the only weapons at hand— bricks and broken-off Coke bottles. They fought off their attackers long enough to grab a car and flee—to New Brighton, Port Elizabeth's main black township, where the Watsons always know they'll be safe.

· Two different times, Valence was attacked while alone. Once it was by three men when he was coming out of a café. One of the men was armed with a sharpened screwdriver. "I caught the ringleader a few days later and I beat him. Honestly, I was so mad I beat him senseless, absolutely. And it came out he was a railway policeman."

· A white man carrying a .22 pistol and working alone (he should have known better) attacked Ronnie Watson in Ronnie's hotel room while Ronnie was on a trip to Botswana. Ronnie managed to tackle him and get the gun. The attacker is currently serving a five-year jail sentence.

Scattered along the way have been telephoned death threats, an attempt to set Valence's apartment on fire, and other harassment the brothers now regard as merely routine. The press "asks us for a comment sometimes," laughs Valence, "and we say, 'Comment? You mean every time there's a smear pamphlet, we've got to comment? Forget it!' "

The Watsons' most extraordinary experience came at the height of the consumer boycott. Valence, his wife and children, and the Watsons' parents were all living in the family's large house in Port Elizabeth. The other brothers were in and out all the time. The house was also a place where black activists knew they could always find food and a bed for the night.

One day all the Watsons went away for the weekend. They had asked Archie Mkele and another friend who worked in their stores, Geoffrey Mocanda, to stop by and check their house. As the two men parked outside, they were pulled out of their car and knocked unconscious by half a dozen men in face-concealing balaclava ski masks—the standard costume for South Africa's nighttime death and terror squads. The house was shaken by a huge explosion and burned to the ground. Mkele and Mocanda were slapped in jail. Cheeky, Valence, and Ronnie Watson were arrested and charged with arson, fraud, and trying to murder Mkele and Mocanda. I ask Gavin why he wasn't arrested.

"Well, you can see *I'm* not a criminal!" he says. All the brothers laugh uproariously.

The police claimed that the Watsons had arranged for Mkele and Mocanda to burn down their house so they could collect insurance. While holding three of the four brothers in jail for six months, they tried to torture Mkele and Mocanda into testifying as state witnesses. Mkele was repeatedly half-suffocated with a plastic bag over his head, but he wouldn't give in. Eventually the police gave up on him. Mocanda finally did agree to testify, but smuggled a letter out of jail saying that he was testifying only under extreme duress.

"Gavin takes the letter and gives it to our attorney," says Valence. "Leon's a nice liberal, who believes, well, you know, 'things aren't so bad.' You know liberals, that's how they are. So he warned him, 'Be careful, Leon.'"

Leon Schubart, the Watsons' attorney, put the letter in his suitcase and went to Johannesburg to consult another lawyer about the case. En route, his bag was "lost" by the state airline. When it reappeared the next day, the letter was gone. Despite this loss, the state's case collapsed in court. Among other things, the Watsons proved that before the fire, they had received an offer to buy the house for more money than it was insured for.

The Watsons were found innocent. A crowd of several thousand blacks carried them shoulder-high through the streets of Port Elizabeth, even though, under the State of Emergency in effect at the time, such demonstrations were banned. "Cheeky gave an interview to the BBC in the middle of Main Street," remembers Valence. "The cars and buses just stopped. It was fantastic."

"The captain of police came to me," adds Gavin, "and asked me to please stop the crowd from breaking down the doors. The court doors. *Asked* me! He said they couldn't control the crowds. Emotions were built up so amongst the black community, because what was happening to us had been happening to them *for years*."

Recent times have not been easy for the Watsons. Without them there to manage it, their clothing business failed while they were in jail. They've had to scramble for other jobs. Under the strain of what they've gone through, Cheeky's and Ronnie's marriages both collapsed. Ronnie shows some of the pain of that, still, on his face. He is living with Valence and his family now.

But in the end, the brothers still have each other. They still coach rugby. And, in all their burly exuberance, they do not give the impression of people who have suffered. During our conversation they repeatedly poke fun at "white liberals" like their attorney, the sort of people who believe "it can't happen here."

Now, of course, it *is* happening here: death squads, midnight arrests, fire-bombed offices, the whole bit. "Now," says Gavin of the liberals, "the amazing thing is: guess who phones us when it happens to them? *They* phone us, and they're crying over the phone! So Ronnie goes to them and says, 'Can't you stop crying? Laugh like we've been laughing!' "

As I look back on what happened in and near this city 150 years ago, it is clear that a further tragedy compounds the obvious injustices of South African history. It is that so much of that history itself is not recorded. "The struggle of man against power," writes Milan Kundera, "is the struggle of memory against forgetting." The Boers who lived along the coast from Cape Town to Port

Elizabeth, and the British colonists who followed them, left abundant records of their lives. But from the Africans they conquered in the Eastern Cape the history is mostly indirect: filtered into song or oral poetry and legend. Trying to sense the experience of these conquered black civilizations from such faint traces is like straining to see something through glass that is almost opaque.

Sometimes, however, the scene on the other side of the dark glass glows with extraordinary brightness, with characters so striking that they both passed into black legend and forced themselves on the awareness of white conquerers. One such group of men and women forms a thread that runs through South African history of the last century and this one: that of the prophets. Just as whites claimed divine sanction for their conquests, so did the peoples they conquered turn to the supernatural to express their despair and to ask for aid. These appeals were given eloquent voice by a series of black visionaries, almost all of whom came from the Eastern Cape.

The first major prophet of whom we have record is Makana Nxele, or Makana the Left-Handed, a Xhosa religious and military leader of the early 1800s. He fought in the wars against the British, who were based at Port Elizabeth and nearby Grahamstown. Although up until that time the Xhosa had had no pantheon of gods, Makana preached of one. He taught that Dalidipu, the god of black people, was vastly superior to Tixo, the god of white people. Dalidipu would turn the invaders' bullets into water, Makana said, and would bring the old heroes back from the dead and lead them to victory over the British.

After a British raid on Xhosa territory in 1819, Makana Nxele led ten thousand men against the British fort at Grahamstown. As they marched, they sang:

> *To chase the white men from the earth*
> *And drive them to the sea.*
> *The sea that cast them up at first*
> *For the Xhosa people's curse and bane*
> *Howls for the progeny she nursed*
> *To swallow them again.*

But when Makana's soldiers tried to storm the fort, the British mowed them down in swaths with grapeshot. A thousand were killed.

Three months later the British again attacked Xhosa country, killing people and burning homes. Hoping to stop the slaughter, Makana came to the British camp and gave himself up, saying, "Let me see whether delivering myself up to the conquerors will restore peace to my country."

He was sentenced to life imprisonment. Soldiers took him shackled, in the back of a wagon, to Port Elizabeth; from there he was sent on the brig *Salisbury* the remaining four hundred miles to Robben Island, off Cape Town. On the island, he found other Xhosa prisoners, and slaves who had been jailed for their part in rebellions. On Christmas Day, 1820, Makana led an uprising. He and his comrades overpowered guards and seized their guns. Thirty men jammed themselves into a small whaleboat and headed four miles across the water to the nearest part of the mainland. The overloaded boat capsized in the surf. "Makana," writes Edward Roux in his pioneering history of black struggles in South Africa, *Time Longer Than Rope*, ". . . it was said, clung to a rock for some time, encouraging the others with his deep voice, until he was swept off and drowned."

Makana was followed by many prophets from this region. In the 1850s appeared the most famous of them all, Nongquause. Like Joan of Arc, this sixteen-year-old Xhosa girl claimed to have heard voices urging her to save her people. The voices ordered that cattle be killed and the land lie fallow; then, they said, on an appointed day two blood red suns would rise and battle for control of the sky. A great wind would sweep the whites into the Indian Ocean, fat cattle would rise from the fields, and Xhosa grain pits would overflow.

Nongquause's message raised great hopes, and when the day came, crowds faced the horizon, waiting, but in vain. Their cattle slaughtered and their fields unplanted, some 25,000 to 50,000 Xhosa starved. But prophets predicting a rising of the dead, a sweeping away of the whites, and millennial abundance appeared again and again in later years, even in this century. In the 1920s, a prophet named Wellington Buthelezi told his followers to sacrifice all their pigs and white fowls, and preached that on the Day of Judgment American blacks would arrive by airplane and bomb the unfaithful with burning charcoal.

Makana Nxele himself is remembered today as an early martyr in South Africa's liberation struggle; I have heard his name evoked on the ANC's Radio Freedom, whose call sign is a fusillade of rifle shots. His name also survives in that of a hill overlooking the site of his brave but futile charge against the British; it is now called Makana's Kop, or Makana's hill. Makana's Kop today is the site of a South African military post that monitors the African townships of Grahamstown, the scene of much fighting against police and soldiers in the mid-1980s.

The other prisoners who escaped from Robben Island with Makana in 1820 were all swiftly recaptured. Three of them were hung. Their heads were cut off and put on stakes on the island, as a warning to other would-be escapers. Rumors swept the country that Makana was alive, and would return. People waited for him. "But he did not come back," writes Roux, "and the expression 'Kukuza kukaNxele' [it is the coming of Nxele] has now become proverbial. It means 'deferred hope.' "

November is the start of summer below the equator, and as the holiday season begins, Port Elizabeth is like Fort Lauderdale at spring break. A harbor tour boat company advertises a "sundowner cruise" with music and cocktails. A tinkling bell announces an ice-cream vendor's cart as it rolls along the beachfront esplanade. Day-Glo boards shine out from the windows of a surf shop. A bumper strip reads SCUBA DIVERS DO IT DEEPER. On a bright Sunday morning, the open-air terrace of the hotel where I'm staying seems to be a favorite pickup spot: black waiters are bringing round after round of Castle and Lion beer to young white clerks and college students on vacation who are laughing and flirting, bare arms and legs soaking up the sun.

The small car that stops here in mid-morning to pick me up has three people in it: Rory Riordan, a local white activist who organized the Human Rights Festival that ended last night; his nine-year-old son Dominic; and LaDoris Cordell, a black judge from San Jose, California, who spoke at the festival.

We are going to church.

We pass through a district of factories and wasteland that sep-
arates downtown Port Elizabeth from its African townships. Almost every major South African city has such a buffer zone. At
one level its purpose is military—it lets the government contain
the black revolt outside white areas. At another level, the reason
for this band of vacant lots is psychological: it is easier for white
South Africans to forget blacks and deny that their problems exist
if they can't *see* them.

In Port Elizabeth's half-dozen African townships there are no
parks, no working swimming pools, and 3,000 library books for
470,000 people. Dozens of people have been killed on these dirt
streets in the uprisings of the last few years. Port Elizabeth has
always been the heartland of black militance; although Robben
Island prisoners come from all over South Africa, it is the Xhosa
language, spoken here, that is the island's lingua franca. In the
heady early days of the 1984–86 uprising, the consumer boycotts
here were better organized than almost anywhere in the country.
When they and other forms of resistance were crushed, thousands
of Port Elizabeth Africans were jailed. Evidence of the continuing
war is on every side: passing yellow police trucks—known as
*"kwela-kwelas,"* or "mellow yellows"; the ruins of a shop that had
belonged to a municipal councillor, despised as a collaborator; the
blackened rubble of a school, a senseless target it would seem,
burned to the ground by militant "comrades."

At the door of New Brighton township's Church of the Ascen-
sion, the minister is waiting. The church belongs to the Order of
Ethiopia—an independent black group loosely affiliated with the
Anglican Church. Impatient with missionary paternalism, it chose
its name because Ethiopia was mentioned in the Bible and, when
the order was founded in 1892, was one of the few parts of Africa
not colonized by Europeans. A congregation of about two hundred
fills the simple, cinderblock building. Men and women sit on separate sides of the aisle, and as we walk in, they are singing. Feet
shuffle and stamp, waves of song echo from one side of the aisle
to the other, a hymn fragments into half a dozen parts in harmony,
then flows back together to end in a great cataract of sound. The

*a cappella* music fills the building to the rafters and thunders out through the open windows and across the desolate township.

Out these windows we can see an expanse of jerry-built, dirt-floored shacks, a vacant field strewn with stones and windblown newspapers; an occasional cow or goat; piles of trash in midstreet (garbage trucks make few pickups here); and a single cold-water tap in the middle of the street, serving some fifty houses. Only 15 percent of the homes in New Brighton have electricity. How, how, from that desolation, from these dirt streets with a single faucet, have these two hundred people emerged clean and in their Sunday finest, the choir in bright white robes? And how can their hands so strongly clasp mine, the color of the world which has shunted them into this slum, shot at them, tear-gassed them, failed to send trucks to pick up their garbage? How can they welcome us with such warmth?

As the singing goes on, we are ushered to seats in the front row of the benches that face the pulpit from the side. Young Dominic Riordan is sitting next to me. Facing us in the front row on the other side of the pulpit is a black boy of about his age. Living here, in one of these tin shacks, is that boy likely to ever have talked to a white person who is not a policeman? But he catches Dominic's eye, gives a luminous smile, winks, and makes a "thumbs up" sign.

The minister greets us "in the two official languages—English and Xhosa. Afrikaans is not an official language!" He then introduces a lay preacher who gives a twenty-minute sermon in Xhosa. At the start, someone translates each sentence for our benefit. But then, frustrated with the pauses, the preacher waves the translator away and continues full-speed, pointing at the ceiling, pointing out the door. I can recognize only a few words, *"amandla!"* (power), "situation!" and "Isaiah!"

After the sermon, the minister says he is particularly glad we've chosen this church to come to, because one member of the congregation "is the wife of Raymond Mhlaba, who has been more than twenty years on the Island, with Mandela. Would . . . she . . . please . . . *stand!*"

With great dignity, she stands, and is applauded long and loudly.

Her husband was a long-time trade unionist, organizer of a 1949 bus boycott here, chair of the ANC in Port Elizabeth, and, until he too was captured, Mandela's successor as commander of the ANC guerrillas. [Mhlaba was finally released from prison in late 1989.]

The minister leads prayers, and then comes a long period of singing while members of the entire congregation circulate around the church, rhythmically bouncing up and down, embracing each other. Dozens of people dance up to us, give us the freedom handshake or a rib-cracking hug, saying, "Peace be with you!"

LaDoris Cordell is introduced, and the congregation whispers with excitement: she is young, female, and black—any one of which is almost unheard of for a judge in South Africa. She says that the black churches in the United States were a center of the struggle there, too. "It's where we met and we sang and we talked . . . and we *won*. We still have racism in the United States. But apartheid is now against the law. And I know you will win, too. We are with you in our prayers." She says that her great-grandparents were slaves, and the congregation gives a low "*OOOOaaahhhh!*"

After she speaks, Rory Riordan rises and explains that we must leave early, for Judge Cordell has an appointment with Govan Mbeki. The congregation goes on with the service, singing a thunderous, multiparted hymn in Xhosa. As we slip out the door in mid-song, two hundred hands shoot into the air to wave goodbye.

# Place of Weeping

By 1837, large Voortrekker caravans were kicking clouds of dust into the air as they headed north from the country near Port Elizabeth.

"We see their high-wheeled trek wagons," writes James Morris,

> plunging through rivers and over ravines, the long ox-teams slipping and rearing, the driver with his immense hide whip cracking above his head, the black servants straining with ropes on the back wheels. We see them camped in laager within the circle of their wagons. The men in their wide-brimmed hats are smoking long pipes beneath awnings, or lie fast asleep upon the ground. The women are imperturbably suckling their children, mending their clothes, or preparing heroic Boer meals of game, eggs and violent coffee. Hens scrabble among the propped rifles and powder horns, a tame gazelle, perhaps, softly wanders among the carts. . . .

These covered wagons were lighter and narrower than the prairie schooners then crossing the American West, for the steep mountains the Voortrekkers knew they would have to cross were tougher going than the Great Plains. Getting a team of sixteen oxen to pull a wagon up a rocky, roadless mountain was hard enough; coming downhill was still worse—especially in a torrential winter rainstorm. When heading down mountainsides, men shoved boulders out of the way, than hauled back with all their weight on leather straps attached to the back of the wagons to keep them from careening downhill on top of the oxen. On the steepest hills the Trekkers took the back wheels off their wagons and chained big logs onto the axles as brakes. Even these efforts were sometimes not enough: paintings and drawings of the Great Trek show many wagons overturned and shattered on the rocks.

The Trekkers reached a major landmark at the Orange River, today the northern border of South Africa's Cape Province, and then the boundary marking the travelers' entry into a little-known land beyond all reach of British rule. The rain-swollen river was three hundred yards wide. "An anxious counsel was held on the bank," writes Oliver Ransford in *The Great Trek,*

> then, while some of the men swam their horses and cattle over the great stream of yellowish water, others hacked away at the Babylonian willows growing beside it and constructed a stout raft. On to it they loaded the wagons and a mountain of stores, next the sheep and goats, and finally the women and children. . . . The children were gay and playful, but presently above their laughter and the sound made by water rippling against the pont, there rose the clear notes of a psalm sung in thanksgiving by the women. The very air and sunlight seemed keener and brighter as the raft approached the farther bank: and when the women stepped ashore there were joyful shouts of "Now we are free."

In the new land across the Orange, game abounded: lions, zebras, antelope, and gnu. "[T]he journey then resembled a voyage at sea since for weeks on end each day was like the one which had preceded it," Ransford continues. ". . . Every occurrence was interpreted in biblical terms: thus a grass fire seen burning on the veld ahead was accepted gratefully as the pillar of smoke by day and the pillar of fire by night, which the Lord himself had placed there to guide them to a new Canaan."

The land the Trekkers moved through immediately across the

Orange was largely unsettled. At this stage of their journey they
fought only one major battle, with the Matabele people. The Matabele chief, Mzilikazi, saw that all these wagons boded something
more ominous than the occasional white trader or missionary he
had previously met. He sent his troops south to challenge the
Boers, who, in the Great Trek's first major test of muskets versus
spears, soundly defeated the Matabele in the Battle of Vegkop.
In another foretaste of things to come, the Trekkers celebrated
their victory, it is said, by reciting the 118th Psalm—proof, as
always, that God was with them:

"I called upon the Lord in distress: the Lord answered me, and
set me in a large place. . . . All nations compassed me about: but
in the name of the Lord will I destroy them. . . . They compassed
me about like bees; they are quenched as the fire of thorns: for
in the name of the Lord I will destroy them."

The Trekkers knew precisely what "large place" God had in mind
for them. To find it today, you need only look at a rainfall map
of South Africa.

Much of the country's interior is dry, with less than ten inches
of rain a year. Finding water during the Trek was an occasion for
celebration—and sometimes for settlement, which is why the
names of scores of South African towns end in "fontein" or spring.
But in the direction the Trekkers were heading, the only place
where there is a wide stretch of land with abundant water is to
the northeast, where the map's shading indicating high rainfall
covers most of what today is the province of Natal. The Portuguese
explorer Vasco da Gama came upon Natal in 1497, and gave it
its name because he was sailing along its coast on Christmas, the
day of Nativity.

The Voortrekkers had no such charts, but early exploratory
treks and a few wandering hunters had brought back word of this
Promised Land that rolled for hundreds of miles under a warm,
near-tropical sun. The problem was getting there. By air today, it
is less than four hundred miles from Port Elizabeth to the middle
of Natal. But the Voortrekkers had to make a journey almost
twice as long. First, the densely settled territory of the Xhosa
people blocked the direct route along the coast. But inland from

the Xhosa lay a different kind of obstacle: southern Africa's highest peaks. The southern end of the jagged, rocky Drakensberg ("Dragon's mountains") range, many of these summits rise more than 11,000 feet and in winter are covered with snow and ice, "scenery as grand as in Switzerland," wrote the enthusiastic Trollope forty years later. No ox wagon could get through.

What the Trekkers had to do, then, was to head still farther north. Only after they had skirted the highest part of the Drakensberg could they gradually swing eastward, find their way through passes across the northern end of this range where the mountains were not so high, and then head downhill into the fertile valleys of Natal. You can trace the arc of their route on the map at the front of the book.

As the Trek's main body waited to cross the Drakensberg, a contingent of fourteen horsemen and four wagons moved on in advance. At its head was Piet Retief, the Boer farmer who had published his independence manifesto in the *Grahamstown Journal*. Retief, then in his late fifties, had graying hair and a fringe of beard. An urbane and polished man, he had even lived in the cosmopolitan seaport of Cape Town, colonial capital of the despised British. He was deeply devout, but fond of repeating, "Next to God, we depend on our ammunition." Back in the Eastern Cape, he had written many petulant letters to British colonial authorities, angry that they wouldn't allow him to deal harshly with African cattle thieves in his district. The Trek promised him and his fellow Boers relief from such constraints.

Retief had a self-confident air of authority that stood him above the feuds which were forever splintering the Voortrekkers into columns of wagons going in different directions. The largest group, those heading for Natal, elected him their Governor. With more than a thousand Trekkers camped in waiting behind him, Retief needed to find a wagon route through the forbidding mountains, cross into Natal and determine that the Boers could settle there, then send back word that it was safe to follow.

On October 7, 1837, Retief and his little band finally reached the crest of the Drakensberg at Mont-aux-Sources, named by two French missionaries a few years earlier for the profusion of streams that spring from the mountain. There he saw one of the finest

views on the continent: a long line of mountains whose eastern
slopes rolled downward into the green Natal of rivers and pastures.
"I saw this beautiful land," said Retief, "the most beautiful in
Africa." Another member of his party noticed how the mountain's
dark shadow swept so quickly across this country as the sun set
behind them, and said that a land so marked must be under a
curse. But Retief pressed on.

From Retief's point of view, the only problem with this lush
new territory was that other people were already there, the Zulus.
White South Africans have worked endlessly to spin the myth that
this was not so. Or that if the blacks were there, they had just
arrived, too. "More than three hundred years ago," said the late
Prime Minister Hendrik Verwoerd, "two population groups
equally foreign to South Africa converged in rather small numbers
on what was practically empty country. Neither group colonized
the other's country or robbed him by invasion." Tom Sharpe's
comic novel *Indecent Exposure* satirizes this mythmaking: an archeologist who finds evidence of iron workings in South Africa
before the Dutch came is promptly arrested by the security police.
Unfortunately for the mythmakers, finds of pottery shards and
other artifacts place black Africans in what is now South Africa
nearly two thousand years ago.

A few Zulus, in fact, were even captured as slaves more than a
century before the Great Trek began. In 1719, a British ship
stopped off Natal and its captain traded brass rings and other
trinkets for seventy-four boys and girls. The captain noted matter-
of-factly that "these are better slaves for working than those of
Madagascar, being stronger and blacker." The slaves were taken
to the Rappahannock plantations of Virginia. It was the first of
many ties linking South Africa and the United States in unexpected
ways.

Some Americans, then, have their ancestors among the estimated quarter to half a million Zulus who already occupied Natal
before the Voortrekkers arrived. Just who were these people, with
whom the Trekkers were destined to fight a string of battles,
climaxing with the momentous one at Blood River?

To try to answer this question is to look again through that
nearly opaque glass. Even our very name for this period reflects

white memory, not black memory: we speak of the Great Trek, not the Great Invasion. Firsthand descriptions of Zulu society in the early 1800s are almost all by whites. Voortrekkers kept diaries; missionaries reported home on the souls they were trying to save; British military officers and colonial officials sent reports to their superiors; someone wrote a volume called *A Narrative of the Irruption of the Kaffir Hordes*; and two British traders, Henry Fynn and Nathaniel Isaacs, who were trying to make their fortunes in Natal, wrote books on their adventures among the Zulus.

For a century, most historians relied on the writings of Fynn and Isaacs, the most extensive accounts of Zulu life before the Voortrekkers arrived. And gory tales these were, filled with reports of vast harems, bloody executions, and Zulu kings who ordered enemies killed for coughing in the king's presence or other such slights. It was not until the 1940s that some correspondence between the two men turned up that showed Isaacs and Fynn to be less than reliable reporters:

"Make them [the Zulu kings] out as blood-thirsty as you can," Isaacs wrote to Fynn, "and endeavour to give an estimate of the number of people they murdered during their reign, and also describe the frivolous crimes people lose their lives for. It all tends to swell up the work and make it interesting." Moreover, it turns out, Isaacs was offering his advice to Fynn as Fynn was rewriting his "diaries" from memory twenty years after losing the original. These two men had a powerful motive for creating a myth of the Zulus as totally barbaric, undeserving of the tempting agricultural paradise they lived in: Isaacs and Fynn wanted Britain to seize Natal. Then they could cash in on the value of land concessions they had bought from the Zulus.

There was, of course, far more to Zulu culture than harems and executions. The Zulus are from the Nguni group, one of the two main ethnic families of southern Africa, and one with a rich tapestry of folk tales and legends. The Zulu language was particularly supple: an early missionary dictionary compiler counted nineteen thousand words. Like other Nguni peoples, the Zulus had an elaborate system of hieroglyphics. The strings of little figures carved in the calabashes you can buy in curio shops throughout

South Africa all have specific meanings, sometimes as precise as
"I saw a lion eat a buck at midday."

In many ways, the Zulus resembled the Boers: they measured
their wealth in cattle; they were semi-nomadic; and they formed
a nation by conquest. Like the Trekker wagons, their dwellings
were suited to a people on the move. They lived in huts of woven
saplings and grass thatch—an entire village of these structures
could be put up in a few days, which made it easy to move on to
new grazing land. Zulu villages owned land collectively, and they
cultivated a wide variety of fruits and vegetables, from melons to
spinach. With a stone as an anvil and a goatskin bellows heating
up the fire, they smelted iron and copper into spear points and
jewelry.

Zulu government was a combination of an all-powerful king
who could sentence people to death by the nod of a head, and,
on the village level, a court system of elders who heard evidence
and made decisions by majority rule. There were special festival
days when royal protocol was suspended and subjects had the
right to question the king's decisions, and, like a minister in a
parliamentary system, he had to give answers.

The Zulus and the other Nguni peoples were different from
many others in Africa in one major way: they did not practice
slavery. Nor, despite a lucrative market for slaves in the British
and Portuguese colonies on their borders, did they sell slaves to
foreigners. The single recorded exception is that shipload of slaves
taken to Virginia. Survivors from a Dutch ship that was wrecked
off the Natal coast in the 1680s complained: "It would be impossible to buy any slaves there, for they would not part with their
children, or any of their connexions for any thing in the world,
loving one another with a most remarkable strength of affection."

Unfortunately for any modern would-be makers of counter-
myths, the Zulus were not peace-loving and pastoral, taking to
violence only in self-defense against the Boers. They had a long
warrior tradition, and fought many battles before the Boers arrived. Only a half century before the Voortrekkers came over the
mountains, the Zulus were a small clan among many others. But
in the late 1700s and particularly under King Shaka, who died in

1828, this changed. Before the whites arrived in Natal, different clans fought bitterly over its fertile land. The Zulus came out on top. Under Shaka they fought a series of wars that left tens of thousands of people dead and sent large waves of refugees throughout southeastern Africa. Neighboring clans who did not flee were subdued and assimilated by the Zulus.

Shaka refined the Zulus system of *impis,* or regiments, and trained his men to follow strict military discipline. He replaced the traditional Zulu throwing spear with a shorter *assegai* used for stabbing, a legendary innovation that would be commemorated a century and a half later in the name chosen by the African National Congress for its underground guerrilla network: *Umkhonto we Sizwe,* or Spear of the Nation. Shaka also devised an oxhide shield with a hooked edge that could be used to tear an enemy's shield aside. He became expert in using spies, smoke signals, and surprise attacks—his men were trained to remain completely silent while waiting in ambush. He found that his soldiers could travel faster and farther barefoot than in their traditional sandals, and so his forces were more mobile than those of his enemies, running up to fifty miles in a day. Shaka also pioneered the famous "ox-head formation" of attack, in which one *impi* of *assegai*-wielding warriors attacked head-on in a dense mass, the "chest," while two other *impis* formed "horns" that sprinted forward and then curved in from the sides to encircle the enemy.

Shaka's changes made his *impis* the most formidable military force in black Africa. But by the time of his death he had seen something of the white traders' strange poles that spat fire and thunder, and he guessed what was coming. As he lay dying, stabbed by two of his half brothers in a palace intrigue, his last words reportedly were, "As soon as I go, this country will be overrun by white men."

As I drive along the freeway that cuts through Natal, spiderwebs of lightning flash on the horizon, over the Drakensberg. Distant streams of rain move along the sky in dark columns. The land that first attracted the Voortrekkers is still green. Normally, the dominant color of the southern African landscape is brown: dry grass, earth, bush, desert. But here, over this one corner of a parched and dusty continent, it is as if someone had spread a vast golf course.

Beside the freeway, I notice that the Trekkers' Promised Land is now laced with rows of electric pylons and double-track railway lines. Piled high on passing freight trains is what turned out to be Natal's most valuable prize: coal. This was only discovered a few years after the Trekkers arrived, when a British officer spied a lump on the ground and sent it to the Cape Colony's governor. The Royal Navy was just then switching from sail to steam and the officer immediately recognized that Natal coal could become "of the utmost importance to steam navigation in the adjacent seas." Today, this same coal generates most of South Africa's electricity, powers one of the world's few remaining fleets of steam locomotives, and has given parts of the country some of the most polluted air on earth. In recoverable energy, this country has more coal than Saudi Arabia has oil—a treasure that has greatly buttressed South Africa against the international anti-apartheid oil embargo.

As the road swiftly takes me past towns and valleys and closer to the distant mountains, on the car radio a talk show host interviews an American evangelist. He is building himself a headquarters and recording studio in South Africa, for he thinks the revival of Christianity "is going to begin here and spread up through Africa into Europe." On the Zulu-language station, the disk jockey introduces songs with the names and addresses of migrant workers who have requested them: a long string of Zulu words ends with "——Hostel, Room Numbah Fifteen!" Back on the white station, the interviewer talks to a psychic. The last question is: what will be the future of South Africa? The psychic predicts peaceful change "progressing through all the races."

Black crews are at work on the road's shoulders, usually watched by a white foreman in sun hat, khaki shorts, and knee socks. The crews live in tents pitched nearby. As everywhere in rural South Africa, many Africans are walking along the roadside. The freeway itself is as modern as any in California, sometimes with three lanes in each direction. In places where the highway winds away from telephone lines, the roadside emergency call boxes are solar-powered radiophones. But for all its 120-kilometers-per-hour sleekness, the freeway sports a revealing sign of South Africa's current economic distress: at several places cranes and bulldozers are deployed across the road. They are building tollbooths.

These toll plazas are going up on what was for years a toll-free road. Even more significant, they are not operated by the government. They are run by a private company which has leased the right to maintain the road and collect tolls. South Africa is in the midst of a huge wave of privatizing its economy. Roads, the national mint, much of the railway network, the national airline, and even part of the post office are portions of a $28 billion package of government assets scheduled for some kind of turnover to private business. There is even a Minister of Administration and Privatization. The company now running this road is part of Sanlam, a big Afrikaner-owned insurance conglomerate.

The main purpose of privatization is to raise money. The South African state treasury is pinched from two sides. The cost of containing the current black insurrection is enormous: the fighting has damaged or destroyed more than 4,100 police vehicles since 1984, for example. In the four years following the outbreak of insurrection at that time, military spending more than doubled; it continues to take a huge share of the national budget. But the economy whose taxes pay for all this is stagnant: the country's per capita income has been dropping steadily for the last ten years, and inflation is soaring—the value of the South African rand dropped from $1.30 in 1980 to 40 cents at the decade's end.

The South African economy has been hard hit by white emigration, by sanctions, by local businessmen who are scared to make long-term investments, and by the sheer expense of apartheid. For example, until the government recently started desegregating public hospitals, it was wasting $300 million each year ensuring that people of different races wouldn't receive medical care in the same place. Privatization is a temporary way to meet bills like this. "It's selling the family silver," says a surprisingly frank white businessman I later talk to. "It's no long-range solution to anything at all." You can only sell a road once.

Privatization has another motive behind it, more subtle and more ominous. Until recently, South Africa has had one of the largest state-owned sectors of any economy in the Western world.

The government has controlled part or all of a wide range of industries, from harbors and power plants to forests and sawmills to iron and steel. But even the most die-hard white officials in Pretoria know that someday, perhaps not too far off, they will have to yield control to a populace that is 87 percent black. But control of what? Thanks to privatization, when South Africa finally comes under majority rule, the government that majority takes over will be one whose cupboard is bare. By then, tens of billions of dollars worth of state-owned wealth will have been put into private hands—virtually all of them white.

As I head farther into Natal on this privatized freeway, I feel as if I have moved into the landscape of a dream, and one that has something to do with white South Africans' attempts to escape their troubles. Far ahead, in the slow lane on my side of the road, is a huge ocean-going yacht. The yacht is much too big for a boat trailer, and is being carried in a framework of girders on the back of a full-length trailer truck. Its keel raises it high above everything else on the freeway; you can see it from miles away. Where on earth is it going? The boat is too big for any inland lake, of which there are no major ones in South Africa anyway. And it is heading *away* from the ocean. Slowly roaring up into the foothills of the Drakensberg, the truck is pulling the vast yacht mysteriously toward the continent's interior. I pass the boat; I can even read the name on the stern: SKEDADDLE. In their cab high above me are the solemn faces of the black truck driver and his assistant. For a long time the image of this huge yacht heading into the mountains haunts me, as does its name, as if reminding me of something. Finally, I know what: the Ark.

When Piet Retief and his companions reached the crest of the Drakensberg and looked down into Natal, they did not have long to live. The story of Retief's adventures and violent death in the months that followed are taught to every South African schoolchild, and are pictured in museum exhibits, in paintings, and on the stone frieze that surrounds the giant Voortrekker Monument in Pretoria. They are at the core of the Great Trek's transformation into legend. The way you almost always hear the story is like this:

Retief knew that the Zulu nation, with its powerful regiments, was the ruling power in Natal. A few dozen British traders and missionaries were clustered in one spot on the coast. But if Retief was to safely settle his stream of Voortrekkers, he had to make a deal with the Zulus. Parts of Natal were only sparsely settled; the Zulus might be willing to cede that land to the Trekkers. The Zulus were headed by Dingane, a strong, immense man who had become king after murdering his half brother Shaka.

Accordingly, Retief set off for Umgungundhlovu, or "the place of the elephant," Dingane's headquarters. Ahead of him he sent a letter. Rev. Francis Owen, a British missionary, was temporarily living at Umgungundhlovu, vainly trying to convert Dingane to Christianity; he translated Retief's letter for the king. According to Owen's diary, the letter expressed the Boers' "desire for peace and good understanding with the Zoolu nation: to effect which it was their wish to have, by means of their chief head, a personal interview with Dingane; who would at the same time also arrange with Dingane the place of their future residence which is to be in some part of the uninhabited country adjoining the Zoolu territories."

Retief and his comrades rode into Umgungundhlovu a few days later. There they found an impressive capital: a town encircled by a palisade of mimosa poles some two miles around. A parade ground provided space for military maneuvers; nearly two thousand huts each held some twenty warriors; more huts housed Dingane's ninety wives. There were concubines, court jesters, dwarfs, and a famous glutton, Menyosi, who, it was said, could consume a pot of beer and an entire goat in one sitting. Dingane's equivalent of PR men were two *mbongos,* or official praise singers, who preceded him everywhere, beating their shields and telling of his heroic deeds in loud voices. Nearby were Dingane's large herds of cattle, some bred to a snow white color.

Above the royal village was Hlomo Amabuta, the Hill of Execution. It was here that Dingane's soldiers killed people whom the king had sentenced to death. This happened every day or two, according to the distraught Reverend Francis Owen, who had to witness warriors using rocks to bash in the skulls of unfortunate prisoners while he was conducting prayer services on the opposite hillside. Owen considered these killings proof of Dingane's total barbarism, evidently forgetting that in England at the time people were publicly executed for a vast array of offenses as petty as stealing a rabbit. Nonetheless, Hlomo Amabuta was a gory spot and over it vultures circled constantly.

When Retief arrived, Dingane had four thousand of his soldiers put on an exhibition of dances and military exercises that lasted several days. Only on the third day did the tall, stout Dingane receive Retief, and warily hear his request to acquire land. To stall him off, Dingane told Retief that he must first prove his good faith. Retief should go and recapture some royal cattle that had been stolen by a rival chief, and bring them back to Umgungundhlovu. At that point, said Dingane, they could talk about land. Retief immediately agreed, and spent some weeks tracking down the missing cattle. Then, in late January 1838, gathering sixty-seven Boer men, three youths, thirty black servants, and an interpreter, he set off to make his final deal with Dingane.

When Retief arrived at Umgungundhlovu, again he was greeted by several days of feasting and war dancing. The Boers tried to do the equivalent by galloping around Dingane's great parade ground firing their guns. Finally Dingane put his mark on a document written in the somewhat shaky legalese of Retief and his British interpreter:

> Know all men by this that whereas Pieter Retief Governor of the Dutch Emigrants South Afrikans has retaken my cattle ... I Dingaan King of the Zoolas do hereby certify and declare that I thought fit to resign unto him the said Retief and his countrymen (in reward of the case here above mentioned) the Place called Port Natal together with all the land annexed ... from the sea to the north as far as the land may be useful and in my possession which I did by this and give unto them for their Everlasting property.

On the last morning of their visit to Dingane, February 6, 1838, the Boers assembled to watch one final war dance. Court officials explained that it was an offense to come armed into the king's presence, and so the Boers piled their guns at the gate. Retief sat beside Dingane's throne, which was carved from a single huge block of wood. Warriors played the drums, offered ceremonial beer to the white guests, and danced around them in a large circle. In Zulu, they sang:

> *Drink, oh drink the beer.*
> *Your burning throats call for it!*
> *Drink as much as you can,*
> *For tomorrow you drink no more!*

Retief's interpreter understood and cried out, "We are done for!" But it was too late. Dingane leapt to his feet and shouted, *"Bulalani abatagati!"* ("Kill the wizards!") It was the prearranged signal, and at these words, hundreds of his troops fell on the Trekkers with their spears. They tied them up with rawhide thongs and dragged them to the Hill of Execution. There Dingane's soldiers beat them to death with clubs or rocks, driving wooden stakes through some of their bodies from anus to chest for good measure. After Retief was dead, his chest was cut open, and his heart and liver ripped out, wrapped in cloth, and buried beneath the road that led across a river toward the land he coveted. This would bar the way, Dingane hoped, to further would-be conquerors.

The death of Retief and his men has burned itself into white South African consciousness. Everywhere it is treated as the very depth of treachery and horror. People speak of it almost as if it were an event like the Holocaust, which lies at a level of evil far beyond the normal brutality of warfare.

"Dingane's conduct was worthy of a savage," wrote Rev. Francis Owen, who witnessed the killings. "It was base and treacherous; the offspring of cowardice and fear."

A book written for the centenary of the Great Trek in 1938 describes Piet Retief as being

of a trusting nature . . . he was slow to think evil of anyone, even a savage like Dingane, whose conscience had never been awakened and who had no sense of responsibility for his actions. . . . [The deaths of Retief and his party] and the manner thereof were a lasting grief to their countrymen. It was also a lasting pride and glory. Each had been a martyr in the cause of civilisation. Though they had been pitilessly cast, after a vain struggle, to the death in which all they could do was to comport themselves like men, upon the rocks and amid the birds of prey, they are held in equal honour with the most renowned warriors who have been borne in pomp to the tomb. They are numbered with those of whom it has been said, "the whole earth is a sepulchre for famous men."

".  .  . the reader is constantly affronted and disgusted by the behavior of this black reincarnation of Nero and one naturally begins to hunt about for reasons why a human being should behave so abominably .  .  ." writes the normally restrained present-day historian Oliver Ransford. "There is a quality about the deaths of Retief and his men which does not seem to belong to an incident in history; rather it is like a scene from Grand Guignol, or the feverish outpourings of an artist with a macabre mind.  .  .  ."

A pamphlet from the Natal Provincial Museum Service which is handed out at Umgungundhlovu today tells visitors: "Dingane won the trust of Retief and the Trekkers and kept it until the last moment when he shouted the treacherous order for their execution. .  .  . If the Trekkers had died in a hostile but open conflict, the events of 6 February 1838 would possibly not still be so emotive and would not have influenced dispositions so strongly, even up to this day."

*Even up to this day.* This is the heart of the matter. For Piet Retief's death gives Afrikaners something that every imperial power needs. It is that necessary incident in an empire's history which can be turned into a guilt-absolving myth—the crucial, remembered moment that allows conquerors to feel that they are victims.

Novelists understand this fixation well. They know colonizers have a curious need to feel wronged. The two great portrayals of the English in India, Paul Scott's *Raj Quartet* and E. M. Forster's *A Passage to India,* both revolve around British characters obsessed with a rare act of violence, real or imaginary, in which an English-woman is the victim.

In the mythology of Afrikaner history, the murder of Piet Retief wonderfully does this job of turning conquerors into victims. Dingane ignored a treaty he had signed; he tricked Retief into believing in his peaceful intentions; and he carried out the mass murder in a particularly horrible way. Just as Retief's manifesto in the *Grahamstown Journal* was the first major document of Afrikaner nationalism, so has his betrayal and martyrdom been a key ingredient of that nationalism's constant note of victimhood.

Curiously, despite the breadth of its conquests, Afrikanerdom's rhetoric has never been that of a master race. Instead, it is the complaining tone of a persecuted, lonely tribe, first oppressed by the powerful British, then struggling for survival in a hostile black sea. Today, when fewer than 3 million Afrikaners control a government that has the atom bomb, rules a nation of 40 million, and economically and militarily towers over every other country on the continent, Afrikaners still talk to you as if they are on the verge of extinction. "We are," an Afrikaner editor in Johannesburg once said to me plaintively, referring to the rest of the continent all being under black rule, "being Finlandized." At times, Afrikaners even sound like leaders of a colony still struggling for its independence: "If there is one question which will have to be resolved in the years that lie ahead," recently declared Andries Treurnicht, leader of South Africa's far-right Conservative Party, "it is that the white man in South Africa has the right to his own homeland."

We are accustomed to thinking of the Afrikaner sense of martyrdom as beginning with the Boer War, when 26,000 Afrikaner women and children died in British concentration camps and the Afrikaners were universally seen as victims of horrendous mistreatment by a much larger empire. But in fact that sense of victim's identity begins much earlier, with the events leading up to the Great Trek, the Trek itself, and, above all, the story of Piet Retief. For he and his men were the victims of such great treachery at the hands of the Zulus.

Or were they? If we go back carefully over Retief's ill-fated journey and try to see it as it must have appeared to the Zulus, the whole expedition begins to look quite different. When I began reading about this period, I thought of it as one of a clash between peoples; I see it now as also a clash between rival streams of memory.

Most important in what the Zulus choose to remember is one fact: treaty or no treaty, the Trekkers intended to settle in Natal. Even while Retief was negotiating with Dingane, the Boers were already moving in. The Trekkers were impatient to reach the goal of their migration, and from the moment of his first visit to Dingane's court, before he had signed any agreement, Piet Retief and his advance guard were sending back encouraging messages to the main body of the Trek behind them. As a result, two months *before* Retief came back to Umgungundhlovu for the second and last time with the deed for Dingane to sign, more than a thousand Boer wagons had already crossed the Drakensberg and fanned out across northwestern Natal. At one point, fully a hundred wagons a day were coming through the mountain passes. Much of the territory the Boers had their eye on was uninhabited, but where there were Zulu settlements, the Trekkers moved in anyway. In the course of a few weeks, five thousand Boers had spread across a hundred-mile-wide swath of land, renaming the Zulu landmarks, measuring out farms, and collecting grain from the clay-lined underground storage pits of the Zulu villagers who had fled at the sight of Boer horses and guns. An alarmed Dingane knew the Boers had already occupied some of the land Retief claimed he wanted to buy: a stream of messengers and refugees constantly brought him news of the Trekkers' advance.

In writing of Dingane's court in the years before the Trekkers arrived, the accounts of traders and missionaries often show a patronizing amusement as they describe his fascination with unfamiliar objects they introduced him to. He showed great interest in such things as telescopes, razors, umbrellas, and watches. With a magnifying glass, he used the power of the sun to burn a servant's arm. At first he was skeptical of writing, and so he made one missionary, Captain Allen Gardiner, give a demonstration. Dingane dictated to Gardiner's interpreter while Gardiner was out of earshot, then called Gardiner and challenged him to read what was written. Convinced of the power of this invention, Dingane then tried to get Rev. Francis Owen to teach him to read. The only thing Dingane did not respond to was Christianity; for a ruler who executed so many of his enemies, there was no appeal in any resurrection of the dead.

To these Englishmen so sure of the superiority of their civilization, Dingane's love of gadgets was evidence of his being a childlike, ignorant savage. But reading between their condescending lines today, we can begin to make out a different figure: a shrewd and worried ruler, confronted with a culture that threatened his own, searching desperately for the key to its power. It did not take him long to decide what this was: gunpowder.

Soon all these accounts begin to record Dingane's urgent attempts to buy firearms. Even before the mass of Trekkers streamed into Natal, his desire had become, understandably, an obsession. Over the years he had rigorously questioned white visitors about guns. The only reason he let Francis Owen preach at Umgungundhlovu, Owen finally grasped, was that Dingane hoped to use him as an intermediary to buy gunpowder. Dingane repeatedly asked, and Owen repeatedly refused. When Dingane tried to get Owen to obtain bullet molds for him, Owen made him a present of some nails instead. The unscrupulous trader Henry Fynn sold muskets to Dingane, but removed the bolts. Other traders sold him more guns, but removed the springs.

Dingane can hardly be faulted for failing to honor the treaty he had signed with Retief. This was far from the first time he had signed a piece of paper granting the same land to white men— and Retief knew it.

Dingane, and Shaka before him, had, in return for various trinkets, already signed various deeds giving identical or overlapping parts of Natal to a long string of other white people. They had twice, in fact, officially signed away Natal to the King of England, once at the urging of an ambitious trader, and once at the request of a missionary who drew up a deed providing for this transfer "with the exception of a district in the Umgeni belonging to me." Dingane had also ceded Natal to three different Europeans who lived at the tiny settlement on the coast; he had even pronounced Henry Fynn King of Natal! Dingane had noticed that all these white intruders collected their ivory, left their beads and mirrors in return, and went away again. None of them ever did much of anything with their supposed ownership of Natal, least of all King William IV of England, who gave no sign of even knowing that Natal existed. These whites never seemed to mind that Dingane was ceding land to them that he had already ceded to someone else. So why should Dingane honor these pieces of paper any more than they?

Finally, one of Dingane's greatest reasons to be wary of the Voortrekkers was that he knew they were slaveholders. Even on their epic, thousand-mile migration, they remained dependent on blacks who were slaves, in fact if not in name. Observing the Boers of the Great Trek, a French traveler named Adulphe Delegorgue wrote:

> And then was it not allowable to bring away three or four young Kaffir boys or girls, taken by force from their families and who by qualified phrase were called apprentices in order to ward off the idea of slavery? These were destined for household service, but the farmers, as if ashamed to admit their weakness, though they wrangled about the possession of these beings, and bartered them as they would horses or oxen, were constantly repeating: "For my part I would rather not have them, but what would my wife say if I did not bring her some? It is so difficult to find servants in Natal."

These, then, are some of the ways the arrival of Piet Retief and the Great Trek must have appeared to Dingane and the people he led. None of them make Dingane's murder of Piet Retief and his men any less brutal. And none of them soften our picture of Dingane as an absolute monarch of a militaristic nation. But in the end, as a ruler trying to preserve the independence of his people, Dingane faced a painful situation from which there was no clear, honorable way out. He knew the Boers were already pouring into Natal, without waiting for any treaty. He knew they were bent on conquest and cared nothing for the lives of Zulus who occupied the land they wanted. He knew they practiced slavery, even if they called it something else. He correctly feared the mysterious power of their guns, and, to the end, was utterly unable to get any of his own. He knew that his only possible weapons against their muskets were trickery and surprise attack. And so he acted. His only alternative would have been a partial or total surrender—or perhaps to lead his people on a Great Trek of their own, in search of some unknown new land away from the white men's guns.

To get to the site of Umgungundhlovu today, you must turn off the toll road onto a smaller highway. This road threads through a political patchwork, as if you are continually driving from the First World to the Third and back again.

Africans own only some 14 percent of South Africa's land. Basically these are the same patches of land onto which Africans were crowded by the turn of the century, after whites had seized the best farmland for themselves. In those days, these territories were called "Native Reserves"; in the 1960s, when they were first given the apparatus of self-government, they became known as "Bantustans"; today they are called "homelands"; tomorrow they will doubtless be called something else. In recent years, a major function of these territories has been to let the South African government claim that millions of Africans whom the world thinks are living in South Africa are really citizens of other countries. You see, they're really not South Africans at all, the argument goes; they have their own self-governing states. So why should they have anything to complain about?

Few of these pseudo-states, however, are one contiguous piece of land. KwaZulu, the homeland for the Zulu people, is some two dozen separate bits of territory, strewn across Natal's white-owned farmland like an archipelago. The highway keeps going from island to sea to island.

In the white sea, where blacks are not allowed to own land, farms are large, with stately trees lining the driveways, and wooden archway gates emblazoned with the farm's name: Balbrougie, Fleetways, Prospect, Springfield, Grasslands, Everglades, Strathview. Few people are in sight, white or black. In these wide green fields are wire-tied bundles of hay left by baling machines.

But each time the road crosses into an island of KwaZulu, it is as if I've passed from England to Africa: suddenly there is less green; the cattle are thinner. The land is much more rocky, with big piles of reddish boulders removed from the soil. Less than 20 percent of KwaZulu is arable, but its density of cattle and population is many times that of the surrounding white-owned land.

One result of the overgrazing is severe erosion, which sometimes has stripped the soil down to bedrock. You can see the scarlike jagged ditches through which more than 200 million tons of red KwaZulu topsoil are annually washed away into the sea.

I pass villages of thousands of wattle and daub huts. Sometimes the houses have roofs of thatch, sometimes of corrugated metal held down against the wind by heavy stones. Scrawny goats wander along the road, and many children have the big-bellied look of the malnourished. Because of the tremendous overcrowding that results from blacks being forced off white-owned farmland, scholars believe that Africans living in rural homelands like KwaZulu today have a sparser and less healthy diet than people who lived in the same less-crowded villages 150 years ago.

On the car radio, Radio South Africa's white channel reports a hamburger-eating contest in Durban. A talk show host interviews two women who've written a book about traveling with children in South Africa: it's *so* important to book *separate* rooms for yourself and your children when you travel, they tell us, for better sleep and privacy. A wine industry representative talks about new "little, interesting wines" from small vineyards. The weekly show, "In Your Garden" today gives advice on "the much requested subject of lilies." A newscaster reports a controversy over shark nets protecting the Durban beaches. Are they killing too many other fish? A spokesman for the Shark Board vigorously answers the critics.

As I turn off the road at the site of Umgungundhlovu, I am thinking again of the two radically different histories of what took place here. Today, I wonder, at the spot where Dingane had his headquarters and Piet Retief met his death, which version will I hear?

"From America? Aha! Mike Tyson!" says a Zulu man who is the first person I run into. He explains that this site is now owned by the Dutch Reformed Church. This is the church to which most Afrikaners, including almost all high government officials, belong. There is a mission station, a church, a museum of Voortrekker and Zulu relics, and a school for teaching the deaf; he shows me a classroom where black women are learning to sew, and tells them in sign language that I've come from across the ocean.

The church itself has two curving wings that come out from the sides and sweep forward. A white woman mission official explains to me: "The church has a symbolic shape: it's based on the ox-head formation of attack that was instituted by King Shaka. The church is built like that because it's also attacking constantly—paganism and the human heart, to win it for Christ." Shields and spears are worked into the latticework pattern of the church's doors. These, too, are symbolic. "You slide these doors open"—pushing the weapons aside—"and then you are free to enter, to hear the message of reconciliation." There are no muskets in the lattice design.

From here it is a short walk to Hlomo Amabuta, the Hill of Execution, where there is now a lectern, for speechmaking on patriotic occasions, such as the visit here a few weeks ago of one of those ox-wagon caravans commemorating the Great Trek. A monument is inscribed in Afrikaans: THE GRAVE OF PIET RETIEF AND 70 BURGERS. REST IN PEACE. Pilgrims have left half a dozen wreaths.

Nearby, across a stream and rocky ground dotted with cactus plants with spadelike leaves, is the site of Dingane's capital. Archeologists have excavated the foundations of some of those two thousand huts, and several have been reconstructed. There are few visitors among these ruins today, but each one is given a black guide. Surely, I think, as a Zulu my guide will have a different outlook than the missionary at the church.

She is a teenage girl with a nervous, uneasy frown. But as she stiffly recites a long, memorized spiel, it becomes painfully obvious that it has been written for her by the white missionaries. She repeats the story of trust and betrayal, savagery and civilization, entirely from the Trekkers' point of view: these innocent Christians made the tragic mistake of sitting down to eat with the pagan, deceitful Dingane. She ends, "And as Retief enjoyed himself at the feast, Dingane stood up and said: 'Kill the wizards!'" This, then, is the final conquest, where the conquered repeat the conquerors' version of history.

Immediately after killing Piet Retief and his men here at Umgungundhlovu, Dingane had to act swiftly. His only hope of making a successful surprise attack on the rest of the white invaders spreading out across Natal was to do so before they got word of Retief's fate. At noon on the very morning Retief and his companions were battered to death, Dingane sent his entire army in the direction Retief had come from. After a running journey of several days, scouts located a twenty-five-mile stretch of Boer encampments. Dingane's Zulu regiments spread out, hid behind hills, and waited a few days for a moonless night. The Boers had no idea they were there.

At 1:00 a.m. on February 17, 1838, the Zulus attacked. Entire extended families of Voortrekkers were almost completely wiped out: the Liebenbergs, the Roussows, the Bezuidenhuits. "Oh! Dreadful, dreadful night! Wherein so much martyred blood was shed," wrote Anna Steenkamp, a sister of Piet Retief and a survivor of the massacre.

> . . . [The dead were] hurled into an awful eternity by the assagais of those bloodthirsty heathens. . . . Oh! It was unbearable for flesh and blood to behold the frightful spectacle the following morning. In one wagon were found fifty dead, and blood flowed from the seam of the tent-sail down to the lowest part. . . . On all sides one saw tears flowing and heard people weeping by the plundered wagons, painted with blood; tents and beds were torn to shreds. . . .

The attackers stabbed children in nightclothes in their mothers' arms, and mutilated the bodies of the dead. When the Trekkers counted their losses they found the dead included 41 men, 56 women, 185 children, and—in these reckonings, slaves had no age or sex or exact number—around 200 black "servants."

The Zulus had, however, underestimated how many Boers had come over the mountains, and they had not found all of the Voortrekker camps. Most Trekkers were camped elsewhere, and they survived. They mourned their dead and planned their revenge on the killers of this new set of martyrs. The night of this massacre has taken a central place in Afrikaner history books alongside the death of Piet Retief and has become known as the Great Murder. Two nearby brooks were renamed the Groot Moordspruit and

Klein Moordspruit, the Great and Small Murder-streams. When
eventually the Trekkers built a settlement in the area, they called
it Weenen, or "the place of weeping."

At Weenen today there is a peaceful, tree-shaded cemetery with
Voortrekker headstones. On the morning I visit the town, people
are grieving, but not over these graves. The battle, however, is
still about what was fought over some 150 years ago—land.

Weenen today is a town of refugees. They are black farmworkers
and their families, evicted from some of those white farms with
elegant names and rows of majestic trees lining their driveways.
The workers have often lived and worked on those farms for
several generations. Many of the dispossessed are living in something called the Weenen Emergency Camp, which I visit several
miles outside of town, in a treeless valley covered with thornbushes. Housing at the Emergency Camp is mud-stained white
tents, in rows, with black numbers painted on their sides. The tent
floors are dirt. Stones hold down their side flaps. A rectangular
ditch around each one provides some drainage, but in heavy rains
the tents still flood. Behind the tents I can see privies, whose
corrugated tin walls don't even reach chest level.

Back in town, outside the Magistrate's Court, some fifty African
farmworkers, who haven't yet been evicted but are about to be,
are sitting quietly on logs and on the ground in the shade of sweet-
smelling eucalyptus trees. The women and men sit separately. I
am here this morning with a white lawyer and some black law
students, who have come to take statements from these people.

Life for black farmworkers in South Africa is hard to begin with:
hardly any belong to unions; health and safety regulations do not
apply to them; and here in Natal there has been a grisly epidemic
of birth defects from agribusiness use of toxic herbicides such as
Agent Orange, which are banned in many other countries. The
rate of poisoning of black farmworkers by such chemicals is estimated to be twenty times that in the United States. Added to
these troubles, since 1950 more than 1.5 million black farmworkers have been pushed off South Africa's white farms. These
farms are consolidating into ever larger units, like corporate agri-

business in the United States, and machines of all kinds are replacing human labor.

One set of recent mass evictions is in the thornveld country—land covered with thorn trees, used for cattle grazing—here around Weenen. A similar cluster is around Ladysmith, some forty miles away, where ten years ago a family named Shabalala was among thousands forced off the land. Joseph Shabalala and his three brothers went on to tour the world as the core of the singing group Ladysmith Black Mambazo, but for many years they returned to sing each year at Christmas for the refugees near their old homestead. "We are homeless . . ." goes one song, "strong winds destroy our home. . . ."

The people at Weenen this morning tell similar stories, but in the form of affidavits taken down under the trees by the law students:

29 November 1988. Client: Amos Majola. "On the first of September, 1988, the landowner, Mr. McIntosh, came to my kraal and demolished three of my four houses. . . . He came alone and threatened to come back and demolish the last house. There was no court order for eviction and he said nothing else and then left. (He had previously asked me to leave his farm). . . . Value of broken down houses: 1) R100, [$40] 2) R120, 3) R100. All possessions are now in the last house."

The Mr. McIntosh involved, who is trying to evict a number of the other people clustered in front of the courthouse today, is a former Member of Parliament for the liberal opposition. According to a Natal newspaper this week,

Mr. McIntosh . . . told *The Witness* the workers' claims were "grossly exaggerated."
. . . He denied that he had evicted any families but admitted that he had "terminated their services."

Tension around Weenen is high; white farmers have been shooting the dogs of black farmworkers who don't leave. Their attitude is summed up by the common Afrikaans phrase, *"Ek is die baas van my plaas"*—"I am the boss of my farm." I talk to one evicted farmworker waiting under the eucalyptus trees who has been living in a tent by the side of the road for eight months.

The lawyer appears before the magistrate inside the courthouse; outside, while the law students continue to take statements, women sing softly. With determined faces and bright-colored shawls and blankets around their shoulders, they intone the same words over and over. Someone translates:

> *They're going this way*
> *And that way,*
> *They are confused,*
> *The Boers are afraid.*

But not today, it appears. The lawyer finally emerges from the courthouse, still in the black robe attorneys wear for court appearances here, and gives a little speech to the people waiting under the trees. He explains that he has succeeded in having this group of evictions put off for two and a half months. But there is no chance of further victory, he warns, and people should use the time to plan where to go when they are forced off the farms. For most, the only choice is the Emergency Camp.

The gathering is over. The women ululate. Everyone shouts three times, shooting their fists in the air, *"Amandla . . . Ngawethu!"* ("Power to us") and *"Izwe . . . Lethu!"* ("The land is ours"). These words are familiar from political rallies, but they have a far more somber ring here, where those who speak them are about to lose their precarious foothold on the land. Gathering their coats and shawls, all of them slowly get to their feet, to begin the long walk back to the homes they must leave, in some cases ten to fifteen kilometers away.

The farmworkers all have put on their best clothes for today, even if it means wearing a thick winter coat for the long round-trip walk in the summer heat. Some of the men have jackets, cast off from the white farmers whose land they work. One man wears a coat much too small for him that must be from a farmer's son:

a teenager's school blazer with a red and gold crest on the breast pocket. In a different life, this coat must have adorned the chest of a senior at graduation, or whirled across the dance floor at a high school prom.

In piecing together what happened at Weenen, Umgungundhlovu, and elsewhere during the time the Voortrekkers invaded Natal, the evidence we have to look at is, as I have said, usually that left by white observers of black culture. But one of the most interesting figures of the time is a black man who made his livelihood as an observer of white culture, a sort of anthropologist in reverse. His story forms a curious footnote to that era.

When the prophet Makana organized his unsuccessful escape from Robben Island by whaleboat in 1820, one fellow prisoner in his boat was another Xhosa veteran of the fighting with the British, who spoke both English and Dutch. His name was Jakot Msimbiti, although he seems to have been known to the whites only by his first name, since it was similar to Jacob. After his escape and recapture, Jakot was sent back to Robben Island in chains.

Several years later, Jakot's skills as a linguist earned him freedom: he was taken off the island and put to work as an interpreter on board a Royal Navy survey ship, H.M.S. *Leven,* that headed a flotilla putting into bays and inlets along the east coast of Africa to make navigational charts. Jakot sailed as far as Mauritius and Madagascar. He heard the groans from the holds of slave ships being loaded in the swampy, fever-ridden harbor of what is today the Mozambican capital of Maputo. Jakot became almostly certainly the first African of his time to see firsthand the workings of British, Boer, and Portuguese imperialism. Not surprisingly, the experience gave him a violent distrust of white men.

Jakot was later transferred to an interpreter's post on a British ship bound on a trading expedition to the Zulu coast. There he was shipwrecked. He made his way to the royal court at Umgungundhlovu, and for the next decade made himself useful, first to Shaka and then to his successor Dingane, as an interpreter and an expert in the ways of the whites. The kings welcomed his advice, for traders and explorers were starting to nose around Natal with ominous frequency. Jakot repeatedly warned Dingane they were up to no good.

The whites hated Jakot, for they knew very well that he was warning Dingane against them. Captain Allen Gardiner wrote:

> He assured [Dingane] that a white man, assuming the character of a teacher or missionary, would arrive among them, and obtain permission to build a house; that, shortly after, he would be joined by one or two more white men; and, in the course of time, an army would enter his country, which would subvert his government, and eventually the white people would rule instead.

The traders bitterly protested to Dingane that Jakot was a troublesome agitator and shouldn't be trusted. In 1832, when the soldiers Jakot forecast hadn't arrived, Dingane had Jakot put to death. And then, one by one, to Dingane's horror, all the things that Jakot predicted began to happen—the missionaries, the houses, the invaders. By a decade after Jakot's death, the British Army was marching into Natal. Unlike the visions of the black prophets, all Jakot's predictions came true.

# Loyal Natives

After the bloody night of the Great Murder, the Natal Voortrekkers regrouped most of their wagons into more tightly fortified camps. They fought several skirmishes with the Zulus, and began to plan an expedition against Dingane. For the Boers, avenging the twin massacres of the Great Murder of Trekker families and the killing of Piet Retief and his men at Umgungundhlovu became an obsession. Their quest for revenge, which finally was to reach its climax at Blood River, would change the course of history in the region. But that was not to come until many months and many battles later. Meanwhile, Voortrekkers both in Natal and in other parts of South Africa warily continued to explore the new lands they had found.

Throughout 1838, ox wagons of the Great Trek creaked and jounced further into Natal. In October, three quarters of the way from the Drakensberg to the sea, one party of Trekkers came over a ridge and saw the Umsindusi River winding across an attractive bowl of land rimmed on all sides by green hills. They were taken with the beauty of the spot, pitched camp by the stream, and decided to make this their capital. Piet Retief had been murdered in February; the man who succeeded him as leader of the Natal Trekkers, Gert Maritz, had fallen ill and died in September, saying with his last breath, "Like Moses I have seen the Promised Land but shall not dwell in it." The Trekkers named their new city after both men: Pietermaritzburg.

Here, for a few short years until the British decided that *they* wanted Natal, flourished the capital of Natalia, or the Free Province of New Holland in South East Africa. The town was a simple one, but for people who had been living in covered wagons for three years, it must have seemed luxurious. The new capital's two most important buildings were the Volksraad, or legislature of the Trekkers' republic, and the church.

As always, the Trekkers were supremely confident that their conquests had God's approval. And so there was a big celebration when the church at Pietermaritzburg opened its doors in 1841. Its first preacher later went on to minister to other congregations scattered across the areas where Voortrekkers had settled, officially becoming the founder of the Dutch Reformed Church in three of modern South Africa's four provinces. A dour, granite-faced man with a long beard, he stares solemnly out of old photographs surrounded by a large brood of his equally somber-looking children. His name was Daniel Lindley, and he was, surprisingly, an American, from Athens, Ohio.

Lindley had come to Africa as a missionary in 1835. But he found preaching to the Africans hard going. The Voortrekkers, on the other hand, were eager for an ordained minister, for there were none on the Trek. Writing home, Lindley described his change of flock:

> I do sincerely believe that the cheapest, speediest, easiest way to convert the heathen here is to convert the *white ones* first . . . or we labor in vain to make Christians of the blacks. . . . [T]he influence of the whites, if evil, will be tremendous. . . . To their own vices the aborigines will add those of the white men, and then make themselves two-fold more the children of hell than they were before.

Lindley spent almost all his adult life in South Africa, where the town of Lindley is named after him today. He learned Afrikaans and proved himself to the pioneers as a marksman, swimmer, and good judge of horses. Fresh from an America in the midst of its own Indian wars, he shared the Trekkers' faith in white supremacy. "He did not humbug himself or anybody else," a contemporary wrote of Lindley, "by saying that the Ethiopians or any other niggers could be washed white."

Pietermaritzburg is still the capital of Natal. The meeting place of the Volksraad is now the site of City Hall, a red rococo structure with balconies and cupolas and stained-glass windows; it is said to be the largest all-brick building south of the equator. Hundreds of air-conditioned tour buses pass through Pietermaritzburg and its surroundings each year, bringing white vacationers to look at the restored Victorian houses, the iron hitching rails, the Annual Horse and Carriage Society Show, and to smell the azaleas in the famous formal gardens. On the day I arrive here from Umgun-gundhlovu, stamp collectors at a convention are giving each other prizes for distinguished achievement in philately. Some of the tourists and convention-goers visit the small white church where Daniel Lindley once preached. It is now part of a museum about the Voortrekkers, filled with lace handkerchiefs, declarations and proclamations, Bibles, and muskets.

When the Trekkers first ruled Natal, it was by force of those muskets. But the British, who took over several years later, came to realize over time, just as they had in India, that more sophis-ticated means were needed to keep the white hold on this territory. It was they who set up a key mechanism of control that has flour-ished throughout South Africa ever since, nowhere more starkly, I discover, than in Pietermaritzburg today. For the metaphor that best describes it, one must move two blocks from Lindley's church to a tall stone obelisk outside Pietermaritzburg's City Hall. The obelisk is inscribed:


THE
NATAL CARBINEERS
MOURN THE LOSS
OF THEIR COMRADES WHO FELL
WHILST TAKING PART
IN SUPPRESSING THE REBELLION
OF THE HLUBI TRIBE

UNDER LANGALIBALELE
AT BUSHMAN'S PASS
NOV 4TH
1873
"GENTLY THEY LAID THEM UNDERNEATH THE SOD
AND LEFT THEM WITH THEIR FAME, THEIR COUNTRY
AND THEIR GOD"

ROBERT HENRY ERSKINE
EDWIN BOND
CHARLES DAVID POTTERHILL
OF THE
NATAL CARBINEERS
ALSO
ELIJAH KAMBULE
AND KATANA
LOYAL NATIVES

The last two words are the key. South Africa's whites are now only about 13 percent of the country's population. By the year 2000, they will be roughly 10 percent. The problem they have always faced is how, with those small numbers, to dominate the rest. A major strategy over the years has been the use of "loyal natives"—who are willing to serve as policemen, as army support troops, as minor governmental officials, and occasionally as figureheads promoting the illusion that blacks are exercising real power. These are the people who have been pressed into service to suppress black rebellions, whether by the Hlubi tribe in 1873 or by the African National Congress today.

Today, safely out of sight of the white tourists crowding the graceful nineteenth-century arcades and narrow lanes of Pietermaritzburg's downtown, the city's black townships are by far the bloodiest battleground in South Africa. This war is something of a test case, from the government's point of view, of how successfully it can continue the century-old strategy of using black force to contain the black revolt. It is a battle that pits the latest wave of rebellion against the government's most important black loyalist—a man who is, ironically, a direct descendant of Dingane.

More than 2500 people have died so far in Pietermaritzburg's civil war, and a far greater number have been injured. More than ten thousand homes have been destroyed. In one particularly bloody six-month period in 1987–88, 528 people, or nearly 100 a month, died in the Pietermaritzburg area—almost two thirds of all people killed in political violence in South Africa during that time. In 1988, more than twice as many people died in political violence in Pietermaritzburg as in all of Lebanon.

On one side in this struggle are sympathizers of the United Democratic Front, the major coalition of opposition groups of the 1980s, and of its most important ally, the Congress of South African Trade Unions. Both the UDF and COSATU strongly support the one-person/one-vote demand of the African National Congress.

On the other side are the forces of the black politician on whom many white businessmen and government strategists have pinned their hopes: Chief Mangosuthu Gatsha Buthelezi, Chief Minister of the KwaZulu homeland, Minister of Police of KwaZulu, and the great-great-grandson of Dingane. Buthelezi is also President of Inkatha, his own political party cum militia, which holds all the seats in KwaZulu's rubber-stamp legislature and operates with the support of the South African government.

Although the conflict had been simmering at a lower level for some time, Pietermaritzburg only erupted into open warfare in May 1987. At that time the UDF and COSATU called a two-day general strike in protest against a whites-only election. More than 90 percent of Pietermaritzburg's 400,000 Africans took part— one of the highest turnouts in the country. This was a humiliating defeat for Buthelezi's Inkatha, which was campaigning against the strike. Hundreds of club-wielding Inkatha members then began raiding townships dominated by UDF supporters. The UDF people fought back, sometimes making brutal raids of their own, or murdering or mutilating Inkatha supporters in UDF-controlled areas. As the violence has escalated, gangsters, feuding clans and people with personal grudges to settle have joined in. As in Lebanon, the conflict has now become so deeply rooted that no truce will easily be able to stop it. The fighters, victims, and refugees tend to be young men, and in Pietermaritzburg's black township high schools, the girls now outnumber the boys.

Chief Buthelezi has used his control of the KwaZulu government—pensions, housing, school admissions, scholarships, hospital jobs, and the like—to build up Inkatha. He has said openly that Inkatha membership is taken into account in civil service promotions. The organization claims nearly two million members, but few people believe it. And many members are there because of coercion. "If Inkatha had wanted to make friends," says Pietermaritzburg mayor Mark Cornell, "they should have gone and helped the people instead of going to them at three o'clock in the morning and saying, 'Sign this [membership] card or we'll kill you.'"

Much is riding on the outcome of the bloody struggle in Pietermaritzburg's townships. The more than 6 million Zulus are South Africa's largest single ethnic group. Pietermaritzburg is one of the country's half-dozen largest cities. Unless Buthelezi can show that its African population is loyal to Inkatha, he cannot claim to speak for the Zulus. Without that claim, he cannot be the key player that South African business and the government want him to be.

Buthelezi's role is an unusual one. As Chief Minister of KwaZulu, the country's most populous homeland, he is the top black collaborator with apartheid. He has urged the movement to compromise on its demand for one person/one vote. Years ago, the government jumped him over an older brother to make him chief of the Buthelezi subtribe, and ever since then it has installed him in successive positions on the way up the ladder to his present one. Pretoria subsidizes $80 million worth of KwaZulu's budget, and staffs key posts in its administration. For much of the 1980s, dozens of other black political organizations were banned from even having a meeting in someone's kitchen, but Pretoria has always happily allowed Buthelezi to address stadiums full of Inkatha faithful. Inkatha is also permitted a paramilitary training camp where new members wear uniforms and are divided into sections, companies, and brigades.

Buthelezi has carefully mixed the trappings of modern power with those that evoke the Zulu military tradition. He arrives at rallies by helicopter or in a convoy of a dozen Mercedes cars, but his bodyguards carry *assegais* and shields. He employs a public relations team of white former journalists, but wears the traditional leopard skin of a Zulu chief.

Inkatha is in effect for Zulus only, and Pretoria loves that kind of nationalism, for it emphasizes rather than minimizes ethnic differences among Africans. By contrast, organizations like the UDF and COSATU, though overwhelmingly black, are deeply committed to the principle of non-racialism, have people of all colors in key positions, and vigorously oppose any tribalism. In fact, most black tribes are far less different from each other than Pretoria's divide-and-rule strategists would wish: a Zulu and a Xhosa can understand each other's speech; an English speaker and an Afrikaans speaker cannot.

At the same time as he is an integral part of the system, Buthelezi makes certain formal gestures of opposition. He loudly refuses the official "independence" Pretoria would like to give KwaZulu. (Although not recognized outside of South Africa, four of the ten homelands are nominally independent countries, complete with coats of arms, flags, and national anthems.) Inkatha has borrowed the African National Congress colors of black, green, and gold. And when making speeches, Buthelezi denounces apartheid as vigorously as anyone. But none of this bothers shrewder heads in Pretoria—for if he did not do these things, they know, he would lose what limited credibility he has as an African leader, both at home and overseas. "For white South Africa," wrote the late Steve Biko, "it is extremely important to have a man like Buthelezi speaking and sounding the way he is doing."

Pietermaritzburg's war zone begins only a few minutes' drive from the Victorian buildings of the city's downtown. Along the way, the road passes the riot police headquarters, which is surrounded by a wire fence. Although it is early morning, already a knot of women are gathered waiting to visit prisoners at the jail. In the building's parking lot are rows of unmarked vans. Some have opaque windows, through which informers can finger people for arrest. Some have no license plates. Some have different numbers on the front and rear plates.

As soon as I reach the city's African townships, the roads are of red dirt. Women walking along them carry on their heads jugs of water from communal taps. A billboard in Zulu advertises a brand of lard. Cocks are crowing. A yellow police truck speeds along a road, raising a plume of dust. Here and there in a vacant lot is a house trailer flying the South African flag, a mobile temporary station of the SAP, the South African Police. Though hilltops still rim the horizon, these lowlands have no nineteenth-century rose gardens; instead, the pervasive rotten-egg stink of hydrogen sulfide from a tannery fills the air—even South Africa's smells have been relocated according to the Group Areas Act.

Almost anywhere you go in these townships, you can find sites of recent killings and a mood of fear and despair. In one home I visit in Nhlazatshe, a COSATU union member was murdered by an Inkatha vigilante squad at 2:00 a.m. recently, and his house damaged. The window frame is still charred black, the empty space covered by a flap of black plastic.

In Ashdown, a strongly pro-UDF area, the Ashdown Advice Office shares a simple corrugated metal shed with a shop that refills cylinders of cooking gas. On the wall are photographs of funerals. As rain drums on the metal roof and turns the road outside to mud, I sit and talk with two fieldworkers in the office. Both are soft-spoken, articulate black men in their early twenties. Like many people in Pietermaritzburg, they don't want their names used. And, though they're eager to talk, they don't want their voices on my tape recorder, in case the tape is seized at a police roadblock and turned over to Inkatha.

"A lot of our people are being killed, chased from their place," one explains. People have been fleeing to Ashdown when Inkatha squads attack their homes in other townships. "Our houses are four-room houses. We haven't got enough space for refugees. We find sometimes that twenty people are staying in one room. When people come here they are very much stranded. Often the clothes they are wearing are the only possessions they have."

The Advice Office keeps track of how much rent the refugees

are paying, to make sure they are not overcharged. And it distributes clothing. Though they are poor themselves, township residents have donated a stack of old clothes and tennis shoes, piled against the wall in one corner, for the refugees.

"Inkatha always comes with more than a hundred people. They even attacked the school. They carry sticks, rifles, homemade guns. You can't predict when it will happen. It could happen now."

Do police ever stop the attacks?

"No. You'll find the Inkatha people just go right past those mobile police vans and attack here. The police *pretend* to be interested in stopping the attacks. But they'll disperse Ashdown people with tear gas after the Inkatha people have left. Inkatha attacked a sportsground near here, where people were playing football [soccer]. They got a guy at the bus stop who was sleeping, drunk. They killed him right in front of the SAP."

A photo on the wall shows three children standing next to a coffin of their elder brother. He was Zenzele Xulu, the breadwinner of his family—the parents are both dead. He was killed by Inkatha "during the war." His sister, the secretary of the Ashdown Youth Organization, a UDF affiliate, was abducted by Inkatha in another township and brought to Ashdown: "They were stabbing her all the way. They killed her here."

The three surviving children "are scared most of the time. Because they don't know how long they will live. They have to live on other people's mercy. They have to go to the neighbors to ask for food. They come here and ask for twenty cents to buy a candle for the house."

The Advice Office fieldworkers are trying to raise money to pay off the brother's funeral expenses. They show me the bill:

### Msimang's Funeral Undertakers

300.00—coffin
20.00—gown
9.00—cross
140.00—cemetery fees
200.00—services
194.00—2 buses

39.48—GST [General Sales Tax]

R902.48 [$360]
R302.48—balance owing

Vusi N., an official of a COSATU trade union, lives in another township. A short man with an intense, deliberate way of speaking, he bends his head down but still looks me in the eye, as he leans forward across a table to tell his story:

"At about a quarter to six in the morning they marched into our area. My wife woke me up. The women were shaking, waving their hands, saying, 'They're coming to kill all the people who won't join Inkatha!' They were coming down the hill in three rows. There were about fifty of them. They burned about fifteen houses. They were carrying sticks, guns, axes. Two people were killed. Shot. Both of them shot.

"When they arrived," N. goes on, "I see them hitting people, asking, 'Where is UDF?' The youth they are hiding. The people are running up to the hills. I was inside locking my house. I hear the guns shooting, *bof!* I never run to the hills. My children say you mustn't run away. But no one saw me. After that incident I know that my name was on a list."

Two hours later, N. says, the police finally arrived—*after* Inkatha had left. Knowing he was a marked man, N. has left this township, and is one of Pietermaritzburg's thirty thousand refugees; he and his wife and their five children now share one room in someone else's house.

Did the police arrest any Inkatha people after this skirmish?

"They don't arrest Inkatha people. What *they* do, Inkatha, is they go to the police and they say, 'Listen, this one was doing this,' and then the police will come and arrest a UDF member. But now when myself I go and I say, 'These people have done this, they killed this person and that one,' they won't arrest them. The people now are scared to go and be a witness for a case because they see that if Inkatha knows you are one of the official witnesses, in the night they will go and kill you. Or in the daytime, even."

At least four such potential witnesses against Inkatha have been murdered. "As soon as someone decides: O.K., they will testify," says a Pietermaritzburg human rights worker I talk to, "then they have to leave the area. It means changing your life." Attempts by COSATU and UDF lawyers to use the court system to restrain Inkatha have had little success, since the government so strongly supports the vigilantes. Seven Inkatha branch chairmen in Pietermaritzburg have been identified in affidavits as participating in violence; not one has been charged. After forty-three members of an Inkatha squad armed with machetes, knives, and sticks were briefly arrested on their way to attack the local COSATU office, the charges were dropped. These vigilantes would never even have been arrested if they had not strayed into the white business district.

Most important, in the last few years in Pietermaritzburg, more than one thousand people have been put into preventive detention—locked up for anywhere from a month to several years, charged with no crime. This is business as usual for South Africa. But the significant thing in Pietermaritzburg is that nearly all these political detainees have been COSATU and UDF supporters, including many senior leaders. Only a handful of Inkatha members have been detained, and they very briefly; the government has detained no Inkatha leaders at all.

The police have made no secret of their support for Inkatha. In January 1988, police and army vehicles escorted an Inkatha raid into Ashdown; eleven deaths followed. Lawyers have dossiers of more than two dozen other instances of Inkatha-police collaboration. The local security chief, police brigadier Jack Buchner, even went on national television to explain that the police were working to "return" control of the townships to their "traditional" leaders.

There have been repeated peace negotiations in the Pietermaritzburg war, but the South African government for years made sure they would go nowhere. On four different occasions, Minister of Law and Order Adriaan Vlok has restricted, jailed, or house-arrested UDF leaders just as they were about to sit down for negotiations with Inkatha. He has not hesitated, however, to meet with Buthelezi, and at one point held a joint press conference with him. And so the killings have gone on.

□

The accretion of details of threats and violence and killing that people in Pietermaritzburg describe to me is almost numbing. For surely the worst kind of terror is a war like this, where there is no clear front line, no clear zone of safety, and where the time and place you are most likely to be attacked is in your own bed in the middle of the night. How does one live under such circumstances? Brave words and defiant gestures count for little. Perhaps the greatest heroes in Pietermaritzburg are those who merely try to live normal lives, against all the pressures to leave, to change sides, or to become paralyzed from fear.

I find myself thinking about these things as I talk to the local UDF president, Rev. Simon Gqubule, the head of a Methodist seminary on the city's outskirts. At the time I'm in Pietermaritzburg, Gqubule is banned, which means, among other things, that it is illegal for him to talk to journalists. But he sees me anyway, without hesitation. A quiet man of great presence, he speaks slowly and forms his sentences carefully, as if each must hold up under searching cross-examination.

All three of Gqubule's children have spent time in detention, one for the first time at the age of fourteen. At one point during the recent upheavals, they were all behind bars at the same time. But instead of dwelling on this, Gqubule talks of the other young people who were in jail as well: "I got an opportunity to go around to the homes of the other children, and I was able to minister to them, which was a new area of ministry for me."

On the walls of Gqubele's office are framed photographs of groups of clergy at church conventions. On his bookshelves are titles like *A Theology of Auschwitz* and *Evil and the God of Love.* Such questions weigh on him heavily. He talks about how he tries to preach against the taking of revenge. "How can we as Christians go and kill?" He says how moved he was at a recent funeral for someone killed in the violence when a UDF official, "this young fellow who had just come out of detention, pleaded with the people and said, 'Don't hit back.' "

Gqubule's banning order prevents him from addressing political meetings, so it becomes difficult to talk young "comrades" into not retaliating for an Inkatha attack. "There's been so much killing," he says sadly. "Far more than you see reported in the papers. You know we've had some terrible things. People were coming out from the cemetery after one of these funerals, and the Inkatha people just stabbed or gunned down people. Children. Young boys and girls."

At one point, Inkatha demanded that Gqubule and another faculty member leave the seminary within six days or it would be burned to the ground. More than one hundred armed warriors marched to the seminary and repeated the threat. The place was in an uproar: the staff held emergency meetings, students were sent home. "I didn't call the police," Gqubule says, "because I knew they wouldn't come." Instead, he simply decided to stay.

The appointed day came. Inkatha did not return. The seminary reopened. "I was so scared, you know," Gqubule says in a gentle voice that reverberates long after I have left him. "They say Christians shouldn't fear death, but . . ."

Although most deaths have been in Pietermaritzburg and its surroundings, violence between Chief Buthelezi's militia and its opponents has now gone on for a decade throughout Natal. More people have died in political violence in Natal in the last four years than in Northern Ireland in the last twenty. Various public opinion surveys show Buthelezi slowly losing support among urban Zulus over the last ten years; this seems only to have driven Inkatha to new heights of violence. When Inkatha didn't like the politics of the play *Asinamali* (it later played on Broadway), which revolves around a rent strike, its vigilantes burst into the theater and killed the promoter. When students at the University of Zululand staged a peaceful protest against Buthelezi's plans to speak at the university, hundreds of Inkatha members carrying spears, shields, clubs, and battleaxes rampaged through the campus, killing five people and injuring one hundred and thirteen. After Durban civil rights lawyer Victoria Mxenge was assassinated a few years ago, several busloads of armed Inkatha warriors charged the funeral, killing seventeen and injuring more than one hundred, while South African Police in Land Rovers and Casspir armored cars looked on. When some of *those* victims were buried a few weeks later, the mourners were attacked by more busloads of vigilantes, this time led by three members of the Inkatha Central Committee. Buthelezi can flaunt his paramilitary power so freely because of who his backers are. The South African government is not the only force behind him; big business loves him as well. He praises free enterprise at every opportunity. And he vigorously opposes sanctions against South Africa. Small wonder that he has the support of the powerful Cane Growers' Association (sugar is Natal's biggest crop), whose head has called him an "asset" that should not be "lost." And when asked why the country's largest corporation, the Anglo-American Corporation of South Africa, supported Buthelezi, its chairman at the time, Gavin Relly, told a reporter: "You can't expect us to run away from the single black leader who says exactly what we think."

Big business is particularly happy with Buthelezi because, in an effort to draw support away from the more militant COSATU, he has organized his own labor union federation. But despite business and government support for this effort, and, it is rumored, some Israeli help as well, he has had little success as a labor leader. You don't have to look far to see the reason: none of the people he first installed as top officials of his United Workers Union of South Africa were workers; they were businessmen. The president was a personnel manager at a large sugar conglomerate owned by Anglo-American. The general secretary was a former president of the black chamber of commerce. The treasurer was a private investor and a director of an insurance firm.

Building up paramilitary groups like Inkatha is a favorite counterinsurgency tactic the world over. Inkatha is by far the most powerful of the vigilante militias the South African government has encouraged, but groups like it exist in many of the ten black homelands. In the KwaNdebele homeland, for instance, I have seen deep, ridged, crisscross scars on the back of a young man *sjamboked* by the notoriously brutal Mbokhoto vigilantes. To foster similar conservative vigilante groups in the black townships of big cities, the police have apparently been arming certain criminal gangs. A long-time Soweto gang named Kabasa has now acquired automatic weapons and tear gas, almost certainly from police arsenals.

Besides being an extremely sophisticated use of "loyal natives" to suppress revolts, supporting Inkatha serves Pretoria in another way as well: propaganda. Because most of the killing in a place like Pietermaritzburg is done by blacks, it allows government spokespeople to shake their heads sadly over "black-on-black violence." Which implies, of course, that these volatile people aren't ready for all the freedoms you mushy-headed liberals overseas want for them. It also implies that the fighting is somehow between rival tribes—even though in Natal, both the government-backed Inkatha forces and their UDF opponents are almost all Zulus.

With dismaying predictability, the American press falls for the line about black-on-black violence. Two months after my visit to Pietermaritzburg, a long *New York Times* story described the conflict in the city. Only one paragraph out of thirty-three made even the slightest reference to police support of Inkatha, and then only to someone's charge that this had happened in one particular case. There was no mention of the Inkatha gangs escorted by police armored cars, no mention of the government's failure to press charges against any Inkatha attackers, no mention of how the government sabotaged the peace talks, no mention that more than a thousand Pietermaritzburg UDF activists have been jailed, and less than two dozen from Inkatha. The headline read, of course: IT'S BLACK AGAINST BLACK IN SOUTH AFRICAN PROVINCE.

A few days after I move on from Pietermaritzburg, I hear a program on the government radio celebrating the city's 150th anniversary. It is a collage of voices, almost all of them white. "It's a city of flowers," says one. "I'm very fond of it. I've been here since 1933. And I'm happy to be a senior citizen here today because they look after us very well."

"I've always enjoyed its *setting*," says another voice. "Its setting is marvelous. You can stand in the middle of Pietermaritzburg and look in any of the four main directions and see green hills."

"It's very British," chimes in another resident. "One of the most striking aspects of Pietermaritzburg is the wonderful people. I'd like my children to grow up here."

# "A Balanced View"

As I see or hear things like that radio program, I begin to understand that just as there are two rival versions of the Great Trek period of South Africa's past, so, too, are there two contending versions of its present.

One version is the present in which I find myself as I continue traveling around the country after leaving Pietermaritzburg. My head is filled with stories of prison, beatings, midnight vigilante raids, police armored cars standing by while Inkatha gangs club someone to death. Visiting black townships, I imagine more such stories behind every fearful glance or locked door.

The other version of the present is that presented by the government on the radio and on the TV screen. At the time I leave Pietermaritzburg, the death toll in the Inkatha-UDF war there is averaging fifteen to twenty people a week. I begin watching for news of this on the government-controlled TV. The hour-long evening news is in English one night and Afrikaans the next; I watch on the English nights for most of my remaining three weeks in South Africa. I count exactly one reference, of one sentence, to these battles. "Eleven people were killed in violence in Natal," the newscaster says, reading a list of headlines, and that's it. I wait for elaboration, but there is none. Soon the two white co-anchors are bidding each other farewell in the American fashion—"Good night, Gillian" "Good night, John"—and the show is over.

All totalitarian societies tend to use the powerful tool of television to bolster those in power, whether by praising a Great and Glorious Leader, or, in the more subtle South African version, by seldom showing anyone *other* than those in power. Half a dozen or more cabinet ministers appear on the news each night, it seems; one survey some years ago found South African Cabinet ministers making ten times as many such appearances as anyone from the opposition—even the opposition in the all-white Parliament. But TV in South Africa has an additional all-important function as well: denial. Denial not of the right of one side of a struggle to be heard, but denial, most of the time, that any struggle even exists. This is what makes TV here so eerie to watch.

The country I see on television while I am in South Africa is that country of white dreams again, the land of the summer folk, Sunny South Africa. There is a token black reporter or interview subject here and there, but usually the proportion of faces on the screen suggests a society 85 percent white. And, except for car accidents, certainly not one experiencing much bloodshed. On the news one night, for example, a twenty-minute feature looks at the country's airports. Are the instrument landing systems as up to date as they should be? Is the new international terminal building at Cape Town underutilized? Animals are popular: we see the oxen pulling wagons commemorating the Great Trek; we see white schoolchildren presenting a birthday cake to a dolphin in the Port Elizabeth Oceanarium and singing "Happy Birthday." And we hear about the tragedy of ill-cared-for pets. "If you go away on holiday and leave your pet with friends, *please* be sure to leave them the phone number of your veterinarian."

During my visit South Africa is negotiating the end of the long war in Angola and Namibia, and the powerful and ambitious Foreign Minister, Roelof "Pik" Botha, is on the screen almost daily. We see him upbeat and jubilant at a press conference with his unsmiling Angolan counterpart. Botha tells the rest of Africa that South Africa is eliminating discrimination and deserves to be accepted. Addressing the people of the whole continent, he calls them "my African brothers."

Aside from such moments, on TV the world abroad is as distant as one of those blobs on the horizon of that famous *New Yorker* drawing of the foreshortened globe as seen from Manhattan. For the South African Broadcasting Corporation, the rest of the world exists only when it shows a positive interest in South Africa. One SABC newscast has a long segment about Pat Robertson, who is making a trip to South Africa to do *his* TV show. We see Robertson interviewing his old friend Chief Buthelezi; we see him talking with a former mayor of Soweto who says, "I think South Africa is the most exciting country in the whole world"; and we see him meeting lions and giant turtles in a game reserve. South Africa is a land of many groups, Robertson says, but "people of goodwill are the dominant group in this country." He declares that "a return to the oppressive racial policies of the past is unthinkable." The SABC correspondent praises him for presenting "a balanced view."

When it comes to entertainment shows, the most popular ones are our own: "The Cosby Show," "Magnum, P.I.," "Hill Street Blues." Some have been dubbed, like the recycled "Misdaad in Miami" and "Die Strate van San Francisco." I watch, fascinated, as black and white cops joke with each other in Afrikaans on Florida beaches and California streets. What is going on here? Why, in this most influential of all media, is a shrewd and powerful government deciding to show all this interracial camaraderie? And to a TV audience both white and black?

*Explanation #1* (offered by a liberal opposition Member of Parliament): the government is softening up the white population, preparing them for the inevitable negotiations and power-sharing between blacks and whites in South Africa's future. Also, one might add, the Huxtables aren't really that threatening, for they are still clearly living in a white-dominated world.

*Explanation #2* (which applies in all countries): TV is the most powerful sedative there is. It doesn't matter what you show. When people are watching TV, they're not plotting revolution. This is all too true. At one point, I spend an evening at the house of a black activist and prison veteran; but our conversation fades in and out frustratingly as his eyes keep being drawn, as if by magnetism, to the new TV set his wife is watching at the other side of the room.

*Explanation #3* (my own): the government knows people confuse TV with reality. After all, Marcus Welby used to get hundreds of thousands of letters from viewers asking for medical advice. This, then, is the real purpose of welcoming the Huxtable family and their like onto South African TV screens. The subliminal message flickering across the country's living rooms is: *Relax. There is no need for drastic change. It has already happened.*

Besides watching TV, I also browse at newsstands. I probably should be analyzing the ebb and flow of censorship, but I find myself drawn to other things. What, for example, do the police read? *Servamus* is the official magazine of the South African Police. The State President addresses the Police College: "The fact that the SAP has become a world leader in the field of crime prevention, said Mr. Botha, is evident in the advances made by the Force." The Northern Transvaal Black Police Ladies Club holds a champagne breakfast, which hears songs by the Atterbridgeville Police Choir and crowns a new Miss SA Police, Constable Linda Dlamini. For police officers with VCRs, a videocassette review column enthusiastically recommends new U.S. imports: *Robocop, Die Hard,* and *American Ninja 2.*

Soldiers read *Paratus,* the magazine of the South African Defense Force. This month it reports on a volunteer Coast Watchers Association, whose members watch the sea for unspecified dangers. A Soviet invasion? Black frogmen? ANC commandos in canoes? *Paratus* does not say, but it visits one Coast Watcher: "Mr. Leppan said coast watchers had become quite aware of the normal shipping and beach activity patterns and would easily notice any suspicious activities on land or at sea."

Another page lists pen pals for soldiers:

Elizabeth Healey (21), P.O. Box 229, Rayton 1001, has grey eyes and brown hair. She would like to correspond with any Christian soldiers of a similar age.

Leslie Mitchell (20), 3 Palm court, London Road, Sea Point 8060, would like to correspond with National Servicemen. Her interests include Reggae music, motorbikes and partying. She has blonde hair, blue eyes and would love to meet new guys. All letters will be answered.

Also on the newsstand is a popular photo-comic series in Afrikaans, *Grensvegter (Border Fighter)*. It follows the adventures of Rocco de Wet, an Afrikaner James Bond, as he single-handedly cleanses Africa of Communists. He has his own loyal natives, black faithful servant types who help him out. The villains are Russians and East Germans, subverting the continent and threatening South Africa. A beautiful blond East German agent defects and falls in love with Rocco.

Most of each newsstand, however, reflects Sunny South Africa. Its concentrated essence is in the government propaganda magazine *South African Panorama,* printed mainly for overseas consumption on paper with the heft and gloss of an art book's pages. Here, in its purest form, with color photos on every page, is that scenic, cheerful country of ballet dancing, bird watching, and flower shows; the South Africa hosting international competitions in sports too obscure to be affected by the boycott (100-kilometer runs; fishing championships; power-boat racing); the country of perhaps the ultimate Sunny South Africa story: "Beacons of Safety"—a feature on the nation's lighthouses and their contribution to safety at sea. How could anybody want to boycott a country of picturesque lighthouses?

I wonder, though, why the government goes to the expense of producing this magazine; instead, it could merely reprint the contents of the daily newspapers. An entrepreneur plans to open a restaurant in the lion's cage of a former zoo. A dress designer charters an airliner and lifts audience and models to a "Flights of Fancy" airborne fashion show. The South African Bowling Association announces it will now permit male bowlers to play with bare knees. Bare breasts, however, are still suspect: TOPLESS CAPE BATHERS "UNDER CLOSE SCRUTINY." ". . . amid much speculation on how police would handle the situation, a police liaison officer would only say that topless bathing has been 'under review' and that a statement would be released by the Divisional Commissioner of Police, Brigadier Roy During, early this week."

Why is it so fascinating to see white South Africans lavishing their attention on all this, when we know their country is such an unhappy time bomb? How, I think, can these people be so *blind?* And yet perhaps the very strength of their denial of South Africa's violent, precarious reality is testimony to some subconscious awareness of it. It is as if that constant drumbeat of sex scandals and rugby matches, rock concerts and horse races, is necessary to drown out the guilt and the dread that would be there otherwise.

In this denial of reality I hear an echo of something familiar, as so often in South Africa. In the United States or Europe or anywhere else, we live in a world of proliferating nuclear weapons, a shrinking ozone shield, a looming greenhouse effect, and a widening gap between rich and poor nations. Are they not, also, time bombs every one? But seldom do we linger long over these problems; almost all of the time we would far rather read about, or watch, something else. And we do. White South Africans are not the only ones who prefer a Sunny South Africa to the real world.

# Journey
# to the North

At the same time as the main stream of the Great Trek in Natal was reeling from the twin blows of the killing of Piet Retief and his men at Umgungundhlovu and the Great Murder of Boer families a few days later, another, far smaller group of Voortrekkers had already headed off in a different direction: to the far north.

The little contingent of ox wagons rumbling northward was under the command of a stocky, bearded, fifty-three-year-old cattle farmer named Louis Trichardt, the great-grandson of an employee of the Dutch East India Company. Trichardt had gotten into trouble with the British colonial authorities for beating his slaves, and for trying to keep them from running away after the British set them free. And so he joined the exodus of the Great Trek, looking for new land as far from the meddlesome British as possible. In his caravan were seven Boer farmers and their wives, thirty-four children, an eighty-seven-year-old schoolmaster named Daniel Pfeffer who gave them lessons by candlelight, and an unrecorded (as always) number of black slaves and servants. Although Trek mythology skips over the fact, there was some friction in the group because one Boer, Isaac Albach, had a Coloured wife.

This small party had an astonishingly large number of animals: 925 cattle, 50 horses, and more than 6,000 sheep and goats. "The animals cut such a wide swath of grass through the veld and so

pulverised the ground beside every water-hole," writes Oliver
Ransford, "that their spoor could still be followed several years
later. At the end of each day's journey several hours were devoted
to rounding up the livestock . . . to an observer on one of the
mountain tops which flanked the march it would have looked as
though a brown caterpillar was crawling over the slight undulations
of the veld, surrounded by a swarm of ants. . . ."

The daily diet of mutton eaten by Trichardt and his people was
varied by an occasional wild kudu, eland, or rhinoceros. Driven
equally by the desire to get away from the British and by that
peculiar Boer *trekgees,* or wanderlust, Trichardt's long travels earn
him a place as the Trek's boldest explorer. In contrast to the
Trekkers bound for Natal, who had advance reports from scouts,
hunters, and traders, Trichardt knew almost nothing about the far
north. A map carried by the old man Pfeffer had only a blank
space for the territory they were heading into.

Retracing part of Trichardt's journey is the last of my visits to sites
on the Great Trek. Along the highway that follows the route of
Trichardt's wagons, the kudu and rhinos have now given way to
white-owned farmland irrigated by huge, circular center-pivot ir-
rigation systems. Today, the route of Louis Trichardt's journey is
strewn with the refugees of a much larger, more painful contemporary journey—and one made by people against their will. I had
known that this part of the country, the northern portion of the
Transvaal Province, had been the scene of many "forced removals"
of Africans to the homelands, but still, nothing I have read has
prepared me for the sight. You drive along for many miles through
that irrigated white farmland where there is barely a person in
sight; then, when the road cuts through a corner of the Lebowa
or KwaNdebele homelands, suddenly there is a vast town: tightly
packed rows of huts holding fifty or sixty thousand people—dirt
lanes, communal taps, tin roofs, a pall of acrid smoke from thousands of coal stoves, a few stores, and a bus stop. Then the white
farmland, almost empty of people, begins again.

Since 1960, more than 2 million black South Africans have been
forced to resettle in these dismal, camplike dumping grounds far
off in the homelands. Except for China and Cambodia, South

Africa may be the only country in modern times that has forcibly removed a significant part of its population to the countryside. These "removals" are part of its effort to make more distinct the black and white squares of the apartheid master-plan checkerboard. There is a ghoulish precision about this design that ignores not only human feeling but also such facts as that in the homelands there are few jobs. In Dimbaza, in the desperately poor and overcrowded Ciskei homeland, when a new job was advertised some years ago, one quarter of the town's adult population applied for it.

Not only are jobs scarce in the homelands, so is food. In the Bophuthatswana homeland, seven barren, isolated pockets of land strewn across three of South Africa's four provinces, the hospitals are among the only places where a poor person can count on getting a decent meal. I once visited a Bophuthatswana hospital where a young black nurse told me one of her patients was an eighteen-year-old with severe pellagra, a disease of malnutrition, common when people eat nothing but corn. "Then one day this boy's brother came in to visit him. Now *he* looked fit and healthy. So I asked this brother, I said: 'How can you look so well when your brother, from the same family, is here like this?' And he said: 'I was in a car accident and was in hospital six months. That's why.' "

On the drive north today along Louis Trichardt's route, I am with a friend, Francis Wilson, an economist who is South Africa's leading expert on rural poverty. As we pass through one of the homelands, Wilson points at the dry, low hills, thinly tufted with brush, like a scalp that has lost most of its hair. Overcrowding and overgrazing is turning some of this land to desert. A few years ago he spent five days hiking through this region, sleeping in its villages. "When we walked through here, people told us that twenty years ago these hills were covered with trees. Now there are just those stray bushes. There are too many people for the land, and the trees get chopped down for firewood.

"There is no word in the English language really to describe our black population," he goes on. " 'Urban' implies that you're part of an urban economy, with jobs and infrastructure and all the rest of it. The moment you talk about 'rural,' then you start thinking about rolling hills and land. But there are millions of people packed into small areas in these homelands, and a lot of the land is too barren to cultivate anyway—that's why the whites didn't want it. Most rural black people are landless. A large proportion of black South Africans are living in areas that you cannot describe either as urban or rural. They are rural ghettos."

The Xhosa poet St. J. Page Yako writes:

> *This land will be folded like a blanket,*
> *Till it is like the palm of a hand.* . . .
> *They will crowd us together like tadpoles*
> *In a calabash ladle.*

After months of traveling across these dry plains, Louis Trichardt and his caravan at last halted at some good grazing land in the shadow of a mountain range, the Soutpansberg or "Saltpan Mountains." Uneasily, Trichardt saw that this territory would have to be shared with Africans already living there. He built wattle and daub huts, a trading post, a blacksmith's shop, and a crude schoolroom where the octogenarian Pfeffer could instruct his pupils. The Voortrekkers planted vegetable gardens and Trichardt's wife Martha gave birth to twins. He had stopped only a few miles short of the Limpopo River, which today forms South Africa's northern border.

It had been a long journey, from the very bottom of the continent, past the snow-capped peaks of the Drakensberg, to within the Tropic of Capricorn. Trichardt himself was later to restlessly trek on elsewhere, but by the time he had reached the Soutpansberg, he and his companions had already come so far they thought they were approaching the other end of Africa. When they saw a river flowing north with crocodiles on its banks, they called it the Nyl, believing they had come to the source of the Nile.

At the end of a day of driving, the steep slopes of the Soutpansberg loom up before us, blue-shadowed in the late afternoon light. We have reached the site where the Trekkers built that settlement, which today is a town called Louis Trichardt. The town and the district around it, I find, have something of a frontier feel about them; in the last few years this border area has gone on a war footing. There are a few military vehicles about: the army is constantly looking for African National Congress guerrillas who try to infiltrate across the Limpopo. A number of white landowners and black fieldhands have been killed in land mine explosions near here; some ANC fighters manage to get through, despite floodlights and the 3,000-volt electric fences that reinforce the border. Soldiers are stationed on some farms near here, farmers are linked by military radio, and more soldiers escort white children to school. A new air base just outside of town houses a squadron of Cheetah jet fighters—made in South Africa, with Israeli help.

A few miles away from Louis Trichardt, in the Gazankulu homeland, Wilson and I visit the village of Mbokofa. We climb a hill to see the workshop and shrine of a local preacher, healer, and sculptor, Jackson Hlungwane, who makes beautiful carvings out of tree trunks, some as tall as fifteen feet: birds; rhinos; Janus-headed human figures; Adam with Eve, Cain, and Abel growing out of his body. His wife brings us a mug of the sharp-tasting fermented juice of a green fruit called marula. At the sculptor-healer's hilltop shrine, he and his followers have built a strange series of interconnecting rooms and passageways with walls of small, round, brown stones stuck together with mud plaster. But the walls are only chest-high and there are no roofs; it feels as if we are standing in Roman ruins. Hlungwane is not here this afternoon, so I cannot ask him about it, but I wonder if these ruins are a representation, conscious or unconscious, of what he feels apartheid has done to his community.

As the sun goes down we stand looking out on a scene of great beauty. The village stretches down the steep hillside to a valley, with the mountains opposite us in deep shadow; there are round huts with mud walls and thatched roofs; three brown goats wander by. Friendly children in bright clothes smile at us; the sound of drumming and singing comes from the valley floor. I smell corn meal cooking—a woman is stirring a big iron pot of it that bubbles over a wood fire. Other women walk up the hill with jars of water on their heads. It takes several minutes of looking at this picture-postcard scene of Africa before you notice that only one thing is missing: men.

Approximately 75 percent of men in Mbokofa between the ages of sixteen and forty-five are migrant workers. Many work in the gold mines around Johannesburg, which is an overnight journey south by train or bus. Each year they return home only for several weeks' vacation, and one long weekend at Christmastime. Here, as in every rural community in South Africa, a big cluster of babies is always born nine months after the Christmas holiday.

The 13 percent of South Africa's land reserved for black homelands is overflowing with far more people than it can feed. Hence the migrant workers. "In rural South Africa," explains Francis Wilson, "a key element in any family as to whether they are going to be destitute or able to survive is whether there is somebody in that household earning money as a migrant." A thoughtful, energetic, deeply religious man, Wilson's concern about migrant labor is far more than just academic. He once led a small group of white men on a march halfway across South Africa, to the steps of Parliament, to dramatize the distance between black migrant laborers and their families.

A hundred years ago, before self-sufficient black agriculture had been shattered by the white land grab, the problem for white industrialists was *getting* blacks to leave the rural areas and work in the cities as low-paid migrants, especially as miners. The mine-owners proposed special taxes to solve this problem. "It is suggested to raise the Hut Tax to such an amount that more natives will be induced to seek work," said an 1893 report of the Committee on the Native Labour Question of the Mine Managers' Association. Another bill sharply limited the amount of land each African family could own. These measures, said Cape Colony Prime Minister Cecil Rhodes, would "remove these poor children out of their state of sloth and laziness, and give them some gentle stimulants to go forth and find out something of the dignity of labour."

Just as the use of "loyal natives" has been a principal tool of white governmental control, so has the use of black migrant labor been a major tool by which whites have controlled South Africa's economy. Today, roughly 2 million out of the country's 5 million industrial workers are migrants, the largest percentage in any economy in the world. What that means at this end of the system, in

Mbokofa and thousands of other towns, is that women must learn to do without men for much of their lives. I interviewed a migrant worker's wife in a remote village near the Botswana border a few years ago. She was thirty-one and had five children; her husband was a railway worker near Johannesburg. I asked her how much he earned. She laughed sadly: he wouldn't tell her. "I feel lonely most of the time," she said. "We don't love each other as much as we used to. So each time when he is here, it is not a matter of welcoming each other. Although I miss him when he is not here. Sometimes it feels as if I am not married at all. Or only partly."

After watching the sun set in Mbokofa, we drive to the railway station in Louis Trichardt. There I am to catch the night train for Johannesburg, where I will spend the second half of my time in South Africa. Many migrants are also boarding the train. Beneath some trees next to the station, I watch others get on board one of the large buses that take migrants directly to the mines. Women crowd up to the open windows to sell food for the journey to the men inside. A sign on the bus says: "Non-whites only. Capacity: 73 sitting, 18 standing." For some reason, perhaps because this gives it a larger capacity, the bus is not on a single chassis but is a trailer truck, with all the seats in the trailer. This gives it an eerie resemblance to those big trailer trucks used to haul livestock. Beneath the shouts and hubbub of departure, the men's faces are somber. Perhaps they are thinking ahead to the long months of separation, to the bunks in crowded cinderblock barracks, to the industrial accidents and the underground rockfalls in the mines, which make this a trip from which some men never return.

For South Africa's migrant workers, this journey is their Great Trek. For all their working lives, the 2 million migrants are sentenced to this cycle of travel, danger, and long separation from home, as most of their fathers were before them. Like the more famous Great Trek of the Afrikaners, this one, too, has given birth to hundreds of poems, stories, legends, and songs. They are not of celebration but of mourning and fear. And they are found all over southern Africa, for the South African migrant labor system has cast its net across the entire lower third of the continent. Here is one poem, about the start of the migrant's trek, from the Mozambican writer Gouveia de Lemos:

*Put on a clean shirt*
*It's time to work the contract.*
*Get into the wagon, brother*
*We must travel night and day.*
   *Which of us*
   *Which of us will come back?*
   *Which of us*
   *Which of us will die?*

*Which of us will come back*
*To see women*
*To see our lands*
*To see our oxen?*
   *Which of us will die?*
   *Which of us?*
   *Which of us?*

*Part Two*

# CITY OF GOLD

# The Play
# Within the Play

Most visitors from abroad first see Johannesburg as a cluster of skyscrapers, studded with hotels, boutiques, and restaurants, encircled by freeways. But for millions of Africans over the years, such as those making that long journey by trailer truck bus from Louis Trichardt, the first taste of this city has meant the mine shafts and corridors that reach far beneath it, and many miles to the east and west of it. *Egoli,* the Africans call Johannesburg, the City of Gold. Gold mining is the key to modern South Africa; it is, in the words of one scholar of the industry, Frederick Johnstone, "the play within the play." And so in understanding Johannesburg, the place to begin is with the gold.

Some two dozen of us, mostly foreign visitors, are on today's trip to the Libanon Mine. The mining industry runs these tours for all comers several times a week, and, surprisingly, all South Africa's recent mass killings and arrests haven't interfered. Our group is outfitted in boots, white jumpsuits, and helmets with lights on top, then is packed tightly into a metal cage for the long journey downward. The elevator shaft is deeper than the Grand Canyon. Two thirds of the way down, we stop, get out of the elevator, and travel almost a mile laterally, in a small diesel-powered train about four feet high. Over the years, each mine gradually develops enormous multilayered webs of tunnels like this. The combined length of tunnels in any major South African gold mine would stretch from New York to Chicago.

White supervisors, almost all of whom are Afrikaners, shepherd us along the way. There have been sporadic newspaper reports of fights between black and white miners underground, and the national white mineworkers' union chief has urged his members to wear guns to work. I ask one supervisor if there has been any violence here at Libanon. No, he says emphatically, "We get on with each other here." As I take notes, his eyes narrow: "Are you one of these *reporters?* Who write lies about South Africa?"

We get off the train and walk toward the edge of the gold seam. Gold comes in a piebald ore, a thin layer of which is squeezed like a sandwich between two masses of much harder rock. What the miners have to do is to break up the ore and get it to the surface without the hard rock collapsing on top of them.

Gold mines usually work in three shifts: on the first, miners drill long holes in the ore; on the next, they plant dynamite in the holes, retreat, and explode it; on the third, they use shovels, conveyor belts, trains, and elevators to bring the vast quantities of loose ore back up to the surface. There, more machinery crushes it so the tiny particles of gold can be separated out. Most of South Africa's gold ore is of low grade and deep underground, which is why mining it profitably requires large amounts of low-paid labor. It takes 5 tons of Libanon's ore to make a wedding ring's worth of gold.

In the section of the mine we are now entering, one white supervises one hundred and forty blacks. White miners, who are almost always skilled or semi-skilled workers or supervisors, are paid an average of four to five times as much as black ones. Along the walls of a corridor where we are walking are padlocked red storage boxes for dynamite. Although this rule is at last now crumbling, the job of inserting the dynamite was for nearly a century strictly reserved for whites only. Supposedly only they were capable of such "skilled" work. In 1922, hundreds of whites died in a bitter strike, one of whose issues was the preservation of such white privileges. Some strikers were Communists, who marched through Johannesburg under a banner: "Workers of the World Unite, and Fight for a White South Africa."

After clambering down a ladder and squeezing through a narrow, jagged rock passageway whose walls are warm to the touch, we reach the "face," the edge of the gold seam. The sandwich filling of gold ore is three and a half feet high here, and several hundred feet wide. It thus forms the back wall of a low, wide room of jagged rock. Thick wooden posts keep the three-and-a-half-foot-high ceiling from collapsing. But when you've pictured this room, tilt the picture sideways, for here the gold ore sandwich rises from left to right at about a 45-degree angle. Perched every thirty feet or so on the steeply slanting floor of this rock chamber, crouching black miners are holding big drills powered by compressed air, making holes in the ore for dynamite sticks. Their sweaty faces and arms are coated with rock dust. The noise is absolutely unbelievable. I had been in African mines years ago, but I seem to have suppressed all memory of the sound. Imagine half a dozen pneumatic jackhammers the size of those used to dig up streets, all operating within a rock-walled room, beneath a ceiling so low you can't stand.

The drills stop, leaving just the compressed air hissing in the hoses, so that we can hear the supervisor explain what goes on here. Then the inferno of noise resumes. On the way out, the supervisor says cheerfully: "Those chaps, they don't like to stop work. When all those drills are going at the same time, like this"—he makes a motion of gripping a vibrating drill with his hands—"with all that noise—now, *that's* what they like!"

Soon the metal cage whisks us back up to the surface. After changing out of the helmets and boots, we are taken by bus to various full-size models of mine shafts and corridors. "This is where we teach the blokes about winch driving." "This is where we teach them safety." And: "This is where we teach them Fanakalo."

Fanakalo is a tongue invented solely for giving orders. Black miners at Libanon, like those at most mines in South Africa, come from different ethnic groups speaking more than half a dozen languages. Many are even from other countries in southern Africa. Hence Fanakalo, which means "Do it like this." Fanakalo has a simplified syntax and a vocabulary of some one thousand words drawn from English, Afrikaans, Zulu, and other African languages.

From the seats of a classroom, we watch a black instructor shout at a trainee miner in boots and work clothes, who acts out orders that clearly mean: "Get up!" "Get that tool over there!" "Bring it here!"

Libanon's 750 white employees live near the mine with their families, but all but a tiny fraction of the 6,250 black miners here—as at all mines in South Africa—are migrants. At Libanon, the contract period is forty-five weeks. Then they have a month or so at home to visit their families, then they board one of those trailer truck buses for forty-five weeks back at the mine again.

The compound where Libanon's black miners live is surrounded by a high fence, with a watchtower and gate. Gate and watchtower are unmanned at the moment, but both can be used at times of labor unrest. As we pull up to the black miners' dining hall, the white bus driver quips, "Don't have lunch here!" In a pantry is laid out an exhibit of the food served here: a table of samples, each item labeled: "Chicken," "Beef," "Mealies," and "Blacks Beer" [*sic*]. "We issue it to them three times a week," explains the white compound manager. "This is their traditional beer." In the cafeteria itself, a long line of black miners, many still in helmets and dusty jumpsuits, snakes past a counter to get meat, vegetables, and mealies (a cornmeal porridge), which a worker dishes out with a trowel-like scoop from a huge tub the size of a laundry cart.

Finally, the compound manager takes us inside a "hostel" where the migrant miners live. There are sixteen bunks to a suite of rooms, with a simple cupboard for each man, and a few tables. "We've got shower rooms for them here," the manager explains, "and over there are TV rooms. We show them videos when they're off duty." The rooms have the spartan, right-angles look of an army barracks; they are certainly far better than the cement-slab bunks and hole-in-the-floor toilets that thousands of South African migrant workers must live with, especially the non-unionized.

But the amazing thing, I notice with a guilty shock, is that the room is in use. Black figures stir and half rise on several of the bunks; they are night-shift workers, sleeping by day, who have been woken up by this invasion of white strangers, male and female. The manager has simply marched us in here, unannounced, without knocking. Some visitors on the tour wander around the room snapping flash pictures as the manager stands amid the bunks to lecture us and answer questions for ten or fifteen minutes. He has brought us all here as if our skin itself entitles us to intrude, just as a white-coated doctor and medical students have the right to make the rounds of a hospital ward.

What I do not see underground at Libanon, but can only imagine amid the jumble of rock, noise, and machinery, are the accidents. Statistically, there are likely to be half a dozen deaths at this mine this year and more than a hundred serious injuries. Underground mining is dangerous work anywhere, and nowhere more so than in South Africa. In South African coal mines, for example, the accident rate is eight times as high as in Britain. In one single mining disaster in 1960, 437 South African workers were buried alive. Today, more than 700 South African miners are killed and 12,000 seriously injured each year. A hundred of the injured become paraplegics. A study by a group of black divinity students some years ago reported of one mine: "The hospital is very beautiful and clean. But . . . [t]he mortuary is too small . . . and as a result of the high death rate, many corpses are usually packed on top of the other on the small shelves which are 7 in number. The corpses are treated just like chicken in the fridge."

On top of all this, South Africa's migrant miners now face a new disaster: AIDS. In Africa, the disease is spread largely by heterosexual contact. Separating men in their twenties and thirties from their wives for nearly a year at a time inevitably means rampant prostitution. Prostitutes slip into the hostels themselves, or set up business in the shantytowns full of drinking places that grow up near the larger mines. Already, one out of every ten black miners comes down with a sexually transmitted disease of some sort each year. As AIDS in South Africa spreads, its most devastating impact will be among migrant workers—and their wives and girlfriends.

Because migrant labor is so central to South African blacks, it takes on the aura of an epic experience, a rite of passage into manhood in which a man leaves his rural village for a long journey to unknown perils. Some of the dangers are from mine accidents; some are from con artists who work the miners' trains and hostels.

The illiterate country bumpkin miner, fleeced by fast-talking city slickers who charge fees for imaginary permits and the like, is a common figure in black South African fiction.

Some miners at the Libanon mine are Sothos, who travel across the Caledon River, called Mohokare in the Sotho language, to come here. In the old days the entire journey was made on foot, and took weeks. One song the miners still sing goes:

> *Wash me clean, Mohokare, and make me a pure man.*
> *Make me a man who is fit to go to heaven.*
> *Cleanse me from my sins because I am going to*
> *The dangerous place where I may lose my life.*

The 2 million black migrant workers of South Africa spend their entire working lives apart from their families. In a way, what is saddest of all about this pattern is that everyone involved begins to consider it normal. An Anglican minister in Johannesburg who has worked a good deal with migrants tells me:

"The woman ritualizes the absence of her husband. When we get down to how women define work—when we ask them to define it—they define it as taking a migrant job. Gardening, cooking, farming, etc. is not work. Work is going away for eight or nine months. Over three or four generations now there has been an acceptance of this system—men, women, chiefs, mine officials, border-crossing guards, and of course the people in mining company boardrooms. In the boardrooms, you have [white] men whose only living experience of being away from their families was the army or boarding school, things like that—which may have been very good, adventurous times for them, full of male fellowship. So they think of these migrant laborers as having a good time, escaping from their wives, and so on."

Another problem, he adds, is that even though the migrant generally returns to the same mine, that mine may have twenty thousand people on it and he may not come back to the same work gang or the same hostel. "In friendships, the migrant cultivates forgetfulness. He can't afford to form close relationships; it is too painful when they end."

Philip Dixie, a South African sociologist, reports a story he heard

many times from black miners, a myth or fable. In it you can see
the traces of tours by white visitors like the one I took, and also
a haunting image of mining as an earthly hardship from which only
the supernatural offers escape.


Every so often on an appointed day white women enter the
mine. While underground one of the party will slip away to
an abandoned part of the mine: there to have discourse with
a ghost. On parting the woman leaves a large amount of money
at the place of meeting. . . . Later the men of the night shift
enter the mine. . . . It is then that the ghost chooses one of
the black workers, and while they are alone, passes the money
on to him with these words: "You must not tell anyone about
this—not your relatives, not even your closest friends. Take
this money, go home, use it for your children's education,
and never return."

The migrant labor system was started not by Afrikaners, whom
foreigners always blame for everything about South Africa, but
by British industrialists. The practice of separating men from their
families for their entire working lives grew up for one simple
business reason: it costs less. A mine can house a migrant worker
in a hostel bunk for one fifth the cost of building him even the
simplest family housing. And it is that basic logic, calculated at
boards of directors' tables in Johannesburg and London for over
a century, that has separated husbands from wives, fathers from
children, across southern Africa. "If you take a man, a married
man, from his wife it's tantamount to castrating him," says a hostel
dweller in "To Kill a Man's Pride," a short story by Mtutuzeli
Matshoba. "A bullock is castrated to make it strong for labor
purposes."
    If you talk to white mining executives about the migrant labor
system, as I have, they will shake their heads, agree that it's a
terrible thing and someday must go, but then mutter something
about "competitive labor costs" and "lack of infrastructure." The
only recent change in the system is that some mines, including
Libanon, now have special cabins where a small number of miners

at a time can get short "conjugal visits" from their wives, in the same way that some countries of the world grant this privilege to long-term prisoners.

These black laborers of the South African mines produce 44 percent of the Western world's gold, four times as much as any other country. Even that is a deceptively low figure, because some gold mines in other countries are South African–controlled. In Brazil, for example, South African companies have been able to find even lower wages and higher profits than at home. South Africa's own riches in the soil will last for decades to come. Whatever this week's price for an ounce of gold is, remember that that ounce cost less than $300 to mine in South Africa. The rest is profit. An underlying part of the struggle in South Africa today is not only about who gets the land and who gets the vote, but who gets the gold.

Who now owns the gold? Just as the Dutch East India Company economically dominated the first century of white rule in South Africa, so has another single company dominated the country's economy in this century. It controls the Libanon mine; it controls or owns scores of other mines comprising more than two thirds of the capital invested in South African mining; it controls nearly half the value of all shares on the Johannesburg Stock Exchange; and, off the coast of Namibia, it is building dikes and pumping out seawater in order to strip-mine the ocean floor. The last operation is the largest civil engineering project in the Southern Hemisphere. All told, more than 600 companies employing 800,000 workers on six continents are ultimately owned or controlled by one giant corporation: the Anglo-American Corporation of South Africa.

Despite the name, Anglo's ownership is mostly South African. "[It] looms larger in its home economy," according to *Business Week,* "than does any other company in any country." It looms large in many other countries as well. For much of the 1980s, Anglo was the largest single foreign investor in the United States. Through a long-standing cartel arrangement with the Soviet Union, it effectively controls the world diamond market. And it has a complex web of subsidiaries and associated companies all over the world; Anglo's control of the Libanon mine, for example, is via shares it owns of other companies in Johannesburg, London, and Luxembourg. Given such concentration of wealth, it is not surprising that the African National Congress, the black consciousness movement, and the major black trade unions have all generally favored nationalization of key industries, especially the mines. Anglo's holdings are the size of an entire national economy already: inside and outside South Africa, Anglo has assets worth more than the gross domestic products of the nine other states of southern Africa combined.

At the top of the Anglo-American empire, officially retired but still jetting about the world to open factories, engineer takeovers, and confer with heads of state, is Harry Oppenheimer, a genteel, soft-spoken man now in his eighties, who breeds racehorses and collects first editions of Byron. His family's controlling interest in Anglo and its vast network of affiliates has made him one of the world's wealthiest men.

One paradox I have often noticed in South Africa is that the white person who tells you blacks are no better than chimpanzees is likely to be a farmer, his boots deep in manure, or a garage mechanic in oil-stained work pants. While the white person who says apartheid is perfectly ghastly, really quite dreadful, and simply *must* be ended, is often saying so while a black maid serves him or her tea on a silver tray. Harry Oppenheimer is a good example of this, for his position, and that of men like him, makes a certain kind of liberalism quite painless. Oppenheimer and other mining executives long opposed, for instance, the "job reservation" laws which reserved all skilled jobs for whites. White workers fought ferociously for job reservation, hoping to keep those jobs for their sons. But for the mineowners the law was only a costly nuisance. When hiring skilled workers, what businessman wants to be restricted to a pool that is now only 13 percent of the population?

Oppenheimer has brought to its most sophisticated level something at which many white South African businessmen excel: criticizing apartheid while lavishly profiting from it. He declares himself, for instance, in favor of one person/one vote. But top executives of several companies in the Anglo family have sat on the government's Defence Advisory Council, which, until it was disbanded in a recent bureaucratic reshuffle, helped the military

plan more effective ways of suppressing people who are demanding, above all, votes. Oppenheimer's entire gold-mining operation
depends on migrant labor, yet when you talk to him he is the soul
of broad-minded enlightenment.

I interviewed Oppenheimer some ten years ago. In an anteroom
outside his office was a bronze statue of an African miner with a
pneumatic drill—it felt strange to see this sweaty, deafeningly
noisy operation turned into art and silence. An old grandfather
clock stood against one wall; a secretary was on the telephone
making arrangements for someone to fly to Zambia on an Anglo
corporate jet. At the end of a long, thickly carpeted corridor lined
with antique maps of Africa was Oppenheimer's own private office.
The walls held bookcases and a family portrait; it felt more like a
living room than the apex of a global business empire.

Oppenheimer himself was a short, smiling, urbane man, gracious
and friendly, wearing a dark gray suit that matched his heavy
eyebrows. He answered questions for an hour or so, artfully skip-
ping across the political terrain, and almost always staking out a
liberal-sounding position. He had great praise for Chief Buthelezi.
He insisted that the government could not impose a new constitution without black agreement: "It's always fun making up a constitution, but in the long run you arrive at that by negotiation."
He showed only the slightest flicker of uneasiness about living
under majority rule: "Where you have a heterogeneous country
of this sort you've got to make jolly sure by provisions of the
constitution that no one lot is going to oppress another lot."

What about ending migrant labor? This was the only point where
Oppenheimer shook his head. "I don't think that in the mining
industry we could really get rid of migratory labor completely.
When you think there are four hundred thousand black people in
this industry and they all have their wives and the people who are
necessary to service the community, it's a big move. The cost of
it would be quite enormous."

Oppenheimer did, however, speak forcefully on another point
then under much debate: whether blacks should be allowed to
form effective trade unions.

Of course they should, Oppenheimer said in crisp, Oxford-
accented sentences. "It is much better than to have no one to talk

to. I mean nowadays, if there's great discontent, there's a tendency to have a riot. And that's the first you hear of it. And then you say, 'Now for goodness' sake explain this to us, what you want,' and very often there is no one to explain it to you, although there may be a very good grievance all the same. [The mineworkers] say that everybody wants to come, so they try to arrange for a negotiation to take place at a mass meeting, which is not very easy. So I do think it is important for there to be an organization which they can really trust to represent them."

For just these reasons—the 1970s in South Africa saw widespread labor violence and wildcat strikes—Anglo and other companies gave the nod to new labor legislation that permitted the formation of the black National Union of Mineworkers in 1982. But relations between Anglo and the black miners' union soon soured, especially after a 1987 strike. Since that time, the union has charged, Anglo has distributed thousands of smear pamphlets aimed at discrediting the union and has hired white mineworkers to moonlight as security guards. These guards regularly stage surprise searches of union shop stewards' hostel rooms when the miners are underground. Anglo now videotapes union meetings on company property. At most Anglo mines, workers must use an ID card with a magnetic strip to get in and out of their living compounds or move from one compound to another, which gives management a computerized record of the movements of each worker.

Mine labor rebellions are quickly put down by the South African Police, some of whose units are actually stationed on mine property. But just in case they're not enough, Anglo maintains its own company police force, which includes dog squads, horse patrols, and a fleet of armored cars. For a time, until a public outcry forced their removal, Anglo even fitted out some of its mining compounds with tear-gas dispensers operated by remote control.

South Africa's gold rush began when an itinerant prospector named George Harrison stumbled on an outcrop of ore in 1886. In the tumultuous decade that followed, Johannesburg turned from a patch of bare *veld* into one of the continent's most important cities. In its rough-and-tumble early days, Americans played a surprisingly major part. By 1896, more than half of South Africa's gold mines were run by American engineers, and the United States was the country's largest supplier of mining equipment. Johannesburg soon played host to another American invasion: tempted by the prospect of men with money in their pockets but no families, hundreds of pimps and prostitutes flocked to South Africa from New York.

In a way, of course, South Africa's gold rush is still going on. At the same time, its early years are being transformed into legend. It is a legend that serves the purposes of those in power and becomes yet another brick in that wall of denial between Sunny South Africa and reality. "The past is full of life," Kundera says, "eager to irritate us, provoke and insult us, tempt us to destroy or repaint it."

And repaint it they have. Nowhere has this happened more dramatically than at Gold Reef City, South Africa's major theme park, on Johannesburg's southern outskirts. A re-creation of the city at the turn of the century, Gold Reef City has obviously taken some ideas from Colonial Williamsburg. The little yellow signs throughout the complex, KODAK PHOTO SITE, recall Disneyland. But this celebration of the raw pioneer days blends seamlessly into South Africa's rough-and-ready present. At the entrance, security guards give all visitors (perhaps a quarter of whom are black) a pat-down body search and ask, "No firearms?"

Everywhere at Gold Reef City, today mixes with a sanitized yesterday. A white country-and-western band, in Wild West getup, strums electric guitars and sings in fake American accents. Under the broiling midsummer sun, two sweating Africans stroll around dressed in loincloths, feather headdresses, and sheepskin leggings: they are supposed to look fierce and native to advertise the "Mine Natives Dancing Competition" scheduled for this afternoon. Walking past them, looking equally uncomfortable in the heat, comes a young white woman in an old-fashioned dress with a laced-up bodice: she is supposed to look "Gay '90s" to advertise one of the bars here. There is a brief moment of camaraderie. "Howsit?" she says to the two blacks, in the usual South African slang greeting. "Hot!" says one.

Gold Reef City has a blacksmith's shop, a general store, an old newspaper office with a linotype machine, and Barney's Tavern, with the actual bar counter over which the great 1922 white miners' strike was planned. You can take horse-drawn carriage rides between them all. But nowhere, not in the large scale model of a mine, not in the photos of nineteenth-century mining engineers with handlebar mustaches and old soccer teams of white miners, not in the replica of a mine manager's spacious home, or anywhere else, does a single word or picture even hint that this entire industry was and is founded upon the labor of black men, living in communal barracks for twenty years of their lives, separated from their families for ten or eleven months of each year.

But perhaps an American should not be too self-righteous. For the first four decades of its existence, Colonial Williamsburg was entirely built around several central concepts, such as Opportunity, Individual Liberties, and the Integrity of the Individual. Not until the 1970s did any exhibit acknowledge that more than half the population of the real Williamsburg had been slaves.

# Johannesburg
# Notebook

The first white settlers to cross the site of what is now Johannesburg were in caravans of the Great Trek that came in the wake of Louis Trichardt's long journey to the north. While the embattled main body of the Trek remained to the east, bogged down in the struggle with Dingane over Natal, these northbound Voortrekkers fanned out across what are today South Africa's two interior provinces, the Orange Free State and the Transvaal. The restless Boers wanted to put as much distance as possible between themselves and the British. Lumbering across mountains, deserts, and trackless plains, in their cumbersome wagons whose oxen had to rest in the midday heat, they traveled as little as four miles a day. Nonetheless, small parties of Trekkers roamed amazing distances into the continent, as far as today's Zimbabwe, Angola, and Mozambique.

Oddly, they didn't see the prize. Because no one found large deposits of gold until decades later, the Voortrekkers did not know that they were crossing or settling on the richest parcel of real estate in the world. Johannesburg itself was not founded until half a century after the Trek began; the whites who settled on its site before then were only a few scattered farmers. When Trollope passed through the district in 1877, there were not even any roadside inns, and, a bit petulant, he had to stay in Boer farm-houses.

By two decades after the start of the Trek, more than eighteen thousand Boers had settled in what are today the two interior provinces and what were then—following some internal squabbles and some fighting with the British—independent Trekker republics. The early years of Voortrekker settlement in the interior followed the same pattern as their arrival in Natal: a thirst for land, and a trail of blood left by repeated battles with the Africans.

During the Great Trek, no recorded fighting took place where Johannesburg now lies. But the Trekkers did fight one extraordinary battle some miles to the north. It seems to foreshadow something about Johannesburg because, like the gold mining which was later to shape the city, it took place underground.

In the Transvaal district of Waterberg, a Trekker named Hermanus Potgieter went to the *kraal* of a Matabele chief named Mokopane to barter for ivory. A quarrel broke out. Potgieter was a hot-tempered, excitable man, widely feared for his raids on black villages to capture children as slaves. Chief Mokopane's people had suffered heavily from these raids. When one of Mokopane's sons said something insulting to Potgieter, Potgieter shot the young man dead on the spot.

Mokopane's people rose in fury and murdered the twenty-three men, women, and children in Potgieter's party. Potgieter himself was pinned to the ground and skinned alive. And so, just as the Natal Trekkers had had the Great Murder and the massacre of Piet Retief's force to avenge, now the Transvaal Trekkers had martyrs of their own. Recalling the mutilated and dismembered bodies of Potgieter's group, another Trek leader said, "This frightful spectacle, which filled my soul with horror, induced in me the fixed resolution to punish the barbarians, even were I to lose my life in consequence."

The Trekkers raised a commando force of some 550 men for this punishment expedition. But they found that Mokopane and his people, along with some allied clans, had left the scene of the murder and taken refuge in some nearby mountain caves. The largest of these was believed to be over 2,000 feet long and up to 500 feet wide. Mokopane had a small supply of rifles, and he made good use of them. The Trekker commando charged into the mouth of the largest cavern, storming forward over the rock floor. But from the cave's recesses, Mokopane's men opened fire, killing one Boer. For both sides, the battle must have been one of total terror, for it took place in a darkness illuminated only by the muzzle flashes of the guns. The explosions echoed off the rock walls, and the cave filled with gunsmoke. The Boers were unable to see their opponents and finally retreated, carrying out their wounded.

The Trekkers tried unsuccessfully to collapse the caves with dynamite, crushing those inside. Then they tried to smoke Mokopane's people out of the caves. They failed, and one of their two commanders, Potgieter's nephew, was killed by a bullet fired from inside the cave. Furious, the other Boers put to work fifty teams of oxen and three hundred black laborers dragging trees and stones to block off the cave mouths. It took five days of exhausting work to seal the cave, except for one entrance deliberately left open.

Mokopane's people had some food, but soon they began to die. The siege continued for three weeks, and only then did most of those who were still inside try to leave the cave. The Boers let women and children go, but every time a man showed himself at the one remaining cave entrance, to dash toward the nearest stream for water, the Boers shot him dead. The Trekkers killed nine hundred Africans in this manner, and a much greater number died of hunger and thirst inside the mountain. Finally, the Trekkers charged into the cavern again. Despite three weeks of starvation in the dark, the surviving members of Mokopane's band inside put up enough of a battle to wound four Trekkers. In all, several thousand Africans were killed in revenge for the two dozen Voortrekker deaths.

Today, the city that has grown up a few hours' drive from where that battle took place is South Africa's most important. Even though government ministries are in Pretoria and Parliament meets in Cape Town, Johannesburg is South Africa's true capital, its New York. And so for the rest of my stay in the country, I will be based here.

One of the youngest of the world's major cities, Johannesburg is among the few with no harbor and no river. Its only river is the underground one of gold, which even the street names do not let you forget: Claim Street, Nugget Street, Wanderers Street. Above this subterranean river a city has grown up which seems to contain both new empires being born and the remnants of those past. Gleaming new hotels and office buildings with atriums full of greenery and glass-walled elevators are interspersed with Portuguese groceries whose owners fled here from Angola and Mozambique when Portugal let go its African colonies. A freeway leads to Johannesburg's international airport; ten minutes away from it homeless Africans are living in abandoned mine tunnels. The city even has (a very few) white beggars cooking and sleeping in parks and vacant lots, and (a very few) blacks driving BMWs. In the midst of all its modern splendor and poverty, though, Johannesburg still flaunts reminders of the Great Trek that first brought white settlers to the region. The city's Afrikaans-language university, for example, is seven stories of glass and concrete. But its buildings are all one—oddly linked in a huge, jagged circle with no breaks, a design that mimics the Voortrekkers' *laager,* or fortified ring of ox wagons.

One could write for a lifetime about this city. Here are just a few images of Johannesburg at this moment in time, with Blood River 150 years in the past and a fully democratic South Africa an unknown distance away in the future:

## SERVANTS

Sixty-nine percent of white South African households, I read, employ one or more black servants. And 98 percent of these employers, I unscientifically estimate, will, at some point in a conversation on the subject, use the phrase, "*Ag,* man, she's like one of the family."

But not too much like one of the family. For whites have always made sure that blacks are differentiated from the family in clear ways. Eighty or ninety years ago, it was by means of clothing. White Johannesburgers of that time anxiously debated whether servants and other blacks should be allowed to wear "white" clothes. "No native should be allowed to wear ordinary European dress during working hours," said one letter to the editor of the Johannesburg *Star* in 1911. ". . . European dress gives him an inflated sense of importance and equality."

Today, denial of that sense of importance and equality takes different forms, and, as far as servants are concerned, I note one strange form of it on the city's roofs. One large section of Johannesburg is filled with apartment buildings for whites, ten to twenty stories high. Through their picture windows in the evening you can see lamps, glowing TVs, silhouetted figures with drinks in hand. Even white apartment dwellers have live-in black servants; they live in quarters of their own, on the roof. But these rooms are universally built without normal windows. On this top floor the windows are always very small, and at transom height, seven or eight feet above floor level. Thus, the servants are sure not to have what whites would surely get if *they* were on that floor—a view.

## SOWETO

At the Dube Village police substation this morning, some fifty black riot police are forming up into a column, two by two. They carry short batons in their right hands and shields in their left. A parents' meeting about conditions in the Soweto schools is scheduled for this afternoon, and surrounding it with police is merely standard procedure.

A few blocks away, Dr. Nthato Motlana sits in a paneled study off his consulting room. A veteran of banning and several spells in prison, he has been a spokesperson for black rights since the 1940s, and is the chair of the Soweto Civic Association. A small, intense man with a beard and a quick, humorous smile, he is wearing his white doctor's coat. He interrupts our discussion once or twice to answer a knock on the door and dispense advice or medicine to a patient. At first he is restless: yet another foreigner with the same old questions, when he has his patients and that

schools meeting to worry about. But once he gets going, he quickly
warms up.

"Fly over South Africa and look," he says. "The rains fall on
only one side of the mountains, and every time there's a rainless
spot where nothing grows, that's where you'll find the blacks. All
the river valleys in South Africa, and I mean *all,* except for maybe
a few in Natal, are part of the white land. Look, when the white
man came here he found us occupying all those fertile valleys,
because we were herders; we had cattle and we needed the water:
by the riverbed is where there is grass, grazing, water.

"I'm a Tswana. My people occupied this whole area before the
white man came. These gold fields, that's where we were. This
fellow van der Merwe, an Afrikaner archeologist, has done work
to show that villages, sophisticated societies in terms of those days,
existed around the years 300 to 400 A.D. around this area. I have
no doubt that with improved carbon-dating methods he'll in fact
show that we were here in 400 B.C., not A.D. But despite the fact
that this Afrikaner has showed this kind of thing, all the maps still
show those damn little arrows! Man, you must have seen those
maps, streams of blacks moving from the Central African lakes
downward and white arrows moving up from the Cape of Good
Hope, and we all met in the middle of this country and fought
over who would get this empty land. Shit! Crap! We were here
first. This has been shown. Everybody knows this."

When it is time to go, I ask Dr. Motlana if I can use his phone
to call a taxi. He shakes his head. No good, he explains: black
taxis, like the one that deposited me here, do not have radios.
White cabs won't come here. Embarrassed, I wonder what to do.
None of the people I know in Soweto have a car. Could I call a
friend from outside to come and pick me up? No, he says, because
of that schools meeting there will be a police roadblock on the
highway into Soweto by now. Motlana begins to look annoyed:
he may have me on his hands for some time.

Just then, his doorbell rings. It is two white visitors in ties and
pinstriped suits, accompanied by a black man. Motlana had forgotten this appointment. He beckons the three of them into his
study and shuts the door. Waiting outside for these newcomers,
whoever they are, is a sleek Mercedes with a uniformed chauffeur.

I sit amid the medical instruments in the doctor's examining room until the visitors emerge. I introduce myself and ask if I can get a ride back to downtown Johannesburg. Both the white men look slightly askance, as if a stranger in a restaurant had asked for some food off their plates. But, in the presence of Dr. Motlana, it would be impolite to say no. They ask, "You are going to the Carlton?" (The city's fanciest hotel.) No. "A journalist—you are a Washington-based correspondent?" No. But still they say they will give me a ride. They introduce themselves. They are West German diplomats. One is based at the embassy in Pretoria; the other drops the name of his American counterpart, thereby establishing that he is on the Assistant Secretary of State level. "I'm on a familiarization trip here. Before this I served in black Africa for five years." There is a slight emphasis on "black," for the benefit of the listening Dr. Motlana.

We get into the Mercedes: myself, the chauffeur, the two diplomats and the black man with them, a minister of a local church who has been their guide on a tour of Soweto this morning. The two Germans cheerfully ask the minister many questions about the houses we pass, and about life in Soweto. They want to appear sympathetic, but not, of course, to the point of making too many commitments. The minister seems to be hoping for a German foundation grant for a self-help project he works with.

As we drive along, the bluish haze of smoke that spreads over Soweto from tens of thousands of coal fires makes it hard to see more than a mile or two. It is easy to see why many Sowetans suffer from lung troubles. The tan brick houses we pass have privies in their backyards; each four-room matchbox home holds an average of seventeen to twenty people, and sometimes as many as thirty, sleeping on couches and floors. More than 2 million people live in Soweto now; once a family has a foothold here, friends and relatives from the countryside come flooding in to stay, hoping for work. The houses are in even rows on streets deliberately built wide enough for armored cars to make U-turns. Children thus use these streets as soccer fields, daringly stepping just a few inches out of the way, like nonchalant bullfighters, as the diplomats' limousine hurtles by.

The two Germans are sitting in the rear seat; the black minister and I are on jump seats in front of them. There is something worn and pained in the minister's face. When the conversation pauses, I ask him if he was in prison recently. He says yes. Was he tortured? "Yes," he says. Then it all comes pouring out: "If you *prepare* yourself for the worst, then you can take it. You must always think of the worst in advance, and then when it comes—the beatings, the electroshock—you can survive." He speaks with great feeling. "My wife, though, did not fare well. She was in prison at the same time, and they did it to her also. In the morning, when she went to wash, she could see what they had done to children she knew, students, who were in the same prison. Now she wakes in the night shouting. She fears any knock at the door. She has pernicious anemia. The doctors say it is from tension. They can do nothing for her."

We are on the freeway heading into Johannesburg now. The Germans say nothing; they seem embarrassed. This talk was not on the program. They shift about in their seats uncomfortably and confer in German about where to have lunch. When we arrive at the Carlton Hotel, a smiling doorman in top hat and tailcoat opens the car door. The two diplomats hop out with relief; they quickly shake hands with the minister and me, and hurry off into the hotel's spacious lobby.

## SECURITY

If South Africa ever runs out of gold, it can export burglar alarms. In the Johannesburg Yellow Pages, a full sixty pages are devoted to alarms, locks, security services, or fencing. Alan Fencing (Pty) Ltd advertises itself as specializing in

"• Rocket and Grenade Fences
  • Alarm and Electronic Fencing
  • Burglar Proofing."

In one morning's *Sowetan,* the daily paper for blacks, more than one third of listings under "Situations Vacant (Male)" are for se-

curity guards. The South African private security business employs
more than 250,000 people. You can hire guards ranging from
Super Cops, who wear uniforms like the California police on TV,
to German Special Security Advisors, whose insignia has an imperial eagle and something that looks like a Nazi SS symbol.

Most cars seem to have some sort of burglar alarm or security
lock, including varieties I've never seen in the United States: but-
tons hidden in ashtrays; combination locks; pocket transmitters
you push while approaching the car, that make the headlights flash;
coded computer chips that have to be plugged into a slot on the
steering-wheel column. On windless nights, the part of town
around my hotel echoes with the sound of all these car alarms
going off by mistake, an erratic symphony of warnings in a society
on edge, like the watchmen's whistles of Gorky. The alarms are
in the white areas only, however, for I see and hear none of them
when I stay overnight at a friend's house in Soweto.

Some of this array of guards and alarms is likely anywhere in
the world where the very rich live near the very poor. But much
of it is also white South Africa's anxiety response to the ANC
guerrilla war. A raid on the Sasol coal-to-oil conversion plants
some years ago set storage tanks on fire and sent a heavy pall of
smoke over Johannesburg for several days. Guerrillas have made
other attacks in the city itself: explosions at police stations, in
sidewalk garbage cans, in a hotel lobby. The attacks are not numerous enough to be a real threat, but are enough to make whites
uneasy.

Some of their defenses, however, seem mainly symbolic. Everywhere in the white suburbs, for example, are eight-foot-high fences
or cement walls. You see all these fortifications and think they
must be protecting a military post, then come closer and find it's
only somebody's backyard. Yet except for the ones with razor
wire, the fences are easy enough to climb over—a friend and I
do so with no trouble once when trying to get to a political meeting
whose main entrance is being watched by the police. Other forms
of armament seem equally irrational. Driving past a railway yard
on the city's outskirts, I even see an armored car on rails. Is this
for suppressing insurrections of railway workers? Of passengers?
Of rebel-held trains?

## YUPPIES

One morning I wake in my hotel room and find that during the night a telex for another room has been slipped under my door by mistake: GILTS HAVE DOUBLED IN VALUE SINCE PURCHASE APPROX 5 YEARS AGO. MOST GRATEFUL YOU PROVIDE COMMENT AND ANY DOCUMENTATION REQUIRED WHILE I AM ON SAFARI. EARNINGS SHOWN ARE TAX FREE AND SHOULD BE GROSSED UP TO ESTABLISH MAXIMUM MORTGAGE ENTITLEMENT. It strikes a note that echoes on all sides, for a sizable slice of white South Africa is in a frenzy of moneymaking.

CREATING WEALTH IS ONE OF THE MOST RESPONSIBLE THINGS YOU CAN DO reads the headline of a magazine advertisement,

Because wealth generates employment. It makes development possible. It provides housing. It raises everyone's standard of living. And it is the single most important thing you can do to ensure the future of our country and its peoples. Through the consolidation of your financial services, greater efficiency and further opportunities may be realized. The United is fully geared to offer you such a range of services. With banking, borrowing, investment and insurance all under one roof.

Another magazine profiles some local high achievers:

All Grant Dunbar ever wanted to do in his twenties was make a million before he hit 30. The baby-faced majority shareholder (over 80 percent) in FastFax, leader in the fax supply and service field by a long shot, he is worth far more than that at only 31. But you know what they say about people who peak early: that they can only go downhill. "Not me," he says. "Far from it. I've just started. I think my company has the potential to be as big as Altech." Still, he sees his thirties as a time to catch up on the things he neglected during the years he was carving a path through the high-tech jungle. . . . Marriage is NOT on the cards, so don't even think of it, girls. Admitting that he can't be told what to do, that "compromise" is not a word he understands, Grant says: "I'm quite happy with the idea that relationships are transient."

The place where such people are spending their grossed-up earnings is Johannesburg's northern suburbs, an expanse of elegant shopping malls, sleek mirror-glass corporate headquarters with courtyard fountains, and restaurants where the waiters ask, "Would you like some fresh-ground pepper on your salad?" Here, also, are the comfortable homes on quiet, winding streets lined with plane trees or the brilliant blue flowers of jacarandas. Here are the great estates, like Brenthurst, the well-guarded fifty acres belonging to Harry Oppenheimer, who flew in Peter Duchin's orchestra from New York to play for his wife's sixtieth birthday. And here are the spacious supermarkets where whites shop, pausing at the butcher's counter to buy cheaper cuts—separated out as "staff meat"—for their servants. To the summer folk in this upward-bound part of Sunny South Africa, the black townships are even more invisible than usual, not present even in the white subconscious. I meet several psychotherapists and ask them: how does apartheid enter the dreams of your white patients? They all agree: generally it doesn't.

The pinched government treasury is spending little money on building in the black townships these days, and so in Johannesburg the big real estate deals are here in the northern suburbs. A forest of construction cranes is silhouetted against the horizon. More than $3 billion has been staked on five gigantic projects in this area. One is a huge American-designed "airpark"—a shopping and entertainment complex build around a runway for light planes and helicopters.

Business is booming here, rather than in downtown Johannesburg, because downtown is increasingly filled with blacks—people who are living illegally in officially "white" apartments, and shoppers who take the train in from Soweto on weekends. And so corporate offices are moving out to the suburbs, for some of the same reasons their U.S. counterparts flee Manhattan for Connecticut or Westchester.

Throughout these green suburbs dart vans and buses bringing in from the townships the Africans who work in the shops and restaurants and department stores. The customers they serve are mostly white. But not entirely: blacks are welcome also—as long as they've got money to spend. Advertisers have targeted this category as a growing one. They are, in the words of a local business newsletter, people who are "yearning for World City, dressing, driving and grooving to outsmart, but still locked in family traditions such as mealie meal, a visit to iKhaya over long weekends and vestigial respect and care for the elders. But . . . these cats believe they're Born Beautiful and their place in the sun must surely come." South African marketing experts have labeled this group of potential customers BLUMS—Black Upward Mobile Sophisticates.

## RHETORIC

In the nearly thirty years since I first visited South Africa, the distribution of power has not changed. But, I notice, it is now clothed in radically different official rhetoric. In the old days, white politicians talked of blacks as no more fit to take part in political life than children. Today, by contrast, cabinet ministers speak highflown words about progress and power sharing and about how rapidly apartheid must be dismantled—if, indeed, there is any left at all. Human rights for all? Of course! Democracy? A splendid idea! At times, the government's rhetoric is hard to distinguish from that of the liberation movement. Frederick W. De Klerk, the country's new President, says he wants "a South Africa free of domination or oppression in whatever form."

If, then, all these blacks shot down by troops and police and armored cars are not being killed for protesting domination or oppression, why, in fact, are they being shot down? The answer is clear: they're Communists. Or terrorists. Or manipulated by Communists and terrorists. Members of Parliament fulminate against the Cubans and the Russians and *die rooikomplot* (the red conspiracy). Professional anti-Communists are flown in from places like the Heritage Foundation and the U.S. Naval War College to give solemn speeches of warning. And the South African government has eagerly supplied sites, tanks, trucks, and troops to film producers making Rambo-type movies for the American and European market, such as *Mercenary Fighters* with Peter Fonda, and *Red Scorpion,* where Dolph Lundgren plays a disillusioned Soviet assassin sent to Africa, who betrays his Kremlin masters.

The real audience for all this anti-communism is overseas, where South Africa has worked long and hard to forge bonds with conservatives in government and the military in the United States and Europe. "Government jargon makes much of the 'total onslaught' of Marxist forces against the West in Africa, of the 'Soviet threat,' " wrote *New York Times* columnist Flora Lewis on a visit to South Africa. "But when pushed for details, nobody seems to take it seriously except Washington."

Maintaining this official anti-communism has become much harder since the sea change in the Soviet Union and Eastern Europe and recently, for the most part, it has been quietly abandoned. But in South Africa itself, years of such rhetoric have left a peculiar, dual legacy. Among young township blacks, few of whom have read a word of Marx, the word "Communist" has come to mean someone who is fiercely dedicated and determined. (It is not the only word the liberation movement has stood on its head. One imprisoned ANC leader named his daughter Treason.)

Among most whites, on the other hand, "Communist" can mean anybody who is upset about black poverty. One day in Johannesburg I have lunch with a forceful, matronly white woman in her fifties who works for the Red Cross; she tells me about her organization's work combating rural hunger. As we walk out of the restaurant, we overhear a white couple whispering to each other at another table: "Could you hear? That girl's a *Communist!*"

## ALEXANDRA

In the 1950s, a talented generation of black writers romanticized the "shebeens" of Johannesburg: the unlicensed township speakeasies where drinking, music, and fellowship could be interrupted by a police raid at any moment. For some whites, too—like the naive American journalist in Nadine Gordimer's short story "Open House"—these were places of exotic appeal, with the promise of interracial sex and the furtive thrill of the illegal. But the reality may be closer to a shebeen I visit in Alexandra township, the desolate black slum surrounded on all sides by white Johannesburg, at the unromantic hour of nine o'clock in the morning. It is basically just a table, surrounded by corrugated tin walls and a tin roof. Already at this hour, several men are sitting here talking, drinking liter bottles of Castle beer. Every once in a while one staggers out unsteadily to urinate in a corner of the dirt yard next door. From time to time, a man or small boy shows up at the door, coming from home to return empty beer bottles.

Ever since the first settlers at the Cape of Good Hope traded brandy for cattle more than three hundred years ago, liquor has been a powerful tool of white colonization. The conquerers came "with bible and bottle," writes the poet S. E. K. Mqhayi. The extraordinary thing was how deliberate this was. In 1891, a Johannesburg *Star* editorial brazenly said: "In alcohol is to be found the only influence which may be trusted to sap the fund of seemingly infinite vitality [of blacks] which will overcome civilisation if civilisation does not overcome it." Two years later, an observer in the countryside wrote: "Many farmers hold that canteens do good; they make the labourers work for drink, they absorb their wages rapidly, and compel them to work for more to supply the craving . . . one farmer said it ensured him a good supply of labour." Some white-owned vineyards in the Cape region today still use the infamous "tot" system, where black farmworkers are paid partly in drink: five cups or "tots" of cheap wine at fixed times throughout working hours, adding up to more than a quart per worker every day.

Looking into old tavern records and police files, the social historian Charles Van Onselen has shown how the mineowners of the turn-of-the-century Johannesburg gold rush found what he calls "a double delight" in encouraging blacks to drink. First, several major mineowners jointly owned the main distillery. And second, the black workers who drank could save little, and so had to remain at the mines instead of returning to their families in the countryside.

Mineowners lobbied hard against restrictions on drinking. "Nearly everyone is agreed," stated a Mining Commissioner, "that total prohibition would be disastrous to the native labour position." Only when alcoholism reached the point where up to 25 percent of black laborers were too drunk to work in the morning did the owners let the authorities partly crack down. Today the alcohol and mining industries remain tied; South African Breweries, which controls the beer market, is part of the Anglo-American empire. At the time of my visit, it is saturating the airwaves with a gauzy pre-Christmas TV commercial showing well-dressed families of all races joyfully welcoming returning members at a railway station before, presumably, going home to start drinking.

The owners of this Alexandra shebeen are uneasy at my presence. With my American accent, they must think, I'm probably not a police agent, but still I'm a white man asking a lot of questions. The woman serving beer looks at me with an expression that suggests she is thinking: how can we get this guy out of here? She proposes to her husband that he drive me on a quick tour of the township in his *bakkie,* or pickup truck. And so he does.

He is a wizened black man in his fifties, who owns a plumbing business as well as the shebeen. He tells me his name, and, with a nervous eye on my tape recorder, proceeds to say how things are just wonderful in Alexandra, absolutely splendid, and getting still better all the time:

"Streets are being tarred, paved, storm drains, sewerage and everything! Look, it's something you can't do overnight. It takes years. It's working fine." He refers only briefly to "that unrest business" of several years ago, when, I remember, police killed some two dozen people here in a single week. "But now everything is solved." I remark on the crowded shacks around us. Everywhere in the world it's the same, he insists. "You've always got difficulty in housing people. I'm not a politician, hey? I'm not interested in politics. No."

I sit next to him in the cab of the *bakkie.* We pass a rough field with cattle, goats, sheep, and pigs, then head down a dirt road. "Our black people have a tradition here," he explains. "Like now, you see, here's a graveyard. That's why people have the cattle here. If somebody dies, the day of the burial, you buy goats or sheep and slaughter them, for the people who come to the funeral."

The road we are jouncing over has been made muddy by rain

last night. The tires slip. Something in the man seems to change. "I'll get through," he says in a changed, weary voice. "Yesterday morning it wasn't like this when I came down to the graveyard. To my son's grave."

"Your son?"

"In 1986, he was shot by the police."

"I was here then," I say, "and I went to that funeral. It must have been painful for you."

"We couldn't cry anymore, because such a lot of kids died. He was twenty-two, and a quiet boy and hardworking. He was finished with his schooling. That Monday morning, I said to him, 'Let's go to work,' because he was working with me in the plumbing business. 'Daddy, I can't,' he said. 'Look at what's taking place. Mummy will be alone here.' So he stayed at home. Only to die. But you never know your time. He was standing at the gate—up there, at home, when the bullet hit him. I can't say whether it was a stray bullet or not."

We pass the cemetery and leave the dirt road for a new, paved, divided street. He makes one final try to resume his previous voice: "They're going to do the streets like this—every street! Divided, yes. One way up and one way down!"

Then he asks me not to use his name. "Lots of them were scholars who were killed. He was just looking at the kids running on the street when that bullet hit him."

## A CASE OF THEFT

Amid the well-tended green parks of Johannesburg's northern suburbs, along those quiet streets that rustle with fallen leaves in the autumn, it is sometimes hard to remember that this whole shimmering edifice is built upon conquest. Not all the bloodshed was between black and white. As recently as the start of our own century, the two great white tribes of South Africa fought each other in the Boer War, partly over the question of who was going to get the gold under this soil. Today such thirst for wealth is sublimated into the socially acceptable channels of executive trainee programs or MBA degrees. But every once in a while there is a reminder of it in its earlier, more direct form. A friend tells me a story of something that happened, he says, on one of these tree-shaded streets a few years back:

In a certain elegant mansion behind its eight-foot-high wall, a Johannesburg mining magnate's son and his wife gave a dinner party. Their guests were a dozen or so friends: wealthy young whites from the city's elite, home for the holidays from Oxford or Cambridge or the London office of the family firm. The talk was of yachting, horse racing, holidays in the Mediterranean. The young woman decided to show her guests a new ring her father-in-law had given her, made from an unusual diamond with a yellowish tint. "Look how beautiful it is!" she said. "I'll pass it round." Guests in tuxedos and evening gowns began passing the ring from hand to hand around the dining table. Food and wine were served, toasts were drunk, and some time later the hostess noticed that the ring had not yet come around the table and back to her.

"Can I have my ring back?" she asked. No one spoke.

"Who has the ring?" she asked more urgently. But each guest claimed to have passed it on to the next person, or not to have seen it at all. *"Who has the ring?"* she asked again.

The ring was never recovered.

# The Truth Room

Although other streams of Voortrekkers continued to explore other parts of the country, the beleaguered main body of the Great Trek in Natal still had not resolved its conflict with the Zulus over land. It was this bitter fight that would finally culminate in the Trek's greatest battle, the event that would leave the greatest imprint on the collective memory of that time, among both blacks and whites.

That battle was still nearly a year away, though, in the early months of 1838. The Boers who had made the long journey over the Drakensberg were bloodied and thirsting for revenge. First King Dingane had tricked and slaughtered Piet Retief and the band of seventy men who had gone with him to Dingane's court to obtain land. Then Dingane's regiments had quickly fallen on Trekker camps and, in the Great Murder, had massacred nearly five hundred men, women, and children in a single, terrible night. To top it off, the Zulus who attacked on the night of the Great Murder had made off with some 25,000 cattle and sheep—a substantial share of the Trekkers' wealth. The Boers still did not think of themselves as invaders, but as good Christians who had arrived in the Promised Land. They felt sorely beset by heathen hordes whom God had sent to try their courage and determination.

The two massacres had taken place in February 1838. As the

year passed, groups of Voortrekkers and Zulus fought a number of skirmishes, but the major part of the Zulu armies remained intact. Among the Trekkers, morale was low; living in fortified camps and fearful of more Zulu attacks, they had a hard time finding enough protected land to graze their remaining cattle and horses. Food was rationed, ammunition ran low, and illness swept the crowded, muddy camps.

Dingane remained with his court at Umgungundhlovu. He knew that several thousand Trekkers had come over the mountains into the edges of his kingdom, and that small streams of them were pushing farther into Natal. But he also knew that the decisive showdown with them had not yet taken place. Dingane was, however, acutely, bitterly aware that the Trekkers had guns, and that it would be almost impossible for him ever again to have the advantage of a massive surprise attack. For him, it was an ominous year of skirmishing and waiting. He received some reports from his scouts, but many did not return: they were caught and executed by the Boers.

Dingane also had to deal with thousands of refugees who fled toward Umgungundhlovu from the areas where the Trekkers had their camps. They abandoned their crops and villages, and the Boers took spoils. Once again, the only writings are those left by the conquerors. Behind their records of these seizures can be imagined the Zulu despair:

"News came from the patrol harvesting the gardens of the Kaffirs," said one Trekker account, "that more wagons must come there in order to carry to our camp millet, maize, pumpkins and calabashes." The Boers, low on food, grabbed whatever the Zulus had abandoned, and as usual took this as a sign of divine approval. "This is indeed through God's care a great blessing for these poor emigrants, that the Lord has in the wilderness prepared a table for them," wrote Erasmus Smit, one of the Trek leaders. "May God make us all thankful for his fatherly care!" There are no surviving descriptions of Dingane's court during these months, but as he and his people received news of their villages plundered, their crops stolen, their scouts killed, they can only have felt a sense of impending doom.

□

During my visit to Johannesburg, I find the resistance movement
suffering from a similar sense of devastation and fear. As in Dingane's time, it is the whites who have the more powerful weapons,
and in the last decade they have been using them with a vengeance.
Recent South African history has always moved in cycles of upheaval and repression: The massive civil disobedience of the late
1950s was met with the Sharpeville massacre. The Soweto student
revolt of 1976 was followed by police killings of hundreds and
the banning of black consciousness organizations. The township
upheavals that began in 1984 have been met with the bloodiest
state violence of all, with more than five thousand people killed
so far. Now, at the time of my visit, South Africa is trying hard
to stamp out the last flickers of this revolt. There will undoubtedly
be more cycles of repression and upheaval, freeze and thaw, in
the decade ahead. I am surely here at a low point, however, for
it is hard to imagine a more harsh crackdown than I see around
me.

One stark symbol of the repression is in the middle of downtown
Johannesburg: the shell of a six-story building. All its windows
are shattered, and its floors strewn with rubble. Owned by the
South African Council of Churches, Khotso House provided office
space not only for church groups, but also for a wide variety of
other opposition organizations, from women's groups to a multiracial photographers' collective.

Near midnight on August 31, 1988, Khotso House was destroyed by a carefully planned bombing. Someone apparently
drove a vehicle packed with high explosives into the building's
basement garage, and left it near an elevator shaft that would carry
the blast to upper floors. Eighteen people were injured, and the
building itself was rendered useless. Floors buckled, walls collapsed, and fragments of glass and concrete were blasted all over
the street. As I walk past Khotso House some three months later,
workers are dumping blast debris from the upper floors down a
long chute.

In the last few years, close to a hundred other mysterious night
explosions, fire-bombings, or burglaries have hit the homes of

activists or the offices of unions, student groups, black newspapers, and church organizations. Because hardly any bombers are ever caught, they are generally thought to be off-duty policemen, particularly those belonging to a neo-Nazi right-wing group known as the AWB—the *Afrikaner Weerstandsbeweging* (Afrikaner Resistance Movement).

Another, even more crippling form of repression has been mass jailings. Since 1984, more than 51,000 people have been imprisoned without charge or trial. South Africa has always locked up anti-apartheid activists whenever it felt like it, but in June 1986, clues appeared that something out of the ordinary was under way. Startled common criminals serving sentences all over the country found themselves amnestied. All prisoners not serving time for political offenses got six months off their sentences. This was to make space in the jails. Then, the day *before* the government proclaimed a State of Emergency (which would have alerted people to go into hiding), it arrested some one thousand key activists. Thousands more arrests followed. Most difficult for the victims and their families was that they never knew whether they were going to be kept behind bars for a few weeks or—as happened in many cases—more than two years.

Such crackdowns have an impact on far more people than those arrested, because for every person jailed, two or three more fear it can happen to them next. "I always have my trousers and everything packed," Azaria Ndebele, a human rights worker, tells me. "If there is knocking on my door at night, I get fully dressed before I answer. They have come more than four times this year. They said, 'Why's your bag packed? Why are you all dressed? We've only come to search.' " Others decide to flee to the countryside. At the height of these detentions, a friend who worked in Khotso House before it was blown up tells me, people would slip into the building with little more than rags on their backs, hungry and desperate from hiding out in the mountains or on the *veld,* and begging for help. Con men would come, too, claiming to be activists on the run from the police, and you could not always tell the difference. Quarrels erupted within organizations between those who went underground and those who stayed visible, and there was much backbiting.

Depending on the political climate of the moment, hundreds, sometimes thousands, of people throughout South Africa intermittently live underground. A black activist in the arts tells me, "If I come to Joburg, sometimes it's two or three days before I can find somebody." Sometimes he himself drops out of sight and stays at others' houses for several weeks at a time: "If you're on a small committee and they start arresting the other members, say. If we hold a public meeting, we make sure that not all the committee members are on the platform."

The crackdown of the late 1980s was aimed at all the principal forms of resistance. Black labor unions, for example, were especially hard hit. An estimated four thousand of those jailed were shop stewards or other unionists. In 1987, at the time of a black railway workers' strike, police stormed through COSATU House, the headquarters of the Congress of South African Trade Unions, a few blocks from Khotso House. They smashed more than $20,000 worth of windows and furnishings, beat office workers with billy clubs, and arrested four hundred people. A few weeks later, COSATU House was attacked by two massive bomb blasts. As with the Khotso House explosion, police sealed off the ruins of the building for "investigation," denying union organizers access to their files. In the following months, more than a dozen other union offices around the country were hit by arson attacks, police raids, or burglaries of files. After that, the saboteurs mostly sat back and let the free market take over: many unions were evicted from their offices, and had trouble renting new space. What landlord wants a tenant who'll be fire-bombed?

The consumer boycotts that burst into life in the Eastern Cape and elsewhere in the mid-eighties were met with similar force. Police arrested Mkhuseli Jack, the key boycott organizer in Port Elizabeth and one of the country's most talented young black leaders. Trying to get him to call off the boycott, they beat him severely while he was suspended upside down from a crossbar, his wrists shackled together. Jack refused. They eventually crushed the boycott anyway, and Jack stayed in jail several years.

I talk to Ike Tshitlho, a bearded, articulate man of thirty-six, who helped organize a consumer boycott of the central cattle slaughterhouse in Bloemfontein, in support of some fired workers:

"We held a meeting and we decided since the buying power is about eighty percent black, the best thing for us to do was to organize the black butchers and shopkeepers to only buy chicken meat." But before they could launch the boycott, the police arrested three hundred of the city's black activists, keeping some in jail up to three months. Tshitlho and sixty other people were crammed into one large cell with a single toilet. The boycott failed.

"Street committees" also were singled out for attack. These informal governments had flourished in various black townships as the official structures crumbled. In places where the street committees were particularly strong, like Johannesburg's Alexandra township, the committees actually collected the rent that people were refusing to pay the government, and spent it on community services. "People's courts" settled disputes. Mamelodi township, outside Pretoria, even had an appeals court system. But the authorities hit back, hard. In some townships, virtually every known street committee member was arrested: in East London's Duncan Village township, for example, 256 street committee members were thrown into the city's Fort Glamorgan Prison; almost all were still there a year later. In the township of Zwelethemba, near Worcester, the police mounted searchlights on towers, playing the beams on streets, and letting them come to rest on the front doors of particularly well known activists.

The police in Bloemfontein, according to Ike Tshitlho, "intimidated church leaders not to give us any church premises for holding meetings. The police would go to an employer and tell them that you should never employ this type of person. They have gone to schools and made sure someone will not be accepted."

Some organizations not banned outright, I find, still work in fear of having their files stolen, their offices fire-bombed, their staff members jailed. And so even people doing things that are fully legal sometimes operate half-clandestinely. Such secrecy creates organizational chaos and great opportunities for misuse or embezzlement of funds, of which one hears many stories.

And so the aura of repression spreads everywhere. People I talk to worry even about an everyday act like opening the mail. I notice a poster in the office of a black official of the Council of Churches:

---

### LETTER BOMBS
#### PUBLIC AWARENESS CHART

*Balance.* Any letter should be treated as suspect if it is unbalanced, has loose contents, or is heavier on one side than the other.

*Restrictive Markings.* CONFIDENTIAL, PERSONAL or other restrictive markings might indicate a letter bomber trying to ensure that the package is opened only by a target individual.

*Protruding Wires or Tinfoil.* Letter bombs can be loosened or damaged in the post causing fuses to penetrate the envelope.

*Excessive Weight.* If it seems excessively heavy for its size it should be treated as suspect.

---

Though letter bombs are a recent invention, other kinds of violence in South Africa are not. White farmers, for example, have long assumed a right to beat their black laborers—and court decisions often support them. At the time of my visit, a farmer named Jacobus Vorster, near the town of Louis Trichardt, is let off with no prison time at all for tying a farm laborer to a tree and beating him to death. He is only required to pay the man's common-law wife a pension for five years.

The state, also, lays on the lash at will. More than forty thousand South Africans—98 percent of them black—are sentenced to whippings each year. "Whipping is not more humiliating than imprisonment and will teach a short, sharp lesson," according to J. A. D'Oliveira, Attorney General of the Transvaal. The figure of forty thousand excludes several of the homelands and it also does not count minors, who are sentenced to caning rather than whipping.

One twist of South Africa's reign of official violence is that these days the person who administers it—the whipping, the interrogation, the baton wielded against a crowd—is often black. It is jarring to see black policemen with pistols or shotguns patrolling through the townships alongside white cops, or standing guard at the township police stations that are ringed with walls of sandbags. I wonder: how can they do this? The best answer comes from Primo Levi, who asked the same question about the Jews he saw collaborating at Auschwitz:

> [I]f one offers a position of privilege to a few individuals in a state of slavery, exacting in exchange the betrayal of a natural solidarity with their comrades, there will certainly be someone who will accept. He will be withdrawn from the common law and will become untouchable; the more power that he is given, the more he will be consequently hateful and hated. . . . Moreover, his capacity for hatred, unfulfilled in the direction of the oppressors, will double back, beyond all reason, on the oppressed; and he will only be satisfied when he has unloaded onto his underlings the injury received from above.

Another type of violence in these last few years has come, unfortunately, from the movement itself. Terror begets terror, and there has all too often been a nasty, coercive underside to the opposition in the townships. At times during the consumer boycotts, when no one was supposed to buy anything in downtown shopping areas, gangs of young men searched people returning from downtown and forced them to drink the cooking oil or detergent they had bought there. At other times, "people's courts" got carried away and sentenced people to death. In Soweto one Christmas, gangs of enforcers went from house to house smashing the light fixtures of those who didn't observe a "black Christmas." Sometimes in the townships, young men come door-to-door or stop cars collecting money "for the struggle," but no one knows where it goes.

The worst of the violence from the movement has been the "necklace" killings of suspected police informers (a few of whom later turned out to be innocent). Sometimes burning people to death in this manner was called "Kentuckying," after Kentucky Fried Chicken. The United Democratic Front leadership condemned these executions. But they could do little, for most respected black leaders of any note were, at the height of the necklace killings, in detention or banned from speaking publicly. Their voices could not be heard, and necklacing continued.

One Sunday morning in Soweto, without knowing it at the time, I meet someone who will shortly become the best-known victim of this violence from within the movement. The occasion is just before a church service in the Orlando West district. Rev. Paul Verryn, a white Methodist minister who lives in Soweto, introduces me and several other visitors to nine or ten teenagers who are temporarily living here in his house—mostly boys who have recently been released from detention but who for one reason or another cannot go back to their families. One boy is a short, bright-eyed fourteen-year-old, Stompie Mokhetsi Seipei. The moment passes; the boys leave; and I think no more about them until several weeks later, back home at the far side of the world. One morning the newspapers report that Stompie Seipei has been murdered, and several of his companions brutally beaten, by bodyguards of Winnie Mandela. The survivors bear scars inflicted, they say, by Mandela herself.

Winnie Mandela's own behavior has been increasingly erratic since the mid-eighties. She gave a speech endorsing necklacing; she hired an American businessman to try to collect fees from people making films or TV shows about her and her husband; and her much-loathed group of bodyguards, the "Mandela Football Club," turned into a gang, roughing up and extorting money from Soweto residents. As the wife of the most revered of all black South Africans, she has caused great embarrassment for the liberation movement, but only delight for the government, which let her alone, hoping she would do more. It has had no hesitation, of course, about muzzling, jailing, or torturing thousands of other black leaders who both preached and practiced non-violence.

Finally, there is the violence that is the most painful of all to hear about, because those who inflict it have their victims so totally at their mercy: the violence of the police against their prisoners. A particularly notorious place for this is the *waarheid kamer,* or "truth room," at the high-rise central police station at John Vorster Square in Johannesburg, the building where, as people say, you "go in through the door and out through the window." The police always have some excuse for why certain prisoners don't emerge from John Vorster Square alive. As the black poet Chris van Wyk comments:

> *He fell from the ninth floor*
> *He hanged himself*
> *He slipped on a piece of soap while washing*
> *He hanged himself*
> *He slipped on a piece of soap while washing*
> *He fell from the ninth floor*
> *He hanged himself while washing*
> *He slipped from the ninth floor*
> *He hung from the ninth floor*
> *He slipped on the ninth floor while washing*
> *He fell from a piece of soap while slipping*
> *He hung from the ninth floor*
> *He washed from the ninth floor while slipping*
> *He hung from a piece of soap while washing*

Most prisoners, of course, are not killed in the truth room, only beaten or tortured. I am shown a desperate but reticent message from one victim, smuggled out of prison on a piece of toilet paper: "My private parts have been swollen for a whole week." I hear black-consciousness leader Peter Jones describe how police interrogators first beat him with a weighted piece of black hose ("they called that black power") and then with a green one ("they called that green power"). I hear his colleague, union organizer Mandla Seloane, matter-of-factly tell how he was kicked and punched at his interrogation: "No electricity or anything fancy, just normal white-black stuff."

This "normal white-black stuff" has gone on in South Africa for a long time. In the early days at the Cape of Good Hope, the Dutch East India Company employed a professional executioner and torturer. His official pay scale listed the bonus payment he received for each job, in rixdollars, the Company currency:

| | |
|---|---|
| Breaking limbs | 12 |
| Pinching with red-hot tongs | 4 |

| | |
|---|---|
| Burning | 12 |
| Decapitating | 8 |
| Hanging | 8 |
| Strangling | 6 |
| Scorching | 2 |
| Quartering and hanging up the pieces | 6 |
| Transporting the body to the place of execution | 3 |
| Torturing | 10 |
| Chopping off the hand | 4 |
| Scourging | 3 |
| Branding with a red-hot iron | 1 |
| Placing the rope around the neck | 2 |
| Putting into the pillory | 2 |

This man's successors today are likely to use more modern techniques. Some they learned from Argentine interrogators, who traveled to Pretoria to give "seminars" to South African security policemen during Argentina's period of military rule.

I hear about some of these methods from a black journalist. He is in his early thirties but looks somewhat older. He sits across a table from me in a cafeteria next to the Johannesburg newspaper where he works. His gaze is steady, his voice low and controlled:

"I was in for eighteen months altogether. All of it was in solitary. I had only a rough idea at the time of who was in the same prison with me. Sometimes I caught sight of someone in the corridors; at night we shouted to each other. For the first interrogation I was taken in on a Monday morning and kept awake until Wednesday night. Every eight hours the interrogation teams change. At first they keep you doing things like standing and holding up a chair for hours at a time. Then come the electric shocks. They would sit me on the floor and cover me with blankets and pour cold water—very cold—down the back of my neck. I was handcuffed, with my hands under my thighs. I could see nothing while it was going on. But I always knew what was coming because they would sit me down opposite an electric outlet in the wall. I never saw the machine or even felt the wires. The water conducted the electricity. I was screaming. They were screaming questions at me. This would go on each time for thirty minutes or more. After each session you are a shivering wreck, man, a wreck. And then they tell you: 'Tell us what we want or next time we'll use it on your balls.'

"These guys are just like machines. They show no emotion. They are very businesslike. They believe they are doing the right thing. They tell you constantly during the torture: 'You are just being used by the Communists. South Africa is a good place for you.'

"Throughout this whole interrogation period you are in leg irons. Even when you go to the toilet you are in chains. I never felt as relieved as I did when they removed those chains from my legs after that first week. The following week I was taken to a magistrate. The very same guys who had been torturing me were with me. They were in his office when he asked me: did I have any complaints? The government will tell you that all detainees see a magistrate each week—which is true. And that they never complain—which is also true.

"My case was one of the milder ones. At the end of the eighteen months I was told to go home. I was never charged with anything."

Emelda Sizakele Nkosi is twenty-three years old, a stocky woman in a red blouse and brown skirt. She is composed and firm, and insists that yes, it is quite all right to use her real name.

Nkosi was a member of the Commercial, Catering and Allied Workers Union, the shop steward at a supermarket. One night in November 1986, at about 4:00 a.m., some twenty-five policemen "just burst into the house, and into the room I was sleeping in. They didn't even knock." They were actually searching for Nkosi's brother, but "they found me with some material of the union. That was why they detained me."

She was jailed this first time for six months. In other cells in the same block she could hear small children. One woman in another cell had a two-month-old baby. Several gave birth in detention—one in the prison's waiting room because the police didn't bother to get her to the hospital in time.

There were worms in the food. The warders "treated us very harshly. When somebody was sick in the cell, we had to call through the windows for two or three hours. We would just call and call. Sometimes they would come, sometimes they wouldn't come."

A single parent, Nkosi has an eight-year-old boy. While she was in detention, he was looked after by her mother, whose small pension fed them both. "Now when he sees a white man, he thinks that person is a policeman. He even vowed that if I'm detained now, I must take him along."

Nkosi is a committed, knowledgeable feminist, aware of the irony that she was arrested the first time when they came looking for her brother. She knows something of the long history of black women's resistance, which goes back to strikes, boycotts, and pass burnings in the 1930s and earlier. She talks about the huge distance women have to go in a society where pregnancy is a legal basis for dismissal from a job, and about the hostility to the idea of women holding positions of power in unions and other black organizations. Her boyfriend, she says, "thinks that women must only be involved in women's organizations, and must play a low profile. And that men must be at the front. But I was involved in progressive organizations long before him."

Nkosi's second spell in detention lasted more than a year. The first five months were in solitary. "I was given a Bible after three months. I was sick, and looked after by men, because there were not enough women who were working at that police station. Sometimes I would faint without being seen, especially if I got an asthma attack. I would be found after an hour, or I would wake up at the district surgeon's or at hospital." She was not allowed the drug that could prevent the asthma attacks. "All cells were searched regularly. So I couldn't even hide a pen."

Finally, the police put her in a communal cell, with thirteen women, one of them sixteen years old. The women sent a protest to the Minister of Law and Order, and finally went on a hunger strike. "We stayed without food for fourteen days, demanding our release or charge." Eventually, officials took Nkosi away and put her in a solitary punishment cell. "They said I was an instigator." Then she got very ill, with a string of asthma attacks. The women she had been with went on another hunger strike for ten days, demanding her release. It didn't work. The women then broke windows, and burned sheets, mattresses, and blankets.

"After they burned them, the wardresses came to extinguish the fire. Then they left. After an hour, they came with men, forty men. These men were carrying batons, guns, tear-gas canisters, and they were wearing tear-gas masks. They came straight to my cell and asked me what was happening. I told them I don't get proper medical care here, and I want to leave, I want to go home. I told them they mustn't use the tear gas because I was an asthmatic person. They told me, 'We're going to take out your asthma today.' Then they tear-gassed me. I was in my cell. I don't know what happened. I fainted. That happened at half past five p.m. About eleven p.m. I woke up. I found myself in another section, another floor, with only one blanket, and I had some blue marks on my body, which means they beat me up when I was unconscious. When I woke up I was only wearing my panties. The other women were calling to me through the windows. They told me that they had been strip-searching all of us in front of the male warders."

Nkosi was finally released. But like hundreds of former detainees, she is "restricted": she cannot be with more than ten people at a time and she has to be at home from 6:00 p.m. to 6:00 a.m. She must sign in at a police station daily. Although she is not allowed to do any political work, she says forcefully that she wants to resume her union organizing. She has medical problems with nervousness, her feet, her asthma, and her eyes. She thinks the problems with her eyes may have to do with the time in solitary confinement, where for months she had nothing to focus on farther than a few feet away.

From the *Cape Times,* March 2, 1988:

> Prison authorities used teargas nine times between February 10 last year and January 31 this year to "calm down" emergency detainees and defuse potentially dangerous situations, the Minister of Justice, Mr. Kobie Coetsee, said [in Parliament] yesterday. . . .
>
> Mr. Coetsee was replying to a question by Mr. Jan van Eck (Independent, Claremont). He said the use of teargas was subject to strict rules and served as an alternative when all other less drastic options to defuse a potential dangerous situation had been exhausted.

□

Late afternoon. Two weeks before Christmas. Downtown Johannesburg is decorated with long strings of winking colored lights. There are Christmas trees in shop windows and merchants have hired small brass bands to play carols, on sidewalks crowded with holiday shoppers. The sound of "Hark, the Herald Angels Sing" and "O Little Town of Bethlehem" drifts up through the window of the small, bare office where Gladys Shezi is talking. She, too, insists that I use her real name.

"They came around one in the morning. They kicked the doors. After that they started searching the house, putting everything upside down. They slapped everybody in the house in their faces and they threatened that they're going to shoot them if they don't tell what my activities are. I told them: 'Don't threaten my family. Just take me. I am the one who is active in the house.'

"They took me to Alexandra police station. They kicked me, slapped me, even hit me with the back of their guns. When I was bleeding through the nose they let me stay for about thirty minutes. They said they are taking a rest, they are coming back. After that, they said I must come and look at what they are doing to my colleagues, who were detained that day with me. They started kicking them, and hitting them with a plank with four nails in the head. When the blood comes out they started laughing. Then they blindfolded me. Then they started electric-shocking. There are marks. They are all over. The marks of the electric shocks, see?"

With a trembling hand, she points at small, round dark spots on her arms, the inside of her thigh, and points through her dress at her breasts and stomach.

"They laugh and they electric-shock me. I become unconscious. And when I wake up I find myself bleeding through the mouth and in the nose. My dress was torn."

After this, Shezi was held in solitary. "The cell I was staying in was in a block of single cells. I was the only person in that block. There were no people around me. I asked permission to see my kids. They said I'm not allowed. I'm not even allowed to see a lawyer, even to read a book. No visitors, no nothing. My visitors were my interrogators, those white men who come to interrogate me. They were my only visitors. [They threatened] to kill my kids. They threatened to kill my father."

Every time she pauses, we can hear the carols outside. "Silent Night, Holy Night," "God Rest Ye Merry Gentlemen," "Good King Wenceslas."

"I just wanted to kill myself," Shezi goes on. "I tried to tie a rope off the roof of my cell. I was too short to reach, I couldn't make it. I tried for almost three days. On the fourth day they find me out and said I must not do that. Then they put me in a cell which is having nothing on top, not even a shower, a cell which is empty, with a bed only. I stay in that cell for three months."

Shezi was released two weeks ago. She is a slight woman of twenty-seven, hesitant to look directly at me. She is nervous and soft-spoken today, shivering slightly, though her voice becomes a little louder as we talk.

Before her detention, Shezi was active in South Africa's nascent black women's movement, an organizer for the Federation of Transvaal Women. She helped organize a protest march on the Anglo-American headquarters by five hundred women. Another demonstration she worked on, against the government's suspension of the black newspaper *The New Nation,* was stopped by the police at the last moment. She also arranged support for the families of people in detention, and started a sewing cooperative to help township women find a source of income independent from their husbands.

"Others object, but we are trying to show that it's no longer in the olden days when we used to be kept in the kitchen. The women now can drive, the women can even do bricklaying. Men are not the only people who are going to liberate South Africa. On the factory floors, they take it as a sin if you get pregnant. We are being fired without pay, without even notice that you are going to be fired."

I ask about the problem of battered women, on which I have just heard Paul Verryn, the white minister in Soweto, preach a forceful sermon. "Yes," she says, "it's a *big* problem. Of women being beaten, and of being chased out of the house by their husbands."

In her own family, she says, her father, a driver, insisted that her mother, a former office worker with a high school diploma, stay home. If Shezi herself went out in the evening, he would lock her out of the house. "But when I was detained, he started now thinking that women must participate. And he even allowed my mother to go and look for work. Now he tells me that 'you must win the struggle.' He is no longer harassing me and shouting and doing all what he was doing before."

After Shezi's release, the police "said when they've got some information about me, they'll come and take me again. So now I'm not staying at home." She stays with friends, but misses her two small children. "I used to visit them during the nights, and see that they are all right. It is very difficult to have a relationship with them, for they are missing me. They can't have a mother next to them. When they are sick, they always cry for their grandmother. It makes me feel guilty, but I've got no alternatives."

Shezi was visiting her children at home recently when the police arrived. There were six of them. But, thinking quickly, she convinced them she was someone else. "When they said, 'What's your name?' I gave them the wrong name. When they said, 'Where is Gladys Shezi?' I said, 'She is in Natal.' When they went away, I just ran again."

This happened yesterday, she explains. No wonder she's nervous.

These last few weeks, Shezi has had trouble sleeping. "During my nights I always dream about those people when they come to torture me. I see them coming with their guns and trying to grab me, then I wake up again. I saw everything what they've done to me, during my nights when I am sleeping."

As she talks on, however, her voice becomes stronger and she stops trembling. Once or twice she looks me in the eye. She finishes by saying that she plans to go back to organizing women. "I'm going to do workshops for the women. I'm going to try to find some information from the old people like Mother Sisulu and the others about what they were doing during their day. Then I'll be able to educate our females. And I'm going to educate them that when they are detained they must know their rights. I can't resume [the organizing] while I am in hiding. When I see that things are cooling off, then I'll start again."

# Survivors

After talking to those who have been through it, it is hard to stop thinking about torture. I find myself looking at faces in the black crowds on Johannesburg's sidewalks, or in political meetings, and wondering how many of these people have had to endure live electrodes touched to their fingers, toes, breasts, genitals. I wonder, of course, if I could endure this myself. Although that is really not the question, for once you are in the torturers' hands, you have no choice. The question, rather, is whether you can survive without being broken or scarred for life. Despite the terrors they have had to endure, ex-prisoners like Emelda Nkosi and Gladys Shezi are, in a sense, the luckier ones. Neither has any doubt that she will keep on, as they both put it, "in the struggle." And it is that commitment that gives each woman such an impressive strength. But many of the countless thousands of victims of prison and torture in South Africa have been physically or emotionally crippled by their ordeals—especially those who are very young. I wonder what happens to them, whether they can be healed, how they can survive.

I pursue this question with a white psychotherapist I meet. Along with a dozen or so of her Johannesburg colleagues, she has been donating her skills to treat former political prisoners. Her name is Ruth Rice; she works as a clinical psychologist. We talk in her home, a modest house with several dogs and a flower garden. She is a quiet woman in a blue print dress, with a bearing of gentle dignity. On the windowpanes of her kitchen dish-cabinet is a homey clutter of pictures of family and friends, postcards from around the world, and a small photograph of Doris Lessing.

Treating former prisoners is not easy, she says. One problem is that traditional psychotherapy encourages people to get in touch with their doubts and weaknesses. But is that appropriate here? "It's not the kind of therapy you can do by asking someone to lie on a couch and feel vulnerable. For me it's always a question of how far you can go in breaking down a person's defenses when you know they may have to go back 'inside' and get beaten up again." She tells me with some optimism, however, about a recent group therapy session where she and a fellow psychologist, a white man, stumbled on a promising new technique:

"[He] and I met together with four people. They all knew each other, they'd been in detention together." The four black ex-prisoners all were depressed, and had the usual symptoms familiar to doctors who've worked with torture victims the world over: sleeplessness, sexual difficulties, inability to concentrate. The other therapist, Rice says, had an idea. "He stood up and said, 'Look, I'm Sergeant Swanepoel [a notoriously brutal security policeman of the 1960s],' and he and one of the guys had an arm-wrestling contest. Some of them were very resistant. But two of them got into it. You could actually see them building up their anger and getting into a thing about potency. [The therapist] got each of the people to actually fight with him, until they were rolling around on the ground, holding him down. 'Sergeant Swanepoel' was using provocative language: 'Come on, you kaffir!' He let them win. He finally got this one guy to fight with him, but it took a lot of doing. This guy was saying, 'No, look, I'm fine, I can cope with the cops, it's all right, it's no problem.' But he was the one who afterwards, when we sat down and talked about it, said, 'I'm absolutely dripping with sweat.' "

Ruth Rice herself has been to Denmark to study at a torture treatment center connected with Amnesty International there. What she and her colleague did here, she says, is contrary to the conventional wisdom; in Denmark, "they are very adamant that one shouldn't re-create the circumstances that a [torture victim] has been in—and so you shouldn't appear to be an authority figure, you don't want machinery around that might look like torture machinery, and so on. But what was so interesting about this was that it *was* re-creating the situation—but allowing them to win.

"The next week," she continues, "these guys came back. They brought another guy. They said they hadn't felt as well before as they had since that last session." The ex-prisoners were upbeat and encouraged; they arranged to meet with Rice and her fellow therapist again the following week.

"But then they phoned to say that one of them had been detained again . . ."

At my request, and after asking the patient's permission, Rice allows me to observe a therapy session. The setting is as different as could be imagined from a psychotherapist's office. We are sitting on metal chairs and a threadbare sofa in the office of a group that aids detention victims and their families. At the other side of the room, someone is pecking out a long list of political prisoners on a manual typewriter. Visitors wander in and out. On the building's front steps sit several people who are probably plainclothes policemen, eyeing everyone who enters.

The patient is a fourteen-year-old Soweto boy whom I shall call Sipho. He arrives with his mother, who wears a kerchief and has two other very small children in tow. Throughout the interview, she breast-feeds and changes diapers; sometimes the children climb onto Sipho's lap as well as hers.

It is the mother, a schoolteacher with a forthright, intelligent face, who first describes the symptoms: "Sipho is having illusions at times. Sometimes at night he talks to himself. Since his detention his attitude has changed. He was a free child, free in speaking. Now he goes away sometimes and doesn't tell us. He stays by himself. And doesn't want to talk."

Sipho wears blue Adidas shoes and a white T-shirt that says GO-MART. He is thin and slightly hunched over; his eyes are downcast. His arms and hands are scarred. "The whole body," his mother says quietly, noticing my eyes.

The boy speaks very low and slowly, looking at the floor, sometimes answering questions only with a nod or a sigh. Sipho's English is hesitant, and sometimes his mother helps him find the right word or phrase. He looks shell-shocked. It takes an hour for Ruth Rice, questioning gently but trying not to sound like an interrogator, just to get his story:

Sipho had been part of a student group that organized a school boycott. He was arrested and put in a cell with seventeen ordinary criminals. During the night, as he tried to sleep, one of them burned Sipho's face with a cigarette, saying, "Here, no one sleeps." He was the youngest in the cell. (Afterward, Rice and I wonder if he was also attacked sexually, but felt embarrassed to say so.)

"I didn't know where he was for three weeks," his mother says. "My husband's cousin is a policeman and he found out."

Soon after he was released, Sipho was attacked in the street by black vigilantes opposed to the school boycott. A friend who tried to defend him was stabbed in the eye. A few days later, while Sipho was in the hospital recovering from his beating, the vigilantes murdered his friend.

"They killed a friend of mine. They stabbed him," Sipho says as if still not quite believing, "the boy who was trying to protect me."

A few months later, Sipho was with a gang of "comrades"— young township militants. They hijacked a truck. The police arrived. The other boys managed to escape, but Sipho did not— they abandoned him in the truck and he didn't know how to drive. The police found a gun in the truck, and charged Sipho with armed robbery. At the police station, he was brutally beaten until he gave his interrogators the other boys' names.

"They kept beating me up. They hit me with their fists. They said they were going to kill me. They said, 'We'll put you away for seven years.' "

Sipho is now out on bail.

By degrees it becomes clear what enormous burdens he is laboring under: rage at the police and vigilantes; guilt at having survived when the friend who tried to protect him died; anger at the "comrades" who abandoned him; guilt at having been beaten into giving their names; fear of their retaliation—and of the horrors that may await him if he goes back to prison.

Steadily, Ruth Rice draws more and more of Sipho's story out of him. There is an unobtrusive wisdom underneath her warmth; he senses it and partly opens up. She speaks so low that I can barely hear her voice, like his. It is frustrating trying to make out all the words, until I realize why she is talking so softly: this is a boy whom white people have been shouting and screaming at.

In the idiomatic South African English that they both speak, Rice tries to help Sipho put his feelings into words: "Did you feel your comrades left you, there in the truck? You must be quite cross with them, hey?" She tries to make him feel that he is not alone: "Every Saturday here we see people who have come from detention. And the same kinds of things that have happened to you have happened to them. They are depressed and sad."

Sipho's mother adds: "He is not just sad; he is bitter. He hates our relatives who are on the police force."

Rice says, to Sipho: "The hardest part must be that you can't go and get angry with the people who hurt you. You can't go out there and be cross with the people who made you cross. You keep it all inside you."

"At night," says Sipho's mother, "he is running in the blankets."

At the end of two hours Sipho and his mother prepare to leave. Sipho says he thinks it has helped to talk, and that he will come back alone and talk to Rice again next week. I feel humbled and awed that this boy of fourteen, to whom so much has happened, is still able to talk at all. It is as if every possible part of South Africa's current storm of violence has fallen upon his thin, stooped shoulders. I also feel moved because of something else. For if Sipho embodies the tragedy of South Africa's present, the quiet woman he met today embodies an unusual piece of its past.

When the Boers of the Great Trek headed into the country's interior, one of the territories they settled first became an independent republic, later a British colony, and finally the province of the Orange Free State. One of its prime ministers was Abram Fischer. His son became chief judge of its supreme court. And *his* son, Bram Fischer, was a highly successful lawyer. Bram Fischer became an outcast to his fellow Afrikaners, however, when they discovered that, underground, he headed the Central Committee of the South African Communist Party. He is the model for Lionel

Burger in Nadine Gordimer's *Burger's Daughter*. In 1966, Bram Fischer was sentenced to life in prison. Nine years later, his body wasted by cancer, he was allowed to come home to die. After his death, the police came and confiscated Fischer's ashes, telling his family they were state property. Ruth Rice, who now sees Sipho out the door and invites the next patient in, is his daughter.

# On Trek

Surprisingly, given what we know today, during the first several years of the Great Trek it was not completely clear that people with gunpowder could defeat those armed only with spears. Our image of such battles tends to come from the Indian Wars of the late nineteenth century, the period of Hollywood westerns. But by that time the American whites had breech-loading, repeating rifles and revolvers. The South African Voortrekkers, on the other hand, had muskets little better than those of George Washington's army. These were muzzle-loaders: you had to insert loose powder, homemade shot and wadding, and then push it all into place with a ramrod. Loading the musket was difficult on horseback and almost impossible in rain.

The Voortrekkers' enemies, the Zulu *impis,* or regiments, of Dingane, were formidable opponents. The Zulus had mastered the principles of maneuvering in large formations; they could run huge distances; and, most terrifying to the small bands of Trekkers, they could mobilize ten to fifteen thousand warriors for a single battle. The Zulus fought with the confidence that they were part of southern Africa's strongest military kingdom, whose successes on the battlefield had completely reshaped this corner of their continent.

The British, fighting with the Xhosa further to the south, had proven the superior power of their muskets. But the circumstances were different: unlike the Voortrekkers, the British had regiments of professional soldiers, plenty of cannon, and a constant supply of munitions and equipment brought in by the Royal Navy. Furthermore, the Xhosa were not as well organized as the Zulus, and much of the fighting between them and the British involved Xhosa attacks on British forts. The Voortrekkers were farmers; isolated forts could not protect the thousands of square miles of grazing land they hoped to find in Natal.

And so during the first few months of 1838 it was uncertain that Voortrekker muskets would prevail over Zulu spears. Dingane and his people were clearly alarmed, however. Despite his two surprise attacks—the massacre of Piet Retief and his men, and the Great Murder—several thousand Boers were still in Natal. Their ox wagons were in heavily guarded camps, or cautiously moving deeper into Zulu territory in columns accompanied by armed horsemen.

In April of 1838, however, something happened that filled the Zulus with hope: they inflicted a brilliant military defeat on the Trekkers. Profoundly angered by the twin blows they had suffered, the Trekkers had organized a commando of 347 men on horseback to seek vengeance on Dingane. This expedition rode to within a few miles of Dingane's headquarters at Umgungundhlovu. But its route led through a narrow, rocky pass. Ndlela, Dingane's best military commander, calculated the Boers' path, and hid thousands of his men behind boulders and in gullies. At a signal, they emerged in several waves and threw themselves on the Trekkers. Because the sudden, wild combat that followed was at hand-to-hand range, the Zulus' spears held their own against the Trekkers' cumbersome muskets. The two columns of Trekkers involved got separated, and some ten of their men were killed, including the commander of one column, Piet Uys, and his fourteen-year-old son.

The remaining Boers retreated, and their disgraced expedition earned the name of the Vlug Commando, or Flight Commando. This defeat was all the more humiliating because they could not blame it on treachery, as with Piet Retief's death, or on an attack on women and children at night, as with the Great Murder. The Zulus won their victory in broad daylight—and the Vlug Commando was the largest armed body the Natal Trekkers had been able to put together. If it could not win a battle, could the Trekkers ever vanquish the skillfully led Zulu warriors? Many on the Great Trek were not sure, and as the year went on, hundreds of Boers actually retreated back through the mountain passes of the Drakensberg to try their luck settling elsewhere.

Those embattled Voortrekkers would be astonished at the fervor with which hundreds of thousands of their descendants are marking the 150th anniversary of the Trek and of Blood River. As the national holiday approaches, South Africa is filled with Great Trek posters, postcards, and key chains; there are Great Trek pens and Great Trek wine. Daily the newspapers and TV screens are filled with pictures of Afrikaners in Voortrekker costumes parading down main streets or receiving the keys to some city.

Afrikaans speakers today form nearly 60 percent of South Africa's white population, and although it is mainly they who are celebrating, they are not alone. One indication of the peace made between the country's two white tribes in recent years is that for several weeks, one of the Afrikaner caravans touring South Africa has been joined by two ox wagons full of descendants of the 1820 Settlers—the first large group of British immigrants.

It is now December, and some of these wagons have been on the road since August in a sort of extended, floating Fourth of July. All Afrikanerdom, it seems, has gotten into the act. The Transvaal Education Department announces that it is integrating the Great Trek into this year's curriculum: "In Mathematics . . . it will be calculated how far the Voortrekkers could travel per day; in Grammar the children will have a glimpse of the Voortrekker language; in Religious Instruction the influence of the Great Trek will be discussed and in Domestic Science recipes and patterns dating from the Great Trek will be tried out." A special brochure on traditional Boer cookery and preservation methods is issued by the Meat Board.

However, beneath the surface of all this celebrating is an angry feud. I had known before arriving in South Africa that there were political tensions among Afrikaners, but I had had no idea how bitter they were. Today's Afrikaners are deeply split:

The ruling National Party preaches a far more sophisticated strategy than brute force alone. With an eye on mollifying sanctions movements and uneasy bankers overseas, and angry blacks at home, it knows that the best way to maintain white rule in South Africa is to pretend it's doing something else. And so it flies the banner of "reform." This has meant a variety of changes, including an end to most "petty apartheid"—segregated park benches, trains, and the like, and much vague talk about a new constitution which will somehow or other give blacks votes without changing anything else too drastically.

Whites still hold all the cards, of course: they have 86 percent of the land; they own virtually all of the industry; and the power of the mining companies and other great corporations remains secure. But the reforms have pushed more conservative Afrikaners into a state of outrage. Since 1983, they have flocked to a new far-right party, the Conservatives, who claim that apartheid has been betrayed and that the country has already almost been handed over to black rule. In white elections now, roughly half of Afrikaners (as well as a sprinkling of English-speaking whites) vote for the Conservatives. The party's campaign poster reads: STOP INFLATION, REJECT INTEGRATION, SAVE THE NATION; another, with a picture of a white family, has the slogan: THIS IS OUR LAND. These right-wing Afrikaners want no more reforms whatever, and want the ones already made to be undone. Outside the political parties, other Afrikaner organizations have split in two, their offshoots aligned on opposite sides of the political divide: churches, fraternal and cultural groups, the student union, and even the once all-powerful secret society, the Broederbond.

Because of this fissure that runs through Afrikanerdom there are, I discover, two rival groups of ox wagons crisscrossing South Africa with great fanfare, and there will be two rival celebrations on the anniversary of Blood River on December 16th. One group of costumed celebrants in lace bonnets and waistcoats is associated with the National Party and the other with the right-wing opposition. Each claims to embody the true heritage of the Great Trek. I arrange to see them both.

I manage to get on board one of these caravans, the one allied with the National Party, within a few days of arriving in Johannesburg. The ox wagon is moving at a walking pace, escorted by a police car with blue light flashing, and by two motorcycle cops with crackling radios. The wagon is painted green, with bright red wheels, and pulling it are several dozen cheerful, brown-uniformed children of various ages who belong to the whites-only, Afrikaans-language version of the Boy Scouts and Girl Scouts—known, of course, as the Voortrekkers. A moment ago they have been told to make way for an *Engelstalige,* an English speaker. Now I'm riding high above them on the box of the wagon, sharing a seat with the scoutmistress, a shy young mother whose children are in this Voortrekker troop. The children are singing and having a great time, for they've gotten off school.

We are rolling through the streets of Germiston, a large industrial suburb of Johannesburg and the site of some of the country's first gold diggings. We pass some black mineworkers in long rubber gum boots and yellow plastic helmets with lamps on them: what must they think of all these laughing white children pulling a wagon?

The wagon and its support crew and I spend the entire day in Germiston. During the morning we visit the Goudrif (Goldreef) School, an Afrikaans-language high school. The students in their striped blazers, plus students from other Afrikaans schools and some white townspeople, have filled a large set of rugby bleachers. In the background are mine dumps—the huge, flat-topped rectangular hills that each contain several decades' worth of the crushed ore that is left when they take out the gold.

The ceremony here begins with the national anthem, which, like everything else in white South Africa, harks back to the Great Trek:

> *From our plains where creaking wagons*
> *Cut their trails into the earth,*

*Calls the spirit of our country, of the land*
*That gave us birth.*

A minister asks God to help the "Afrikaner *volk*" in their future crises, as He did in the time of the Trek. "We don't have to be afraid of times to come, if we have faith," someone translates for me. "God helped us before and He will again." Directly overhead is a sign of one of those crises, South Africa's international isolation. The rugby bleachers where we are sitting are under the approach path to Johannesburg's Jan Smuts Airport, and above us a fat, silver 747 from South African Airways' service to Europe glides down for a landing. Most African countries deny SAA overflying rights, and so the airline's planes must carry extra fuel and detour out over the Atlantic to avoid flying over Africa. And so now, almost lunchtime, this plane is arriving several hours later than the other airlines' overnight flights from Europe.

A group of schoolchildren pull the ox wagon through a square of wet cement, to leave the mark of its wheel for future generations. Finally the oxen are hitched on, and, accompanied by Voortrekker scouts and horseback riders carrying flags, the wagon passes in review before the cheering crowd, then rolls across the rugby field and out of sight.

This trek is run by the *Federasie van Afrikaanse Kultuurvereniginge,* or Federation of Afrikaans Cultural Organizations. But everyone refers to it as "the government trek," because this group is aligned with the National Party. As a result, the trek is well financed, and its path around the country has been paved with a blizzard of bilingual press releases announcing horse shows, songfests, beard-growing contests, and folk dance festivals timed for the ox wagon's arrival in the 182 towns it has visited so far.

Wary of overseas critics and wanting to prepare Afrikaners for the inevitable changes in South Africa to come, the government has made sure the tone of its trek is bland and upbeat, with no crowing about bloody victories in the past. And so the trek's rhetoric must straddle the difficult gap between commemorating a massive slaughter of Zulus and claiming that these celebrations somehow should include all South Africans, black and white. "Mr. Rudie Prinsloo, Festival Director," says one press release,

". . . once again emphasized that it is a national festival and has nothing to do with politics whatsoever."

After the high school ceremony, I stay in the bleachers and chat with Roelf de Beer, a friendly man with a white mustache and goatee who has been traveling with this trek for three weeks, making a video for the government. He asks me how many children I have and what church I go to, and invites me to visit his farm if I'm ever in his part of the country. He is delighted that I've visited the battlefield at Blood River and that I share his side in a dispute over the size and shape of the 1838 *laager* of linked ox wagons there. Using our fingers and the side of his video camera as a sketch pad, we agree that the National Monuments Council has its circle of metal replica wagons arrayed incorrectly at the site.

"Adam," he says, "the *real* reason for the Great Trek was that the Lord wanted His word carried to the black people of the north. Oh, there was the problem with the English, and the problem about the slaves, and so on, but *that* was the real reason." Moving on in history to two Britons of a later era much hated by Afrikaners, de Beer confides in me that Lord Milner, the British governor whose demands ignited the Boer War, and archimperialist Cecil Rhodes, were both Jewish. (This fact seems to have eluded historians, particularly the many biographers of Rhodes, the son of an Anglican clergyman.)

Even when you don't bring it up, almost every conversation with a South African eventually veers onto the subject of race. Soon de Beer is telling me: "You get people who want to push the black people into the sea. That's the greatest nonsense. I'm a farmer. I can't farm without the help of these people. And they can't live without my help. But there was never a desire between our white people and them to *mix* biologically. And they stay separate—the Pedis and the Zulus. I've got Indian friends about two miles from my house and they invite us for lunch and we go there. But they stay Islam." Sensing argument if we go too much further down this road, he says something disparaging about the way Hitler tried to solve these problems—surely we can agree that *that* is not the way to go. We do, and head off to get some lunch.

□

"Thirty oxen have been taught over the past couple of months to cover the long trek from Cape Town to Pretoria in less than four months," an early announcement from this trek's organizers claimed, but during this day in Germiston, I discover that things have turned out otherwise. The old Voortrekkers did not travel over asphalt, and, it soon became apparent on this twentieth-century trek, pavement is very tough on ox feet. In addition, the red and green ox wagon was taking a beating, for it was not as sturdy as those of old; it is a movie prop, on loan from the South African Broadcasting Corporation. By the time these twentieth-century trekkers had traveled one hundred miles from Cape Town, with well over one thousand still to go, a new battle plan was drawn up, which the trek is now following.

Each day, the oxen are trucked to the outskirts of the next town; then the truck goes back and fetches the wagon. Then the oxen are hitched up for a short, triumphal march through town, and then the process begins again. A van carries supplies; relays of spare oxen are leapfrogged ahead by another truck. Various other vehicles, including a mobile home, carry the officials who make everything happen.

To help make sure of things like getting thirty ox-dinners' worth of hay delivered to the right field each night, one of the cars is connected by shortwave radio with the trek headquarters office near Johannesburg. The mobile home is on loan from its manufacturer, and OK Bazaars, a large supermarket chain, provides free food for "the boys"—some ten black laborers who handle the oxen. The trucks are donated by Toyota.

Flip du Plooy is the officially designated Trek Leader. A portly, genial man, du Plooy is sitting in the front seat of the van packed with food supplies. He is in full Voortrekker dress: shirt with ruffles, pants, and embroidered vest, all sewn by his wife and a group of her friends. He echoes the official rhetorical straddle: "I am an Afrikaner. And I'm very proud of it. I learned that on this trek once again. Although we are a multiracial country." He adds vaguely: "Groups want to live up to their own culture when they have a chance." He carefully stresses that black people, too, are welcome at the festivities along the trek route. Although there are certainly none in sight today.

"I know there's two treks," sadly acknowledges du Plooy. "Everybody knows there's two treks. Except for once or twice, we really didn't have any politics at all. We had a slight clash at one place with the AWB," he says, referring to the fanatical neo-Nazi group. The AWB's members, when they are not blowing up buildings and the like, are supporting the rival trek, the right-wing one.

Later, I ask more about the "slight clash with the AWB" when I talk to Pierre van Zyl, a wealthy farmer-businessman who has donated the use of his oxen and laborers, and who has the title of Wagon Commander. It happened only three days ago, he says, some forty miles from here. For more than three months, the two rival treks rolling through South Africa had successfully avoided each other, but last Friday night, van Zyl says, they were both spending the night in the town of Delmas, some forty miles east of Johannesburg. And they both, as it happened, had made plans to quarter their oxen in the same field. But the right-wing oxen got there first, and when the "government trek" arrived, four right-wingers *with drawn guns* refused to let them enter:

"Because," van Zyl goes on, "our ox-lad [the man leading the oxen] was black. The four armed men were at the gate and one of them came up to me and said I'm not to enter unless a European is leading the oxen. I wouldn't. I said they [the blacks] have been leading the oxen all the way from Cape Town." The guns stayed drawn, and van Zyl's animals slept elsewhere.

A sudden storm rains out a planned ceremony with the wagon at Germiston City Hall, and so I end up talking with van Zyl for several hours in the cab of one of the Toyota trucks. The cab smells pleasantly farmlike: of animal and human sweat, damp clothes, and motor oil. It sways a bit as ten drenched oxen shuffle and grunt unhappily in the back of the truck. Van Zyl is tall and husky, grizzled, unshaven, fifty-nine years old and almost completely blind, having lost his eyesight around the age of forty. Whenever he walks anywhere, one of his black laborers—whom he refers to as "coon boys"—remains at his elbow, guiding him.

Earthy and direct, his tone is a refreshing change from the strained upbeatness surrounding this whole venture.

Why is he devoting nearly four months to the trek? I ask.

"I don't want to prove anything to anybody!" van Zyl replies irascibly. He says he has no special interest in Great Trek history. Instead, "I love my animals."

I ask what are his happiest memories of this trip.

"There were none!" he says. "They never clear the entire road for you! There's always cars parked along the road, there's always oncoming traffic, they blow their hooters! They talk about the Great Trek, but there are lots of obstacles today that people on the Great Trek never had. And it's costing me a fortune!" Van Zyl is in a particularly grouchy temper this afternoon because the wagon is scheduled to be at the Germiston cemetery for a wreath-laying ceremony. But these damned city slickers, he complains, have forgotten to provide a ramp, so he can't get the oxen out of the truck. What do they think? That an ox can leap down three feet like a ballet dancer?

After the rain, we transport first the oxen, and then the wagon, to the field where they are spending the night. "It's my blacks," he says, as he and I share the seat of the truck with a black driver navigating this load of animals past downtown Germiston's office buildings and department stores. "They work on my farms and I know them, and they know the oxen. I feel that as long as I can handle my blacks—there's seventy-two of them that work for me—if I can keep them happy and productive, then I feel I succeed. And I expect the same of the government. I can't find fault with the government if I can't handle my own, the few that work for me. But they're a difficult nation to satisfy. They're very obstinate. They don't really trust us yet."

Always, without prompting, the issue of physical closeness comes up: "And if they come and want to talk to me, and it's a lengthy talk and it's seven o'clock in the evening, I don't mind them sitting on one of my chairs. I don't mind it at all."

However, van Zyl goes on, "I like to keep control. If they have their little dances [in the recreation room he has built for the workers on his farm], then I don't leave the premises. I walk around there all night. I can't remember in all my years that I ever called a policeman to the farm. I handle them myself. If I feel he's done wrong, I give him a clout, and that's the end of it. And he can do exactly the same to me if he's got the guts."

Does he? I ask.

"You'd be surprised. Especially these days. There's a youngster here by the name of Michael. He got hold of me the other night. On the trek here. He had a few drinks, and he entered the caravan [the mobile home] and he just went for me. He used his hands. And for that he came out second. But I realized that he was drunk. I gave him a few clouts. I was satisfied that he was out of action, and that was the end of it. The next day he was sorry. But that's the only time I had to be a little hard, on the entire trek.

"They're a little different from the blacks that you people know overseas. I've never been overseas. Your blacks there are a little more educated. But ours I think suffer less. They're never short of anything. Especially those on farms. They always have sufficient to eat. Look at their kids—they're always fat and happy! If you want to live happy, you've got to make them happy too. They're clever little buggers sometimes. But I have less trouble with them than with the Europeans who work for me."

Curiously, for all his grotesque paternalism, on the trek van Zyl has, as the British used to say, gone native. "They do their cooking in my caravan. If there's no accommodation available, I'll let them sleep in the caravan. I wouldn't let them sleep in the rain. I eat exactly what they eat. I eat that mealie pap [cornmeal mush]. It's the quickest food to cook in the evenings. They get up at two o'clock in the morning [to feed the oxen] but I get up with them. If they stand in the rain, I do."

And he does, repeatedly getting out of the truck cab to stand in the downpour, rain pouring down his open collar. Because he can't see, he asks the black truck driver what's happening, gropes his way along the side of the truck to make sure he's facing the right way, then yells orders in Afrikaans at the crew. Even though van Zyl's relationship with his laborers and oxen is carried on mainly in shouts, he seems to prefer their company to that of anyone else. During this day I'm with the trek, he spends all his time around the truck, and none of it with the assorted city coun-

cilmen, school principals, and other officials who show up to greet
the caravan.

The day ends with a *braaivleis*, or barbecue, on the playing fields
of another Afrikaans-language white school. Meat sizzles over
charcoal; families gather; parental camera flashes light up the evening darkness when a procession of children troops in. There are
oohs and aahhs at the sight of the five- and six-year-olds in child
versions of old pioneer costumes; the older children wear their
brown Voortrekker scouting uniforms. The scouts carry flags and
flaming torches; they touch the torches to a pile of wood, which
ignites into a bonfire. In its midst, atop a tall pole, is a wagon
wheel. It bursts into flame as the fire reaches it, once again striking
that familiar note of Afrikaner martyrdom.

Flip du Plooy is busy at a table selling Great Trek maps and
mementos, and instead of joining the dinner here, Pierre van Zyl
is off eating his mealie pap with his black farmhands. And so I'm
left alone with the families who've come to this *braaivleis*, mostly
parents of children at this school. Over plates of salad and grilled
steak, I talk with several couples: they are from the Afrikaner
bourgeoisie, prosperous professionals; one couple is even planning
a month's vacation in the United States, a costly enterprise indeed
given South Africa's weak currency. They talk about their farms
("*Ag*, man, there's nothing like the bushveld!"), but it's clear these
are weekend places now. One or two of those I talk to speak
English without even a trace of an Afrikaans accent, a significant
help in getting ahead in the Johannesburg business world. They
ask many questions about American universities and National
Parks, but they gingerly avoid politics, except to ask in a puzzled
way about farming, which they find hard to imagine without that
reservoir of cheap labor: "But you don't do it . . . with blacks, do
you?"

One mother tells me about her daughter, who is studying in
Germany and who has developed "psychosomatic symptoms" because of all the criticism of South Africa she hears from German
students. The daughter talked to someone in a South African
consulate there who told her, "It happens to all of us." Psychosomatic symptoms, though, usually arise from an internal conflict,

not from an argument in which you're convinced you're right. What internal conflicts must these people feel beneath their unfailing politeness? They are whites who know white rule can't last forever; they are city dwellers who've arrived in their BMWs, who probably don't feel too sentimental about flaming wagon wheels. I wonder what is going through their minds as they listen to the obligatory speechmaking beside the bonfire, by an official of the school: "We need to relive what happened a hundred and fifty years ago," someone translates for me, "and to remember we all live in one country." That awkward straddle again; surely these guests at the *braaivleis* are sophisticated enough to feel its evasiveness.

After the speeches, the scouts sing, and then there are more songs from a group of half a dozen men and women, who read their lyrics by candlelight as sparks from the bonfire go skyward: love songs; folk songs; patriotic songs about "Suid Afrika" that on this warm evening sound gentle, even mournful, rather than strident. The sky is filled with stars and the air with woodsmoke redolent of campfires past.

My hosts overflow with Afrikaner hospitality, refilling my plate for me, insisting I try some homemade *boerwors*, or farmer's sausage, that someone brought from the country last weekend. When it is time for me to leave and I ask driving directions to the nearest freeway entrance, it is all I can do to prevent one of the men from jumping up and personally escorting me there in his own car. "I was never refused anything which I asked of a Dutchman in South Africa," wrote Trollope, who noticed the same characteristic. ". . . A generous Dutchman would lend me a horse or a cart." There are goodbyes all around; Flip du Plooy gives me a Great Trek souvenir pen. I thank everyone for the meal, for the *boerwors*, for letting me join the trek today. "Now write the *truth* about South Africa," someone says wanly. I have studiously avoided voicing any of my own opinions, but as I go, I sense them feeling discouraged: no matter what we say to this foreigner, no matter what we show him, he'll go home and write something bad about us, like all the others.

# "The Light
of Civilization"

Throughout 1838, fighting continued between the Voortrekkers and the Zulus in Natal. The Zulus' April defeat of the Vlug Commando emboldened Dingane and his commanders, and in August, they sent an *impi* of ten thousand Zulu warriors to attack a Boer camp at Gatsrand. One Trekker witness told of "Kafir hordes terrible to see. I cannot describe their numbers; for one would think that all heathendom had assembled to destroy us." The Zulu soldiers set fire to the surrounding grassland and threw burning *assegais* into the *laager* of linked ox wagons. The Voortrekker men defended the *laager* with muskets; women stood by with hatchets, ready to cut off the hands of any Zulus who got close enough to undo the leather straps that linked the wagons together. After three days, the Trekkers beat off Dingane's forces, killing hundreds. But it was a hollow victory. Many Trekkers were wounded; the Zulus took thousands of cattle who had been outside the *laager;* and the stench of the decaying bodies of the slain Zulus forced the Trekkers to move from their camp.

Toward the end of the year, however, the Trekkers' prospects brightened: rain brought new grass for their cattle, supplies of precious items like sugar and coffee arrived from supporters back in the Eastern Cape, and more Boers, in wagons and on horseback, came over the Drakensberg to join the beleaguered groups in

Natal. Most important, there arrived at the head of sixty men on horseback someone who immediately became one of the Great Trek's leading figures, Andries Pretorius.

"In appearance," Oliver Ransford tells us in his history of the Trek, "he tended to an imposing portliness and carried a small paunch in a stately sort of way as though it was filled with securities and bank drafts." An English soldier was less respectful, saying Pretorius "is about six feet high and has a belly on him like a brass drum." Africans named him *Ngalonkulu*—Brawny Arms. In several surviving portraits of him, he looks like a man impatient and self-possessed, supremely confident of his own destiny.

Efficient, meticulous, and a good military strategist, Pretorius was a natural leader. The besieged Boers had awaited his arrival for months. As soon as he came, they quickly elected him Commandant-General of the Voortrekkers of Natal.

For the Trekkers, much was riding on their choice of Pretorius as a leader. They had arrived in their Promised Land, but could not take possession of it. They had learned to form their ox wagons into *laagers*, and were constantly refining this technique. But it was still a defensive tactic. No *laager* of linked wagons was big enough to protect a whole cattle herd. So insecure were they that most Trekkers had built no homes; they were still living in tents and wagons. And they had to remain there as long as Dingane's troops could attack by the thousands at any moment.

Pretorius's first order of business was to muster a commando to attack Dingane, a larger and better equipped force than the Vlug Commando that had been so shamefully beaten a few months earlier. In early December, Pretorius set off. He had a force of 468 horsemen, the usual unrecorded number of black servants, 64 ox wagons packed with supplies and ammunition, and 3 small cannon. Leading his Trekker army toward Dingane's capital of Umgungundhlovu, Pretorius was determined to fight the battle that would decide the standoff between the Trekkers and the Zulus, once and for all.

My day with the modern-day trekkers in Germiston has been a Monday. For the remainder of this week, two events are in the public eye. They seem totally separate, although they will, at one point, briefly connect.

One event is the Great Trek anniversary celebrations, which are approaching their climax, ten days hence, on the national holiday of December 16th. The rivalry between the two treks has escalated: both have now arrived in the country's urban heartland of Johannesburg and Pretoria, and they are competing daily for the attention of Afrikaners. The tension between them represents the struggle between the ruling National Party and the ultra-conservatives on its right.

The other major story that winds among newspaper photos of ox wagons and Afrikaners in pioneer costumes is about the final week of the Delmas trial. The trial takes its name, by coincidence, from the same small town where the two treks had almost come to blows when armed right-wingers drew their guns on the blind Pierre van Zyl. It is the most important political trial in South Africa in a decade or more, and the longest ever—more than three years.

The South African justice system is a contradictory amalgam. The government routinely tortures thousands of prisoners like the boy Sipho, Emelda Nkosi, or Gladys Shezi, and, in times of crisis, keeps thousands of them in preventive detention for months at a time. Yet at the same time the British legal tradition and the Afrikaners' Germanic love of order mean there is an elaborate network of magistrates in white cravats and lawyers in black robes, of hearings, writs, stays, and appeals, and of judges who—only occasionally, but just often enough to add suspense to the process—will actually rule against the state. It is entirely up to the government's whim whether it decides to lock someone up in preventive detention, or charge the same person with something and hold a full-dress trial. Many activists have experienced both.

Some Delmas defendants have been released, but eleven are still on trial, all black, some of them ministers or church workers. The reason the government has put them on trial, instead of merely slapping them in preventive detention, is that it wants to use this case as a public warning to the democratic movement. Indirectly, the crime with which the men are charged is the death of several black municipal officials. The government acknowledges, however, that none of the defendants actually wielded a murder weapon. It claims, instead, that the angry crowd which killed these government collaborators was stirred to action by the calls for a general strike and a boycott of government township structures by the United Democratic Front, of which several of the men on trial are prominent officials. Thus the UDF itself, and its brand of militant but non-violent politics, is in effect on trial for murder. The implications of this are frightening to everyone I meet in the opposition movement here. All the more so because the judge has just found all the remaining Delmas defendants guilty of treason or terrorism. This week, all that remains to be decided, after a few more days of hearings, is how severe will be the sentences.

## TUESDAY

A public meeting is called to protest the Delmas verdict. Feelings are running high. Many of the defendants are well-known and respected figures from the movement, like Popo Molefe, National General Secretary of the UDF; South African Council of Churches (SACC) official Tom Manthata; and Patrick "Terror" Lekota (the nickname comes from his skill on the soccer field), UDF Publicity Secretary, who has already spent six years on Robben Island.

The protest meeting is to be at the University of the Witwatersrand, Johannesburg's large English-language campus. But as I approach the university at dusk, many Africans are walking the other way, quickly. "It's been banned," someone says. "Change of venue. It's now a prayer meeting. Central Methodist Church."

By the time I arrive, the large, downtown church is almost full; perhaps one thousand people are here, about three quarters of them black. Half a dozen TV crews have set up cameras on tripods, on a raised dais between pulpit and crowd. Several cameras are marked with the logos of European TV networks and are aimed at the pulpit, waiting for the speakers. But one camera at the far left has no insignia. It is aimed the entire time at the crowd.

A white bishop, Peter Storey, comes to the pulpit and welcomes everyone, a bit nervously. "We are in a house of the Lord. This is a worship service. A prayer service. This is *not* a political meeting. We are here to pray."

There are prayers and hymns, and a reading from the Book of Isaiah: ". . . We roar all like bears, and mourn sore like doves: we look for judgment, but there is none; for salvation, but it is far off from us. . . ." A black man who arrives late slips partway down the aisle on all fours, keeping low to stay out of sight of the video camera aimed at the crowd.

Rev. Frank Chikane, the vigorous young head of the South African Council of Churches, steps to the podium. From the political generation of the Soweto student rebels, Chikane has been jailed many times. Once he was forced to stand, chained and naked, for forty-eight hours. He was beaten and tortured so severely that on his release he could not walk. Another time police interrogators tore out some of his hair. His house was fire-bombed when he and his wife were asleep: curtains caught fire next to their baby's crib.

Chikane begins: "I understand there are two visiting pastors from England here. Would you please raise your hands?" Two hands go up. "Thank you. And I want to welcome our two visiting Members of Parliament from West Germany. Would you please raise your hands? Thank you." He continues in the same vein, eyes scanning the crowd. At first I am puzzled at this methodical identifying of foreigners. Then it dawns on me that this is a message to the police: Behave—the world is watching.

As Chikane begins to talk, the European TV crews change video-cassettes every five minutes or so, each time slipping a tape out of the camera and giving it to someone who walks it down the aisle and out of the church. They're not taking any chances. The camera at the far left now aims at Chikane, now pans the crowd. But its crew never changes cassettes.

Chikane speaks with great fire and passion. He is clearly wrought up; several of the Delmas defendants are close friends of his. Chikane ends near tears, saying, each word slow and deliberate, stone-heavy: "Those who are in chains would call on those of us who have our hands and feet free to use them to win our freedom."

The next speaker is black churchman Rev. Allan Boesak, known as the finest preacher in South Africa. He talks not only with anger but with humor:

"When I was in court at the Delmas trial, I heard it charged that the SACC was setting itself up as an alternative government. Well!"—he turns to Chikane with mock pomp—"Reverend Frank Chikane—Minister of Law and Order! Popo Molefe—Minister of Justice!" He pauses for the crowd to laugh. "I heard these men described as terrorists. But this is not the Popo Molefe I know. This is not the Tom Manthata I know. They say the UDF was supporting the ANC. Well, the ANC is the oldest liberation movement on the continent. We can't help that. The overwhelming mass of the people regard Nelson Mandela as their leader. We can't help that. For the real terrorists, you must look in Parliament!"

Two white men in sweaters walk down the aisle and sit on the edge of the dais next to the TV camera aimed at the crowd. As Boesak goes on, one man purses his lips, shakes his head, and whispers something to the other, who strides back down the aisle and out of the church. Everyone knows what's coming next.

Two minutes later, Boesak stops in mid-sentence, holding up a finger. Several dozen white riot police in boots and blue jumpsuits, pistols and batons on their belts, come striding down the two aisles. They quickly form a cordon around the dais, separating TV cameras and speakers from the crowd. Stony-faced and motionless, they stand in a row facing the congregation. Other policemen begin confiscating notes and videotape. It is profoundly chilling to see all these leather boots and shiny black holsters in a church. The crowd does not gasp, though; they've seen it before. Bishop Storey, followed by several police officials, mounts to the microphone and announces that the service has been declared an illegal gathering. "Please leave quietly. It would be easy for something to happen. We want to be peaceful. Please leave quietly, and with dignity."


## WEDNESDAY

For the climax of the Delmas trial, the proceedings have been moved to the Palace of Justice in Pretoria—an old, majestic courthouse on Church Square in the middle of town. The trial is now in the very same courtroom from which Nelson Mandela was taken off to prison a quarter of a century ago.

Today is the last day of testimony for mitigation of sentence. Before the court session begins, a curious episode takes place. A uniformed white policeman, speaking English with a heavy Afrikaans accent, approaches a black woman in the audience and sternly upbraids her. Apparently the wife of a defendant, she has two small children with her. "You must leave the courtroom," he insists. "No children are allowed here." She is surprised and alarmed. She pleads: "There's no one who can watch them outside. Please can't they stay? They'll be quiet." The policeman is unyielding. The argument goes on. He points firmly toward the door. Just at that moment, a white man in a black robe, apparently a defense lawyer, appears and excoriates the policeman in a torrent of furious Afrikaans. I catch the words *"drie jare!"* said with great exasperation. Clearly he is saying: For three years children have been allowed in this trial, so buzz off! The policeman meekly retreats. The black-robed lawyer smiles at the children, touches the mother's shoulder and says something comforting. He walks over to the defense table and jokes with the other black-robed attorneys there. But then, when he takes his seat, it is not at that table but directly beneath the judge. To my amazement, he is not a defense lawyer but the registrar—what we would call the clerk of the court.

I'm so struck by his coming to the aid of the mother and children that I ask one of the defense attorneys about this during a break. "Yes, you're right," he says. "This man has been *transformed* in the course of the trial. He was going to go to that protest meeting before it was banned." The court registrar has little power, of course, but there is still something moving in seeing that a person in such a role can undergo an inner change. The word "transformed" echoes in my head, a faint note of hope on a dark day.

As the day's session begins, the very solemnity of the court seems designed to compensate for any doubts one might have about its legitimacy. The courtroom has the feel of a cathedral: high clerestory windows have panels of stained glass, and a canopylike, decorative wooden frame is suspended above the judge's bench, as if over an altar. Lawyers address the judge as "Your Worship." The prisoners are seated with their backs to us, on a long bench with an elaborately carved back, like a church pew.

The judge, Kees van Dijkhorst, wears a red robe. A bald, frowning man, he questions witnesses closely and makes many notes. He is said to be a hard-liner, because of an episode earlier in this trial. South Africa has nothing so radical as trial by jury, but judges in certain cases are helped by two assessors, who hear and discuss the evidence with them. When Justice van Dijkhorst discovered that one of his assessors had once signed a petition supported by the UDF, he dismissed him from the case as politically prejudiced. He made no move against the other assessor, however, even though that man was reportedly a member of the Afrikaner secret society, the Broederbond. Defense lawyers hope this dismissal will be grounds for reversing the verdict on appeal.

The main defense witness today is Dr. Samuel Motsuenyane, one of South Africa's most successful black businessmen; he is the chairman of an African chamber of commerce and a director of various banks and corporations. His is just the sort of position the authorities hope will turn people into its much desired "black moderates," with a stake in the status quo. But if the government wants Motsuenyane to play the role of moderate, he certainly does not do so today. Asked about Nelson Mandela, he says forthrightly: "I still regard him as my leader. Unquestionably so." He cleverly turns aside red-baiting questions. A prosecutor asks him what he thinks about socialism, and Motsuenyane says he thinks there's too much of it in South Africa. "The government owns everything. We blacks own nothing."

The session ends for the day at lunchtime. Thanks to friends I've come with, I end up eating with the defense lawyers. They feel the morning's testimony went well. They plan to spend all afternoon and evening preparing a summary argument they will give tomorrow morning, Thursday. Their argument, they hope, may have some slight effect on the judge, who will then have Thursday afternoon and evening to think over what they say before he is scheduled to pass sentence on Friday.

In the middle of the meal, however, a late-arriving member of the legal team comes into the restaurant with bad news. In the courthouse, she has just heard that police have been asked to turn out in extra force tomorrow (there already are twenty cops and an armored car today) because the defendants will be sentenced then. The lawyers' faces fall: this means Justice van Dijkhorst will decide tonight what sentences he is giving, if he hasn't already done so, and what they say in the morning will be irrelevant. Nevertheless, they still must prepare and speak, because their arguments will be the culmination of more than three years' work.

Why do the prisoners have to be sentenced on Thursday? Because, it turns out, on Friday the horsemen and ox wagons from the right-wing trek will parade through the square in front of the courthouse. The authorities don't want them in the same place as hundreds of grieving, angry supporters of those on trial.

## THURSDAY

More than one hundred policemen, plus dogs and armored cars, keep order in the square.

Inside, the defense lawyers make their plea for mercy.

With barely a break, Justice van Dijkhorst begins a long speech that ends with his sentences: twelve years for "Terror" Lekota; ten years each for Popo Molefe and Moses Chikane. These three, says the judge, were part of the "conspiratorial core" of the United Democratic Front. Six years for Council of Churches worker Tom Manthata; five years for Gcina Malindi. The others get suspended sentences and are restricted from all political activity. The lawyers are still hoping for a reversal on appeal, but that is a year away at the earliest, and these men have already spent three and a half years in jail while on trial.

After Justice van Dijkhorst pronounces the sentences, many in the crowd, including several defense lawyers, are weeping. As the five men he has sentenced to prison descend the staircase from the courtroom to the holding cells, the first stage of their journey to Robben Island, they are singing.

## FRIDAY

The far-right trekkers arrive in Pretoria. Outside the courthouse parades a long procession of carefully restored ox wagons, and well over one thousand supporters in beards, wigs, and bonnets— on foot, in farmers' *bakkies,* and on the backs of several hundred horses. Eugene Terre Blanche, charismatic leader of the AWB, joins the procession on horseback. Some of the horsemen are armed. Boys crack whips over the oxen. These are the true believers: khaki-uniformed supporters of this trek have pulled one wagon by hand more than five hundred miles from Blood River to Pretoria; their feet are now bloody as they near the end of their journey. One elderly right-winger, Mannie Maritz, a white-bearded former professional wrestler and the son of a famous Boer War general, has ridden his horse more than one thousand miles from the Atlantic coast. For these members of the *volk,* there have been no free rides from Toyota.

Concerned for the welfare of the horses, the Pretoria SPCA brings up the rear of the procession with two horse trailers and an animal ambulance.


## SATURDAY

This week's rivalry between the two treks is not only a competition for the allegiance of Afrikaners; it is a tug-of-war over who gets to use the Afrikaner people's most hallowed ground, the Voortrekker Monument.

This hollow cube of stone with its grillwork on the side looks, it has been said, like a huge, old-fashioned radio. After the Pyramids, it is the largest monument in Africa. Visible from miles in all directions, it stands on a hill outside Pretoria. It was to this hillside that 100,000 Afrikaners came, by foot, bicycle, car and wagon, to the centenary of the Blood River battle in 1938.

That gathering surpassed all expectations. South Africa was then in the depths of the Great Depression, which had driven thousands of Afrikaner farmers bankrupt and had sent them, like Steinbeck's Okies, streaming to the cities in desperate search of work, with all their worldly belongings packed into a *bakkie* or a horse cart.

They blamed their hardships on the blacks they had to compete with on the one hand, and, on the other, on the English-speaking white bankers and businessmen who dominated the country's economic life. Seldom had the Afrikaner sense of victimhood run higher. Runners carried relays of flaming torches across the country. Three thousand Voortrekker scouts waiting at the Pretoria hillside tossed more torches on a gigantic bonfire. In another of those symbolic gestures of martyrdom, women rushed forward to burn the corners of their *kappies,* the traditional bonnets, in the flames. At the three-day ceremony, people laid the cornerstone for the massive granite monument to the Voortrekkers.

Now, fifty years later, the question is: who gets the Monument, the pro-government trek or the right-wing one? The government, of course, holds the cards, and reserves the Monument for itself for the December 16th holiday and the preceding week. The far-right trekkers are furious. Professor Carel Boshoff, chairman of the Afrikaner Volkswag (the Peoples' Guard), official sponsor of the right-wing trek, says that the denial of the Monument to his ox wagons on the sacred day is symbolic of "the way the Afrikaner has been estranged from his rights, his freedom and his fatherland." As a sop to angry right-wingers, the government has allowed them and their wagons to camp at the Monument during this week just ending. Today, Saturday, they are to move out, and the government trek is to move in.

When I arrive at the Monument grounds at 8:00 a.m., both treks are actually there. They are separated, however, by the largest security force I have ever seen in South Africa. There are hundreds of police and soldiers, armored cars in camouflage colors, and long coils of barbed wire marking off a 100-yard-wide no-man's-land between the two groups. A yellow police helicopter hovers overhead. When you walk from the field where the right-wingers are pulling up camp to the hill where the government trek people are setting up theirs you have to go through a metal detector. Upbeat Afrikaans folk songs with accordion accompaniment blare from outdoor loudspeakers while all this military hardware keeps the two halves of Afrikanerdom from each other's throats.

Except for their parade into Pretoria yesterday, the right-wingers have been camping, praying, and speechmaking here at the Monument all week. Now they are moving some twenty miles to a farm where they will camp for the week remaining until December 16th, the Blood River holiday. A procession winds out of the field and onto the shoulder of a freeway: an ox wagon; some sixty men, and a few women, on horseback carrying flags of the old Boer republics; and a long line of cars, vans, and *bakkies,* some pulling horse trailers, with hand-lettered signs naming the towns they've come from. This procession of rough-hewn people on horseback with their nineteenth-century flags plods along the road shoulder while several lanes of freeway traffic zoom past. In the background is the skyscraper skyline of Pretoria, punctuated by a huge TV tower.

After seeing them off, I head back up the hill, past the barbed wire and the metal detector, to where the government trek is setting up operations around the base of the Voortrekker Monument. Pierre van Zyl and the green and red wagon are here somewhere, someone says, but I can't find them; they've been engulfed by a huge crew making preparations for the festival that will continue all week in this spot. The government is sparing no expense to make the production a success. Extra electric lines have been laid to the site, and now scores of soldiers in khaki uniforms are erecting several dozen large olive green army tents. Young men with T-shirts in the blue, white, and orange colors of the South African flag are walking about, supervising workmen and busily talking into walkie-talkies.

Although I've often driven past it, this is the first time I've been to the Voortrekker Monument itself. Its massive base is ringed with stone images of scenes from the Great Trek: battles, massacres, thanksgiving services, ox wagons galore. Then the whole story is told again in a series of tapestries, which took nine women, the guidebook tells us, eight years to make. In the marble-walled interior of the Monument is a stone cenotaph, engraved with the words "*Ons vir jou, Suid Afrika*" ("We for Thee, South Africa"). It commemorates the most revered of Afrikaner martyrs: Piet Retief and his massacred expeditionary force, and the Voortrekker families killed on the night of the Great Murder. Some two hundred feet above is a small opening in the Monument's roof, positioned so that exactly at noon on December 16th of each year, a ray of sunlight shining through it, "the light of civilization," will strike the cenotaph.

Outside today, the scene is less solemn. White joggers of all ages are puffing up the hill, with numbers on their chests, in 4- and 8-kilometer runs that are one of the festival events today. They wear Nikes, Adidas, New Balances; family members with Sony video cameras cheer them across the finish line. At 9:00 a.m. the finishers in a 35-kilometer bicycle race charge up the hill, all with the latest in helmets, water bottles, and brightly colored skintight shorts. Comparing these sweating yuppies with the leathery right-wingers on horseback, it is clear that today's split among Afrikaners is essentially one of class.

The limited reforms enacted by the National Party don't undermine the basic structure of white wealth and privilege. But the whites they benefit are those in business and commerce. One of the most visible changes in recent years, for example, is desegregation of hotels and restaurants, most of which are now open to all races. This means more customers for hotel and restaurant owners, who are, of course, almost entirely white. Or, to take another reform, allowing more black students into the predominantly white universities. This also benefits business—South Africa has a sophisticated, increasingly industrial economy with a shortage of engineers and professionals.

These are among the reasons that the National Party draws its support these days from the more urban, wealthier, better-educated part of the white electorate, people like the runners in their Adidas here this morning. The National Party has become, broadly speaking, the party of white capital, both Afrikaans and, increasingly, English-speaking. But what galls the right-wingers no end is that the party rose to power as the party of the Afrikaner lower middle class and farmers.

All the current reforms are sheer horror to poorer, rural, or working-class whites—which in South Africa means largely Afrikaners. For centuries, their white skin has been the one thing that kept them from the abject poverty of blacks. And for decades, jobs in the traditional Afrikaner preserves like the mines, the railways, the police, and the overswollen civil service have been handed down from father to son. Now the sons face black competition for some of those jobs. And with the budget pinch and privatization, many jobs themselves are disappearing. White skin still does secure someone the right to own land in the 86 percent of the country from which Africans are excluded, but big agribusiness, debt, drought, and weak crop prices have, in a replay of the 1930s, forced thousands of Afrikaners off the land.

Even though they are still vastly better off than the great majority of blacks, poorer Afrikaners are now losing ground. Their real wages are slipping, their lack of higher education is a big handicap, and their unemployment rate, though still a fraction of the one for blacks, is the highest since the Depression. Such a declining economic position is a classic breeding ground for Fascist and racist movements—odd as it may sound to talk of such movements in a country that is highly racist and near-Fascist to begin with. Like the followers of Hitler, Mussolini, or the John Birch Society, what right-wing Afrikaners are most stirred by is images of betrayal in the present or of glory in the past, such as the flags of the old Boer republics their horsemen paraded with this morning. These embittered whites of the far right will form a powerful—and well-armed—lobby against the further reforms the government plans for the future.

This right-wing fanaticism is far from the tone of the government trek now busily erecting its army tents at the Monument. Here, the mood is not one of recapturing the past, but of trying to prove that South Africa is fully a part of the Day-Glo, quadraphonic present, as hip and with it as Europe or the United States. Among the events the government trek's PR people have scheduled for the next few days here are evening concerts by local pop stars, skateboard and roller-skating contests, and a series of attempts to win places in *The Guinness Book of World Records* by breaking the records for bubble-gum blowing, bean spitting, ginger beer drinking, and the number of eggs a person can balance on one hand. Exiled from their sacred monument and brooding around their campfires tonight, the right-wingers will be fuming: Bean spitting! Skateboards! Did Piet Retief die for this?

It would be a mistake, however, to associate South Africa's repression with the right wing and its hope of change with the joggers and suburbanites celebrating at the Monument this sunny

Saturday morning. For these are still the people running the country. I am reminded of this when I step into one of the green tents the army has set up, to find out about the festival schedule from several officials sitting inside. One of them is a tall woman, an officer of an Afrikaner women's organization, whom several people come up to and greet in an almost congratulatory tone. One says to her, politely switching to English for my benefit, "What a heavy responsibility he had! You must be so glad it's over at last!"

It turns out the woman is Mrs. van Dijkhorst, wife of the judge in the Delmas trial, who two days ago handed out forty-three years' worth of prison time. But here everyone is happy: the trial has ended in time not to interfere with the celebrations.

# Velvet Glove, Iron Fist

There is a striking photograph from the time of the freeing of the serfs in Russia in 1861. A crowd of bearded peasants is gathered in front of a great country house near Moscow. An official in a military hat and gold braid stands on the columned portico with a scroll in his hand, reading the Czar's emancipation proclamation. The peasants in their tunics listen quietly, as they have always listened to orders. Languidly looking down at the scene from a second-floor balcony, in flowery hats and frilly white dresses, are several young girls from the landowner's family. They clearly know that whatever is being proclaimed down below, their life will go on more or less as it has been.

This image is a good one to keep in mind whenever Pretoria announces grand new reforms—which it will do often in the next few years. Whatever new freedom gets proclaimed, the South African equivalent of those girls in their white dresses will continue to stand on the balcony. Shoring up the balcony and those on it is, in fact, the main reason South Africa makes reforms. The freeing of the serfs, after all, helped buy a shaky empire some sixty-five more years. A similar hope lies behind recent reforms in South Africa, and those yet to come.

White strategy for establishing control 150 years ago seems simple enough. Riding off to seek battle with Dingane, Andries

Pretorius and his commando troop had horses, muskets, and cannon, and Dingane did not. Today, military force is still the mainstay of white power in South Africa, but it alone is not enough. South Africa's rulers now have two strategies for keeping control: the iron fist of repression and the velvet glove of reform. Sometimes one is more visible, sometimes the other. But both these strategies aim at the same goal: maintaining white rule, in fact if not in name, as far as possible into the future.

Many reforms of recent years have one common goal: building up a conservative black elite.

Nowhere do you see this more starkly than in the homelands. Driving into Mmabatho, the capital of Bophuthatswana, you pass the guarded compound where the leadership lives. It is ringed by a barbed-wire-topped Cyclone fence. Inside are tennis courts and U.S.-style ranch houses bristling with TV antennas; outside is a dirt-street shantytown of shacks made of tin, tar paper, and even the doors of old automobiles.

The same pattern exists in most of the homelands. In the Ciskei, one of the poorest of these ministates, the cabinet members a few years ago voted themselves a raise, to salaries of $56,000 a year ($74,000 for the President), placing them on a par with South African Cabinet ministers. They replaced the fleet of official BMWs with eighteen Mercedes-Benz 230s. The homeland has also built two presidential palaces and a $400,000 monument. The South African government pays much of the bill for such extravagance, building homeland leaders gifts of "independence stadiums" and the like, but has generally felt it to be worth the expense: the homeland leaders, most of them traditional chiefs like Chief Buthelezi in KwaZulu, do Pretoria's work of keepir.g their people under control.

The myth of homeland independence is carefully kept up: in the capitals of the four homelands that are nominally independent countries, the usual office building full of white administrators from Pretoria is called the "South African Embassy." But the facade crumbles easily. Bophuthatswana's long-time ruler, Lucas Mangope, a hereditary chief and one-time high school Afrikaans teacher, was toppled by a palace coup in 1988. Three dozen white

South African commandos immediately arrived by helicopter and armored car, shot or arrested the dissidents, and in a single day restored Mangope to office. "Tonight we are back in full control of Bophuthatswana," announced South African State President P. W. Botha in a slip of the tongue. "I mean, the President of Bophuthatswana is in full control."

Recently, Pretoria's homelands system has begun to unravel. Several homeland leaders have declared their support for the African National Congress. Several others, including the high-living leaders of the Ciskei, have been toppled by popular or military revolts that have placed new leaders friendly to the ANC in power. In addition, resentful white voters in the rest of South Africa are beginning to protest paying for all the palaces, BMWs, and the like. However, subsidies from Pretoria still provide a major share of every homeland's budget, more than 80 percent in the case of the Ciskei, for example. This gives the central government a financial stranglehold the homelands will have a hard time breaking, no matter what the politics of their leaders.

Outside the homelands, in South Africa's big cities, it is the growing black middle class that the government is trying to coopt. From the 1970s onward, the government and white business have tried strenuously to make black professionals, skilled workers, and shopowners feel they have a stake in the status quo. "Unless the black man is given a greater share of S.A.'s free enterprise system," declared the Afrikaanse Handelsinstituut (the white, Afrikaans-speaking chamber of commerce) in 1977, "he will be driven into the arms of Marxism and socialism." Several years later, the organization backed moves to open downtown business districts to black traders. The group's president reassured members who were uneasy about this new black competition: "This is an insurance premium we should be willing to pay." Optimistically, the Johannesburg Stock Exchange—where white traders yell bids for gold mine shares and black clerks chalk in prices on a board—prints some of its visitors' brochures in Zulu.

On the political level, a much more elaborate cooptation scheme is the three-chamber Parliament introduced in the middle 1980s. Added to the whites-only house were additional houses of Parliament for Coloureds and Indians, with some control over social service budgets for those communities. Most blacks regard these two houses as an attempt to split the black community by dividing Coloureds and Indians from Africans. The effort has largely failed: less than 20 percent of eligible Coloureds and Indians voted in the last election. Their well-paid parliamentarians are generally despised as collaborators; some, for protection, live in another of those compounds surrounded by barbed wire.

The government can afford to set up Coloured and Indian parliaments because whites outnumber both groups combined. Rural Africans are, in theory, citizens of the various homelands. But Pretoria's thorniest dilemma is how to coopt the Africans in the cities. Even with roughly half the African population crammed into the homelands, there are still over 12 million others left, more than twice as many as there are whites in the whole country. This is what government strategists call "the problem of the urban blacks"—whose main "problem," of course, is that they exist.

The government has tried to create an urban African political elite by staging elections for near-powerless municipal posts in black townships like Soweto. In the most recent elections, though, fewer than one person in ten voted, despite cheerful TV news stories about the joys of political participation. Less than half the municipal posts being voted on were even contested, and for 138 positions, there were no candidates at all. Three races in Alexandra had to be canceled because the only candidates turned out to have criminal records. These problems were an embarrassing setback in the road toward the reformers' long-planned goal of a new constitution with some kind of visible but unthreatening political role for urban Africans.

On the whole, government efforts to pull even the more well-to-do blacks over to its side have been a conspicuous failure. "One of the big miscalculations of this government has been their anticipation that the black middle class will behave in a particular way," says Neville Alexander, the black Robben Island veteran in Cape Town. To the dismay of security planners, black schoolteachers have often supported school boycotts, taxi owners have supported general strikes, and groups of black traders and the like have affiliated with the United Democratic Front.

It's not hard to see why. The relative prosperity of middle-class blacks makes their political powerlessness feel even more humiliating. If you walk into a bank in South Africa, you are likely to see white, African, and Coloured or Indian tellers working side by side. By day, that black bank teller may earn the same wage as his or her white colleagues, eat at the same restaurants and shop in the same stores, and may even, if lucky, be treated with courtesy by them. But by night, it's back to ill-lit, crime-ridden townships with dirt streets, erratic garbage collection, trigger-happy police, and dismal, overcrowded schools where an average of less than 25 cents is spent on each black student for every dollar spent on each white student. In some African schools, this means a shortage of books, desks, and even chairs, and a pupil-teacher ratio as high as 60 to 1. And above all, blacks cannot, in a way that has real meaning, vote.

In the short story "The Music of the Violin" by Njabulo Ndebele, the parents in a middle-class black family aspire to the good things in life. They buy their son enough toys and diversions so that the mother can say of his bedroom, "This room is as good as any white boy's." As a final act of assimilation, they force him to play the violin. He refuses. How can he do this, he thinks, when in school he must answer homework questions like: "How did the coming of the whites lead to the establishment of prosperity and peace among the various Bantu tribes?"

The major pressure against giving blacks the vote in any meaningful form is, of course, the white electorate. The rapidly growing Conservative Party, with its angry accusations of betrayal, won 31 percent of the vote in the last national election. Any South African leader who hopes to pull a "reform" solution out of the hat must navigate the difficult route between these people on the one hand and, on the other, the millions of blacks who are, understandably, unwilling to settle for anything less than one person/one vote.

Big business, interestingly, voices little opposition to extending the vote to Africans. The handful of giant corporations who control South Africa's economy don't much care what color the faces are in the cabinet, or in the electorate, so long as only votes are redistributed, not wealth. The Anglo-American Corporation, after all, happily does business under black governments all over Africa.

Government efforts to nurture a compliant African leadership class continue. Officials have tossed out a variety of fanciful schemes at different times: A fourth house of Parliament for Africans, like those for Coloureds and Indians. Special city-state status, like that of Monaco, for Soweto and other major townships. A federation of white South Africa, the homelands, and other yet-to-be-defined entities. These plans are always given labels like "co-responsibility," "co-determination," "consociational government," "confederalism," "co-operative co-existence," and so on. All these deliberately hazy plans are attempts to share power without losing control. Any time you hear a South African Cabinet minister use a word with "co-" in it, you can be sure he's trying to convince blacks that some dramatic change is coming, and convince whites that he's not giving away the store. Both ways, it's a difficult sell.

This evasive language can also be seen in the name of the government department whose job is to keep Africans under control, which changes with nervous frequency. It is now called the Ministry of Cooperation and Development, after previously evolving from the Ministry of Native Affairs, to Bantu Affairs, to Plural Relations. One of these changes took place during the 1976–77 upheavals, in which the late Percy Qoboza, a prominent black editor, was jailed for five months and saw his newspaper closed down. When released, Qoboza declared: "Let no one tell me there has been no change in South Africa. I went into jail a Bantu and came out a Plural."

While displaying the velvet glove, Pretoria has at the same time made more efficient its iron fist. The person who beats or tortures a prisoner like Gladys Shezi or Emelda Nkosi is likely to be a low-ranking policeman with no more than a high school education. But the blow of his club or the touch of his torturer's electrode has its origins in sophisticated plans drawn up by men in pinstriped suits in wood-paneled conference rooms, men with graduate degrees from European universities, men who personally may never have lifted a hand in anger. By now we know a great deal about their thinking.

The key architects of South Africa's repression have been P. W. Botha, the country's leader from 1978 to 1989, and the long-time Defense Minister, Magnus Malan. They and their colleagues closely studied how other countries suppress insurrection. As a young officer, Malan was a field observer with the French Army in Algeria, and, later on, with the Rhodesian Army during that country's long civil war.

Paradoxically, given the anti-Semitic strain in traditional Afrikaner nationalism, today South Africa's best source of military strategy and techniques is Israel. Israeli officers have trained South African troops in counterinsurgency methods, and the two countries have formed a close, quiet military alliance, comparing notes on suppressing popular rebellions, and together developing a wide variety of weapons systems. The world has paid the most attention to the Israeli–South African atomic bomb. But what may be more important is the new, jointly developed South African guided missile capable of reaching as far as Tanzania—where there are ANC bases.

Although the country's closest military ties are with Israel, one thinker South Africa's counterrevolutionary planners particularly admire is an American: the conservative Harvard political scientist Samuel Huntington. According to the newspaper *The Weekly Mail,* a 1981 speech by Huntington in South Africa "became a manual for government reformers." Using the recent decades of military rule in Brazil as an example, Huntington urged a sophisticated combination of iron fist and velvet glove: tough maintenance of law and order, plus gradual, piecemeal "reform from above." These reforms, Huntington said, should be introduced at the government's own pace, not in response to upheavals—when they could be seen as giving in to popular demand.

Another favorite of South Africa's strategists is a former French general, André Beaufre. A veteran of World War II, Indochina, and Algeria, Beaufre was Deputy Chief of Staff of NATO. In several books, he, like Huntington, argues for a careful combination of ruthless military force and a "political line"; by "thorough-going reforms," Beaufre writes, "we must cut the ground from under the feet of the malcontents." To combat what Malan and Botha called a Total Onslaught against South Africa by Soviet-backed black revolutionaries, they adopted Beaufre's concept of the Total Strategy.

(Since Gorbachev, one hears these terms less frequently in

South Africa, but they survive in the name of a soccer team of workers from anti-government newspapers in Johannesburg, the Total Onslaught.)

"At the top of the pyramid," Beaufre writes, ". . . is Total Strategy, whose task it is to define how total war should be conducted . . . to lay down . . . the manner in which all—political, economic, diplomatic and military—should be woven together." At the local level, this weaving means determining what combination of police violence and carefully doled-out reforms will best pacify a particular township at a particular time.

Over the years, the security forces have sometimes let reporters see nerve centers for the military side of Total Strategy. In the security headquarters for the African townships outside Cape Town, a huge map of the Cape Peninsula hangs on the wall. Some townships are colored yellow, meaning that they are in the "organization phase" of revolution; others are colored red, meaning they are in the "terrorism phase." The command post for Pretoria's Mamelodi Township also has an even larger scale wall map, detailed enough to show individual houses, with the homes of community leaders and activists highlighted. Elsewhere on the wall a board lists every known organization in the township—sports, religious, political—along with its officeholders and the time and place of its meetings.

The authorities are surprisingly frank about the other side of Total Strategy, the use of minor improvements as a key counter-revolutionary tool. According to Major General Bert Wandrag of the South African Police Riot Control forces:

> The outcome of this struggle will not be determined by weapons alone. . . . School boycotts in black townships in Pietermaritzburg were brought to an end merely by paying attention to the grievances of schoolchildren. A major grievance was lack of textbooks. A small capital outlay in good time could have saved the state and the department millions of rands [spent suppressing the boycotts]. . . . The only way to render the enemy powerless is to nip revolution in the bud, by ensuring there is no fertile soil in which the seeds of the revolution can germinate.

Following U.S. strategy in Vietnam, South African planners have even adopted a key American phrase from that war, "winning hearts and minds," known in South Africa by the acronym of WHAM. The South Africans have added a new term of their own to the WHAM lexicon: "oilspots." An oilspot is a strategically chosen township where the uprisings have been suppressed and improvements begun. As this upgrading makes people more content, the theory goes, the calm from this little island will spread outward, like oil over water. Eventually, these expanding pools of calm from many oilspots will merge, and soothe the stormy waters of the whole country.

Full of enthusiasm for the idea, the government picked thirty-four "oilspots," and in the last few years has spent $1.3 billion building new sports stadiums, planting trees, putting in streetlights, and the like. The allure of the oilspot theory is that you don't have to upgrade *all* black townships, just some. Then the effects will magically spread. This appeals to Pretoria because, in the current economic crunch, there isn't enough money to make improvements everywhere. (Unless, of course, you started taking the necessary garbage trucks and schoolbooks out of white areas.)

Johannesburg's Alexandra Township is one of the oilspots, receiving some $40 million worth of "oil"—the township's first post office, new homes, public telephones, home ownership loans, and running water for thousands of houses. The government sees all these changes as part of its military strategy; the cabinet member who says he is taking "personal responsibility" for the upgrading in Alexandra and several other key townships is Magnus Malan, Minister of Defense.

In Alexandra and elsewhere, these improvements are passed out with paternalistic cheer. The government publishes a *Newsletter to the People of Alexandra* filled with uplifting thoughts like "Through development we reach the sky!" Roadblocks, the *Newsletter* explains, are "to keep all trouble-makers out." A redevelopment official is praised as having an "insatiable desire to work for the community." A comic strip, *Alex and Friends,* also helps promote the new era. "Alex" is an enthusiastic, well-behaved citizen who always wins arguments with "Comrade Rat," a disheveled type who carps at everything. Overall, Alexandra's oilspot reform program seems managed with a clumsy hand: Children who bring in a black plastic bag of rubbish for the community cleanup effort are rewarded with a yo-yo with a South African Defense Force insignia on the side, and the inscription: "For our men at the border."

Most government strategy of the last few years, however, has not been about comic books and streetlamps, but about harsher matters. And much of it has been directed toward one key aim: rebuilding the informer network.

When I first was in South Africa in the early 1960s, at political meetings someone would quietly say, "Watch what you say to S—— over there—we think he's working for the Branch [the Special Branch, or security police]." Sometimes S—— himself would come over and strike up a conversation, full of questions. The informer network pervaded the townships. "If three or more Soweto people decide on a campaign," writes Sipho Sepampla in his novel *A Ride on the Whirlwind,* "the chances are that one of them works for the cops." The whole plot of this novel of the 1976 uprising revolves around a group of young militants' obsessive fear of informers—and around the activities of a real one they do not suspect.

We know something about this network of secret agents because, over the years, several have come in from the cold. One of the most important was a long-time spy named Gordon Winter. Winter was a British ex-convict who emigrated to South Africa in 1960 to start a new life as a newspaperman. He quickly made a deal with the police—for nearly twenty years, in return for cash and tips on good stories, he supplied reports and tape recordings of the wide circle of friends he had, both black and white, in the liberation movement. To get movement people to trust Winter, the police arrested him and put him in solitary confinement. There, unknown to other prisoners, he had a cell with a shower, radio, pets, and ample food and brandy. They also arranged for Winter to build up a successful track record of smuggling people across the border without their being caught.

Eventually, Winter says, he had a change of heart. It is always interesting to see what causes such changes. In Winter's case, if we are to believe him, it was a new marriage and the birth of his first child. Suddenly the world began to look different. Although he had betrayed countless people to the police for nearly twenty years, he felt shocked as he saw a black father and his children in a supermarket buying dog food, the only thing they could afford. Soon after, Winter's black maid was arrested and severely tortured, a suspect in a case in which he knew she was innocent. Winter left the country, smuggled out two decades' worth of files, and wrote an extraordinary book, *Inside BOSS* (the Bureau of State Security), giving not only names but also addresses and telephone numbers.

Winter revealed the police slang for different torture techniques: "the Parachute" (threatening to throw the prisoner out of a window), "the Cracker" (a noose around the testicles), and "the Monkey Man" (stringing a prisoner up by the arms). He described the "Key Room" at Johannesburg's Jan Smuts Airport, where police kept keys for searching every known make of suitcase. And, most important, he confirmed that the liberation movement was riddled with informers like himself, both at home and abroad. The police, he said, often shrewdly ignited friends' suspicions of someone who was *not* an informer by arresting all the members of some group and then releasing one of them months ahead of all the others.

During the uprisings of 1984–86, however, the informer network was the first casualty. Of the several hundred people "necklaced" during this period, most were police informers in black townships. It made informing an unpopular profession. When I visited South Africa in early 1986, I heard stories of people being offered houses, cars, release from jail, and payments up to the equivalent of $500 a month to become informers. There were few takers. The network was drying up. Something had to be done.

With the declaration of the State of Emergency in June of that year, the police and army swung into action. A massive show of military force recaptured enough control of most townships to largely stop the necklacing. Show trials like the Delmas case made people think twice about joining any kind of gathering that might turn violent or be judged illegal. In the township of Bonteheuwel, a working-class Coloured area near Cape Town, recruiters went door-to-door asking people to be informers. An activist from Balfour, near Johannesburg, told the Detainees Parents Support Committee, "On the 15 July [1986] . . . I was taken to Moderbee Prison. I was chained around the hands and feet and four policemen began assaulting me. Whenever people went for meals we were assaulted with batons. We were then told anyone who was prepared to become an informer would no longer be assaulted."

A Soweto minister tells me that, now, "they've got informers on every street, like the street committee network used to be. How do they get people to be informers? They torture them. If they target you, they've got you. For if you don't agree, then they'll put out the word that you *are* an informer. Sometimes I think that for people in such a situation the only solution is to leave the country."

Tshenuwani Simon Farisani is a Lutheran bishop who was imprisoned four times and who wrote a harrowing book about his experiences. He was beaten, electro-shocked, and dangled out of a window. At one point he was hung from a stick by his handcuffed arms and legs. He passed out from the pain, then woke up to find himself looking into the face of a man he knew from attending conferences of the opposition movement. This black informer, who now urged Farisani to cooperate with his interrogators, still wore a T-shirt imprinted with a clenched fist and map of Africa.

White groups supporting the movement are infiltrated also. A friend who takes me to a meeting advises me against talking to people there whom he doesn't recognize: "The Branch is getting more sophisticated now. They no longer try to infiltrate our organizations with crew-cut types. They'll send in people dressed like yuppies."

Now that the informer network is reestablished, the police flaunt it, to spread fear. In Langa, an African township of Cape Town, informers known as *impimpis* wear balaclava masks, and accompany police on nighttime raids. People arrested are first brought within sight of the *impimpi;* if he nods, they are bundled into a police vehicle and taken away. In Port Elizabeth, whole areas of townships have been cordoned off at night, and the residents led one by one past police vans with one-way glass windows. An informer inside indicates who is to be arrested. Elsewhere, I hear chilling stories of informers who are *not* masked: young men still in custody, whose faces suggest they have been tortured, are made to stand at roadblocks and point out people they know to the police.

How many informers are there? It's anyone's guess. One former student activist tells me, "We figure it's one out of five people at a small meeting, and one in seven to ten for a larger group." The suspicion-creating tactics Gordon Winter detailed are still in use. The police know everyone will wonder: Why was X not detained, when everyone else in his organization was? Why was Y given a passport, when Z was refused?

"And so," says one person I talk to, "we *all* end up convicting people with no trial."

One tool in South Africa's arsenal of repression has been borrowed from the CIA and the KGB—disinformation. Fake documents intermittently flood the country. Pamphlets over the forged signature of United Democratic Front leader Henry Fazzie circulated in the Eastern Cape, announcing that blacks had to pay a tax to the UDF: "Your sacrifice is our prosperity." Letters making denigrating remarks about blacks were sent out over the faked signature of Peter Kerchhoff, a respected church layman who has been jailed for his work with victims of the violence in Pietermaritzburg. A forged pamphlet raising money for necklace killings was sent out on South African Council of Churches stationery, even using the SACC postage meter. And the South African Air Force has proudly admitted in court that it produced homosexual smear posters against the End Conscription Campaign, telling the judge that such actions were "necessary for the efficient defence and protection of the Republic." The government has also skillfully used disinformation to worsen the sometimes bitter rivalry between the United Democratic Front and the much smaller black-consciousness movement. The police have outfitted black plain-clothesmen with black consciousness T-shirts and sent them to beat people up in pro-UDF areas, and vice versa.

Another major instrument of repression has been censorship. Journalists have operated under a blizzard of government regulations for several decades, but various new restrictions were in force for several years in the late 1980s. Among other things, these banned reporters and photographers from the scene of any township violence. The American television networks were a major target here, because of the way their coverage fueled pressure on the U.S. Congress for tighter sanctions. The South African government knew that without video footage of police shooting at black crowds, U.S. television would greatly downplay the South Africa story. They were right: one before-and-after count of ABC, CBS, and NBC stories found that the new censorship rules cut the number of South Africa stories per month to a third of what it had previously been.

Besides the outright censorship, in more subtle ways journalists are given the message that Big Brother is always watching. A reporter friend had his interview tapes taken when he crossed the border out of South Africa. Police gave them back after a couple of hours, but he found they had been erased.

One more South African Police specialty is surveillance. People assume that the bugging devices are in telephones: several times I see friends unplug the phone before beginning a serious political conversation. Gordon Winter, however, describes security police microphones hidden in pens, lighters, wall plugs, cigarette packs, doorknobs, bricks, and automobile dashboards.

Sometimes, the tapping is so blatant the police clearly don't care if anyone knows they're listening. One man I meet at a party says that picking his phone up to make a call once, he heard two people talking in Afrikaans about a township roadblock. Finally, exasperated, he said, "I can heeeeaaaar you!" and promptly got his dial tone. A union organizer in Soweto says with a laugh that the police don't just tap his phone, they sometimes *answer* it, asking callers who they are and what they're calling about.

Mail is also watched closely. "I think the chap who opens our mail at the post office got promoted and a new man has taken his place," an Anglican minister known for his work with black migrants tells me. "Sometimes now the letter from Sweden comes in the envelope from the United States, and so on."

Gordon Winter tells the story of attending a political meeting some years ago where a plainclothesman sitting next to him was scribbling notes underneath his raincoat. A black speaker was making some literary allusions. "The cop's assignment was obviously to make a note of all the people attending the meeting and to get the names of anyone mentioned by the speakers. . . . He turned to me and whispered: 'I know these Karamazov brothers are commies, man. But do you know where they live?' "

# Stormtroopers

As Andries Pretorius, the new commander of the Natal Voor-trekkers, and his heavily armed commando troop headed off to-ward Umgungundhlovu, it was clear that a decisive confrontation lay ahead. Somewhere along the way, before Pretorius reached the Zulu capital, Dingane's army would come out to do battle. Everyone on both sides knew there could be no truce or com-promise: the Trekkers were determined on vengeance and con-quest, Dingane on defending his kingdom against the tide of armed whites who wanted his land.

Every night as they marched deeper into Zulu territory, the Boers held a religious service—prayers, psalm singing, and a ser-mon. A devout Voortrekker named Sarel Cilliers was the group's religious leader, and he was obsessed with infusing this military expedition with divine purpose. He and Pretorius decided that all the members of the commando force must take a solemn pledge: if God granted them victory in the great battle to come, the Trek-kers promised, they and their descendants would forever honor the day.

"It was on 7th December," Cilliers recalled later;

> . . . I took my place on a gun-carriage. The . . . men of the force were assembled around me. I made the promise in a

simple manner, as solemnly as the Lord enabled me to do. As nearly as I can remember, my words were these: "My brethren and fellow-countrymen, at this moment we stand before the holy God of heaven and earth, to make a promise, if He will be with us and protect us, and deliver the enemy into our hands so that we may triumph over him, that we shall observe the day and the date as an anniversary in each year, and a day of thanksgiving like the Sabbath, in His honor; and that we shall enjoin our children that they must take part with us in this, for a remembrance even for our posterity; and if anyone sees a difficulty in this, let him retire from the place."

This pledge came to be known as the Vow. The Trekkers repeated the Vow each day until the battle itself. To sweeten the bargain for God, they added a provision: they promised that if granted victory, they would build a church. Three years later, they did so. It is the small church at Pietermaritzburg, whose first minister was the American Daniel Lindley.

And so the Vow passed into legend. In his book *The Political Mythology of Apartheid,* Yale historian Leonard Thompson traces how this happened. There are, he points out, conflicting accounts of just where and when the Trekkers first made the Vow and of just what they said. One Trekker remembered Sarel Cilliers standing not on a gun carriage, as Cilliers said, but on a wagon. Someone else recalled the pledge being made in Pretorius's tent. But this, of course, could not have held some four hundred Boers. The account by Cilliers himself makes no mention whatever of the promise about the church. And Cilliers's recollection is scarcely reliable to begin with; it is a statement he supposedly made on his deathbed, decades later, transcribed by several people who had a strong Afrikaner nationalist agenda of their own. Furthermore, the wording of the Vow in Cilliers's recollection differs from the wording in other accounts.

Most surprising of all is that for several decades after the Vow, everyone forgot about it. Nobody observed any solemn day of thanksgiving. Andries Pretorius lived a busy and politically prominent life for fifteen years after 1838, but no one records ever hearing him mention the Vow. Nobody referred to the Vow at the consecration of the church in Pietermaritzburg. And people quickly forgot that the church was built in fulfillment of a sacred promise: the building soon stopped being used for worship and successively became a wagonmaker's shop, a mineral-water bottling plant, a tearoom, a blacksmith's, and a school.

Gradually, a half century later, the struggles with the British leading up to the Boer War began to inflame Afrikaners' sense of victimhood once again. Only then was the Vow resurrected as a great historical event, and the story surrounding it codified to serve as part of a national myth. It was not until seventy years after the Vow, in 1908, that Afrikaners finally organized to rescue the church building in Pietermaritzburg from its commercial uses and turn it into the museum of Voortrekker life it is today.

Rediscovered and burnished, the story of the Vow serves a useful purpose. Just as the death of Piet Retief and the Great Murder became the legend of Afrikaners' great martyrdom, so the Vow and the Voortrekkers' subsequent victory in battle became proof of their piety and reward. It is a fable that proves that Afrikaners are indeed a Chosen People—whose conquest of the Zulus and other blacks was accomplished not by gunpowder, but by God's will. "For the victory no praise or honor should be claimed," declared the official magazine of the Dutch Reformed Church on the Blood River anniversary in 1983, "because it should only be regarded as a miracle." Today, although the national holiday is celebrated on the day of the Battle of Blood River, it is known as the Day of the Vow.

The idea of the Vow's fulfillment as divine sanction for Afrikaner nationalism is, I discover, still very much alive in South Africa 150 years later. Addressing the right-wing trekkers gathered at the Voortrekker Monument, a far-right politician named Jaap Marais blasts Afrikaner heretics who dare to suggest that the Vow is not sacred or does not bind all Afrikaners. These are the same lily-livered types, he declares, who have forgotten the message of the Great Murder: "The more we appease, the more aggression will be aimed at us."

One of these heretics—and a mild one at that—was the object of a strange attack some years ago. Professor Floors van Jaarsveld was a rather conventional history professor from the Afrikaans-language University of Pretoria, very much a figure of the Afrikaner intellectual establishment. One day in 1979, he was delivering a paper about the Vow at a campus symposium, suggesting that Afrikaners were not the only people to believe that God was on their side. As he began to speak, according to a newspaper account at the time, "a gang of about 40 burly men burst into the hall, surrounded historian Floors van Jaarsveld, emptied a tin of tar over him and plastered him with feathers. During the assault, a man who identified himself as Eugene Terre Blanche . . . seized the microphone and swung the tail of a *sjambok* through the air."

A few days later, Terre Blanche told the press: "I led 40 members into the hall with my braided whip in hand. I was prepared to horsewhip anyone who mocked us. . . . On what grounds can Professor van Jaarsveld question Sarel Cilliers's vow . . . ? God fulfilled His part of the contract. What right has anyone, particularly the Afrikaner, to desanctify this day? . . . I want to warn others that if they do not toe the line, their punishment will be as swift."

Since Eugene Terre Blanche and his brown-uniformed followers burst onto the national scene that day, they have become the most dramatic symbol of South Africa's far right and of the power of Afrikaner myth. A farmer and former policeman, the appropriately named Terre Blanche and six others founded the *Afrikaner Weerstandsbeweging,* or Afrikaner Resistance Movement, at a meeting in a garage in 1973. The AWB operated largely in secret until the tarring and feathering of van Jaarsveld. In 1982, police discovered several AWB arms caches, one of them on Terre Blanche's brother's farm. Terre Blanche and several others were charged with illegal possession of explosives, hand grenades, and automatic weapons—a crime that would have put any black revolutionary in jail for decades. The AWB men, however, got off with a suspended sentence.

A few years after this, the AWB profoundly jarred the Afrikaner power structure by barging into several National Party political rallies and seizing the microphone. At one meeting, rampaging AWB stormtroopers prevented the Foreign Minister from speaking. In breaking up that demonstration, the police for the first time in more than half a century fired tear gas into an Afrikaner crowd.

Much about the AWB is deliberately modeled on the Nazis: the red, white, and black insignia which looks like a swastika with one leg missing; the evocation of the heroic *volk;* the profusion of SS-like black- or khaki-uniformed militia groups, known variously as "sentries," "storm falcons," or "blitzcommandos." Terre Blanche himself is a charismatic orator who does a booming business selling tape cassettes of his speeches. He and his handlers have a keen sense of occasion and staging—he appears at rallies on horseback, or leads torchlit processions at night, surrounded by flag bearers and uniformed bodyguards. Terre Blanche can draw several thousand people to a rally, and often many more. A favorite AWB gathering place is the Blood River battlefield site, where memories of wars past are called upon in support of the war to come. "To those who want to sell us cheaply," Terre Blanche has said, "we say, 'We shall fight!' "

AWB followers form the core of support for the white electoral right wing. Terre Blanche's own program centers on a vague demand for an Afrikaner-dominated, all-white *Boerestaat* consisting roughly of the territory the Voortrekkers settled, the northern half of South Africa. This state would be under white rule but not along the lines of parliamentary democracy. Instead, as in Mussolini's Italy, there would be representatives of different professions and occupations. Other details are hazy.

Demagogues thrive, however, not on precision but on enemies, and Terre Blanche's are clear: blacks above all, then Jews, other English-speaking whites (in public he speaks only in Afrikaans), foreigners, and the traitorous reformer Afrikaners in power, who are turning the country over to all these other people. To poorer Afrikaners, facing the loss of their farms or jobs, or only marginally hanging on to them, Terre Blanche offers a clear array of villains to blame.

Terre Blanche's message is reinforced, unintentionally, by the way the South African press and TV prefer reporting black wealth to black poverty. Newspapers give a lot of attention to the high-living homeland leaders and to the mansions and Rolls-Royces of South Africa's minuscule handful of affluent black businessmen. All this feeds the resentful mind-set of economically threatened poor whites, who then project these images onto blacks around them. No wonder they have trouble making ends meet, they think; the government is giving everything away to black millionaires. I meet one white miner who claims that a black man on his shift drives a Mercedes and that another is building himself a five-bedroom house in one of the homelands. He adds, bitterly, "*I can't afford a five-bedroom house.*"

Like the Nazis, the AWB has a vaguely populist rhetoric. Terre Blanche denounces foreign investors, for example, and says they should not be allowed to control South Africa's mineral wealth. The AWB also runs a welfare program, the *Volkshulpskeme* (People's Help Schemes); farmers and other AWB supporters donate food, shoes, and old clothing, which get passed out to poor whites. In Pretoria, vans with the AWB logo on the side ferry unemployed Afrikaners to local factories where they act as strikebreakers or replace black workers who are trying to unionize.

It is no coincidence that Terre Blanche and several other top AWB leaders are former policemen. Police vans sometimes sport AWB stickers; the two organizations are so closely entwined that they are hard to disentangle. White policemen are almost all Afrikaners, and are part of exactly that economically pinched white working class from which the AWB draws its strength. Officially, police are not allowed to belong to the AWB, and in a feeble publicity gesture, a few open AWB members were recently expelled from the police reserve. One of them, Attie Engelbrecht, told the press that more than 40 percent of the police reservists in his part of the country were AWB members. When asked if the organization was trying to infiltrate the police, an AWB spokesperson replied, "Nonsense. One cannot infiltrate one's allies."

AWB members both inside and outside the police, it is widely believed, are members of the death squads whose killings have terrorized the liberation movement in recent years. Since 1977, more than seventy-five prominent opponents of apartheid or black community leaders have been the victims of unsolved murders.

Sometimes they are shot in their homes, sometimes killed after being kidnapped by armed, masked men.

The list of those killed or beaten to death is a lengthening one, including such people as eighteen-year-old Sicelo Dhlomo, who had been interviewed in a CBS documentary about children in detention; and Matthew Goniwe, Sparrow Mkhonto, Fort Calata, and Sicelo Mhlawuli, all UDF activists whose charred and mutilated bodies were found in the Eastern Cape. A number of other people, such as Congress of South African Students chairperson Siphiwe Mtimkulu and an associate, Toksie Madaka, have, in what South African security planners call "the Argentine option," simply disappeared. Some of their bodies may be among the more than fifty unidentified corpses found secretly buried in unmarked graves near Port Elizabeth a few years ago.

By now these attacks are so routine that they often appear only on back pages of the newspapers: MEN SHOT IN RANDOM ATTACK; BURNT BODY FOUND; GRENADE FLUNG AT RENTS ACTIVIST. Sometimes the South African death squad attacks are aimed at specific people; sometimes they are random, and what's targeted is the area—usually a black township known for its militance. In the Transvaal, where the AWB is strongest, "balaclava men," so called because of the ski masks they wear, sporadically cruise at night through black townships in cars with headlights off, shooting at anything that moves. In the industrial town of Krugersdorp, an AWB stronghold just west of Johannesburg, at least one death and fifty injuries have come from these "balaclava" attacks.

In the end, however, there is a crucial distinction between the person who pulls the trigger and the person who gives the nod. In the death squad killings, the masked people happily pulling the trigger may be AWB sympathizers inflamed by blind race hatred. But recent press revelations have now made clear that some death squads have been set up and operated by the government itself, their members trained at a special camp. The people giving the nod have clearly been high up the ladder, signing execution orders with one hand while doling out "oilspot" reforms with the other. Three former policemen, including one who says he commanded a death squad, have now spoken up publicly. Their statements and other disclosures have shown that, whatever additional killings the

AWB and its offshoots may have been doing on their own, the officially sponsored death squads got approval at cabinet level. Even before the scandal broke, Defense Minister Magnus Malan himself declared that South Africa uses "unconventional methods" against its enemies, but that, "like others, we do not talk about them."

Although much of the AWB's business is done by masked men at night, it still is partly an aboveground organization. Getting anybody there to talk seems like a long shot, but it's worth a try. The AWB is listed, I find, in the Pretoria phone book, and so I dial the number. To my amazement, I reach Eugene Terre Blanche on the phone, he speaks almost perfect English, and he says that of course I can come and talk to him. How about tomorrow morning?

The AWB headquarters is in a nondescript commercial district. The second-floor suite has that disheveled feel of political offices everywhere, with ringing telephones and unruly stacks of newspapers and pamphlets on the floor. Terre Blanche occupies a private office to one side. A black maid brings tea. This morning Terre Blanche wears a blue shirt and dark blue tie. He has intense blue eyes and a well-trimmed dark beard flecked with gray. Although a slim man whose detractors say he wears elevator shoes, his muscular, erect bearing as he stands up to greet me, his iron handshake, and his deep voice convey the feeling of a powerful, tightly wound spring. During the hour he spends sitting behind his desk talking with me, his eyes never leave my face. He is the model of courtesy and charm.

On flagstaffs behind his desk are red, white, and black AWB flags. Isn't this intended to resemble the swastika? I ask. He laughs. Far from it, he insists, the flag is three sevens. Seven is the number of the holy day in the week, and after the commandos of Andries Pretorius took the Vow, God granted them victory at Blood River seven days later. Also, three sevens are the antithesis to the three sixes, mentioned in the Bible's Book of Revelation as the Mark of the Beast.

(Such magical overtones loom large for members of the paranoid right here, as they often have for Fascists in Europe and Latin America. The South African Minister of Finance has even felt it

necessary to get up in Parliament to deny that the new electronic
bar codes on supermarket items are the Mark of the Beast.)

During our talk, a faint smile sometimes passes across Terre
Blanche's face. It is the smile of a man far more sophisticated than
the crudity of his message, but who is not about to reveal what
he is really thinking to anyone. It is also the smile of a man who
knows that any foreign journalist will try to get him to say that
he eats blacks for breakfast; who knows that an interview is a game
whose rules are that I must report what he says into my tape
recorder; and who knows that for every move of mine to get him
to say something self-indicting, there is an easy countermove.

"I am not a racist!" he protests, answering one of my questions.
"I don't see a Coloured person as my enemy. I don't see *any*
person as my enemy, even if he is in Technicolor! If he doesn't
want to give me the opportunity to be a *people* in my own country,
then he is my political enemy. But it has nothing to do with color."
The smile flickers; he has blocked my move.

At mass rallies, Terre Blanche denounces the corruptions of the
"British-Jewish" parliamentary system, and says that Jews should be
stripped of the right to vote. But now, faced with a Jewish interviewer, he is all praise: "The Jewish people asked for two thousand
years for their country. For the land which was theirs. And in the
end they have it. It's a wonderful example of a struggling people—
a nation who wants to be themselves." The smile flickers again.

What about all these militia units of his? I ask. Are they vigilantes? Not at all, he declares, only people training for self-defense.
"We must defend ourselves. I am sure there will be a revolution
in the next eight or ten months. I know the black man. I've grown
up with them. I speak to them. I work with them on the farm. I
know them. I know we are moving to a bloody revolution. We
have no other place to go. We cannot go to your country. Your
people won't accept us. And we have no intention to go. We must
stay here. And we will fight."

Terre Blanche moves quickly into a description of his political
program. "I think the Afrikaners, especially the poor people, have
the right to their own country," he says. "Their own *land*. And
with that I do not mean we want the whole of South Africa. We
only want the land which rightfully belongs to *us*. Which our

forefathers paid for in installments of blood. It can be no one else's land than the Afrikaners'. It was rightfully the country of the Boer people. It belonged to us. And the world said so. The English came. They took it away from us and later on they gave it back—but as a union, not as the old Boer republics. I think the solution lies in that we must divide the country. We must take what is *ours*. I feel it's the only way. I just want my Boereland."

On the map, the territory Terre Blanche specifies as "Boereland" amounts to about 40 percent of South Africa (although part of the rest is desert). What's left over, says Terre Blanche, can be for blacks, English-speaking whites, and anybody else. They can figure out how to divide it, he says. "Let them do their sharing there. But they cannot share power in *my* country."

And the cities?

"I think *they* can have Johannesburg," he says, even though it would seem to fall within "Boereland." His dream is of restoring the legendary days before big cities, uppity blacks, and meddling foreigners. He throws up his hands in disgust. "Maybe it will be news for you, but I think they can have Johannesburg and Soweto. I think Americans can have Johannesburg if they are interested."

Sometimes the underlying impulse behind the AWB is displayed with no masks. One day in 1988, Barend Strydom, an AWB member and a former policeman, approached, one after another, twenty-one blacks on the street in Pretoria and shot them all at point-blank range, killing seven and wounding the remainder. Strydom was arrested and eventually sentenced to death. But the AWB stood by him. "There is support, or rather sympathy, for Mr. Strydom," an AWB spokesperson named Jan Richder said. "We do not say what he did was a good thing. But we understand and we are sympathetic ... the AWB is not to blame, the government is to blame for what happened." Terre Blanche himself blamed the shootings on the government's reforms, particularly the repeal of the limits on black migration to the cities: "If influx control was still in force and the police were able to carry out their tasks effectively, people wouldn't feel threatened."

During his trial, Strydom told the court that he regarded blacks as animals and whites as descendants of the ancient Israelites. The courtroom was packed with fellow AWB members. In a striking reminder of the thread linking past and present, some wore Voortrekker costumes.

Strydom's testimony painted a self-portrait of a man for whom the hardships of poorer Afrikaners, faced with black competition for jobs formerly reserved for whites, were a modern version of the sufferings of martyrs of the past, like Piet Retief and the victims of the Great Murder. So powerful was this mythology for him that it allowed him to feel an aura of religious righteousness as he became, in essence, a one-man death squad. Before going on his shooting rampage, he said, he had made a pilgrimage to the Voortrekker Monument to "reconcile myself with the pledge laid down in 1838. I prayed and asked God to do His will and not mine and if He was not pleased, to deflect me from my path with some visible sign."

And then, he testified proudly, he had recited the Vow.

With his usual sense of the dramatic, Terre Blanche and the AWB are planning to celebrate the 150th anniversary of Blood River by staging a pageant of the battle. Such events have been put on before, but on one notable occasion the reenactment turned into the real thing. In 1916, an early South African movie company made a film called *De Voortrekkers,* to be released on the Day of the Vow that year. (The movie is said to have inspired the 1923 Hollywood feature, *The Covered Wagons.*) Producers set up a *laager* of ox wagons, and three thousand black mineworkers on their day off were issued collapsible *assegais* to play the part of the Zulu warriors. White military reservists in period costume played the Trekkers. While the blacks were awaiting orders, the whites jumped their cue and started shooting—and some slipped live ammunition into their nineteenth-century muskets. The filmmakers made halfhearted attempts to stop the firing, but could not resist the chance to keep their cameras rolling. When the fight was over, one black miner was dead and 122 were injured, 35 seriously enough to be hospitalized. The movie was promoted as having "lifelike" battle scenes and was a big hit.

With this eerie precedent in mind, I make plans to see Terre Blanche's pageant on December 16th.

# Shell of the Old,
# Seed of the New

A most unexpected feeling comes over me as I approach the end of my trip, which is also the end of several weeks in or around Johannesburg. Despite everything—despite the AWB, despite the knowledge of what goes on inside police stations, despite the vast gap between rich and poor—I like this city. I could imagine living here. There is an excitement to Johannesburg, a cosmopolitan ease, an unpredictable interweaving of cultures that sets it apart not only from other cities in South Africa, but from most in the world.

Johannesburg owes some of its liveliness to the breakdown of traditional barriers. One cornerstone of South African life has always been strict residential segregation, codified under National Party rule in the Group Areas Act of 1950. Slated for change, the Act until now has rigidly divided all towns into areas for whites, Africans, Coloureds, and Indians, with the whites always getting the best squares on the checkerboard. But far more than any other city in the country, Johannesburg abounds in "gray areas"—parts of town where people of all races are living, sometimes illegally, sometimes exempted from the Group Areas Act.

One entire hilltop shoulder of Johannesburg where I am staying—the Hillbrow district—is a gray area. It is strange to find this expression labeling such a center of vitality. Almost everywhere else in South Africa, blacks have been moved to make way for whites, but here more than fifty thousand blacks live in what was long an officially white area. There is an underside to this: rent gouging by unscrupulous landlords, crime, horrendously over-crowded apartments, and some evidence that as the area becomes more black, the government is withdrawing street cleaners and garbage trucks. But despite it all, from the sheer pressure of num-bers, one aspect of apartheid is crumbling. As a result, the streets, shops, restaurants, and nightspots of Hillbrow have the feel of New York's Upper West Side: the faces are white, black, brown, rich, poor; some couples are interracial. At night the sound of jazz from music clubs and the smell of curry from Indian restaurants spill out onto the sidewalk. This part of Johannesburg gives you the feeling engendered by great cities everywhere; a whole that is greater than the sum of its parts.

Even the language is unique—a protean urban tongue that shat-ters all the government's neat boundaries. While the South African Broadcasting Corporation rigidly tries to preserve linguistic apartheid—separate channels for separate languages; hastily in-vented Zulu words for "terrorist" and "radical"—Johannesburg's Africans have evolved a new language of their own. It is larded with words, phrases, intonations, and in-jokes from Zulu, Sotho, English, and Afrikaans. Americans got a recent sample of this in the all-too-brief U.S. run of the South African film *Mapantsula*. Here is another taste, from a short story by Mbulelo Mzamane:

" '*Kyk hier*,' the third fellow said, '*ons werk hier and jy kom ons goggle soos 'n bloody induna*. Go back to the house, man. *U-sure ukuthi siyadlala la. Sizaku-khipa lobu-situation onabo thina, jou bloody moomish*. Vamose!' "

Some of Johannesburg's diversity has other forms. The city has, for example, an open gay community, with its own bars, clubs, and hotlines. At the bar level, the community is interracial, al-though the organizations are mostly of whites. In a recent white municipal election, the local National Party even advertised in a gay newspaper, offering to build a gay community center and sports field. Party leaders on the national level were horrified. For straitlaced Afrikaners, even acknowledging that South African gays existed would have been unthinkable ten or fifteen years ago.

Also on the streets of Hillbrow, although I can only guess at which faces on the sidewalk are theirs, are numbers of white draft evaders. The mid-1980s were the first time the government sent large numbers of draftee soldiers to help police shoot down township rebels. Thousands of young white men have emigrated to avoid the draft; a surprising number of others changed their names or addresses and dropped from sight. In the January 1985 military call-up, when it was first clear there was no avoiding duty in the townships, more than 25 percent of new draftees simply did not show up. The government then stopped releasing figures, so no one knows just how many young white men in South Africa are living in this uneasy limbo. Some estimates put the number as high as twenty thousand. In any case, it is certain that a high percentage of them are here in Johannesburg, in whose size and relative tolerance it is much easier to be anonymous than almost anywhere else.

Within the political opposition in Johannesburg, the biggest single change I notice from when I was first here nearly thirty years ago is the number of friendships and working relationships that cross racial lines—and do so without people feeling self-conscious or self-righteous about it. When I was here in the early sixties, even an interracial party was a rare event, and if you went to one, the mere fact that it was interracial made it exciting. The rest of the time, it seemed, no matter what their politics, blacks talked to blacks and whites to whites. I remember being present when a white newspaper reporter I knew was interviewing a white attorney who had some black clients. The reporter asked him: "What are the chaps you're in touch with in the townships thinking about, Bill?" The next day the story appeared in the paper: "The mood in the townships is somber these days. Many people feel . . ."

Today, by contrast, many organizations in the opposition—newspapers, law firms, the headquarters of almost all the major church denominations—are racially integrated. It is not that they are without tensions; some are as full of factional feuds, office politics, and personality conflicts as political groups anywhere. But the fissures are generally not along racial lines. And on the staffs of the rapidly growing black labor unions one finds something else new: white professionals and semi-professionals—accountants, administrators, secretaries, editors, publicists—working for black-controlled organizations. Relative to the rest of the white population, most of whom would be appalled at the thought of working for a black employer, their numbers are tiny. But their presence in such jobs is an encouraging foretaste of a South Africa to come.

Surprisingly, the whole apparatus of book banning and censorship has not dampened Johannesburg's cultural life. Books that have been banned, like Gordon Winter's, have always circulated anyway, sent from overseas or brought home from trips abroad. And some books one would expect to be banned seem not to be, such as several much-loved novels by the British satirist Tom Sharpe, who lived in South Africa for a time and was deported from the country.

No one takes on South Africa better than Sharpe. My own favorite is his *Riotous Assembly*. When a melee results in the death of twenty-one policemen and one Zulu cook, the suspect is charged with twenty-one and a quarter counts of murder. When he is sentenced to hang, the official Executioner says he can't do the job: "I've got thirty-two customers that day and besides, I never hang singles. I always do mine in batches of six at a time and . . . I have my reputation to think of . . . if it got about that I had hanged a single man, people would think I was losing my touch." Another character in the book is Judge Hazelstone of the Supreme Court, an apoplectic hard-liner who once sentenced eleven Pondo tribesmen to death for stealing a goat, and "who, in a Minority report of the Commission on Traffic Congestion, had advocated that flogging be made mandatory for parking offences."

Other cultural artifacts circulate unofficially as well. At the time of my visit, the United Democratic Front is not allowed to publish anything, but I'm given a copy of an underground edition of a journal aligned with it, *Phambili* (Zulu for "the Way Forward"), which has no bylines, masthead, or return address. There has been a flowering of oral poetry in recent years; the work of the best-known of these poets, Mzwakhe Mbuli, who recites forceful, highly political poems in a mixture of English and the African languages, has been intermittently censored, but I have no trouble buying a banned cassette of it on the street one evening. And there is a thriving *samizdat* of films and videos. I watch one extraordinary anti-war video, done by a young army veteran who makes his living producing television commercials, about the war in Namibia. The video shows scenes of a minister blessing white soldiers before a battle, of soldiers talking about self-inflicted wounds they have used to escape combat, and of one soldier describing the men of his platoon dipping their hands in the blood of a dead guerrilla and then clasping hands in triumph.

Nowhere is the vigorous alternative culture more striking than in the way South Africans are rewriting their history. It is particularly exhilarating to find this after I've seen the huge expense the government has gone to in order to put forth the official version of history: in ox-wagon caravans, propaganda magazines, school textbooks, and the Voortrekker Monument and a hundred lesser memorials.

But they're losing the battle. In the last twenty years, no country outside the Soviet Union and Eastern Europe has seen such a massive reinterpretation of its past. Some of the writings are scholarly, some are illustrated and designed for use in the burgeoning black adult education classes that scorn government textbooks. Writer after writer is looking at the entire sweep of the country's history afresh, from the point of view of black peasants, miners, and laborers.

Few history books by black authors appeared for most of this century. "The story," wrote one of them, Nosipho Majeke, in 1952, "if truly told, is one of continuous plunder of land and cattle by the European invaders, of the devastation and decimation of people, followed by their economic enslavement." Censorship and jailings soon silenced voices like these. But by thirty years later, the story *was* truly told. A new generation of historians, predominantly white and working in the protected enclaves of the major universities, has been reexamining the South African past. Colin Bundy has shown how nineteenth-century African farmers in the Cape Province were more efficient than white farmers at producing surplus food for the market—until they were forced off their land. Bernard Magubane and others have attacked "the myth of 1948," showing how all the basic building blocks of apartheid were put in place by English-speaking mineowners long before the National Party took power. Charles van Onselen has written a fascinating series of studies of the underside of Johannesburg during its Gold Rush: the prostitutes, the horse-cab drivers, the domestic servants, the criminal gangs. His classic essay on alcohol in that era (see p. 137), "Randlords and Rotgut," was made into a play by the city's multiracial Market Theater, a rare fate for a historical monograph.

Thirty years ago, novels, poems, and stories by black South African writers were widely banned, and, if they circulated at all, it was as single copies smuggled in from abroad or as manuscripts in carbon or Xerox *samizdat*. Unable to publish at home, many of South Africa's best black writers stopped writing or went into exile. But today a rich array of such writing is allowed, much of it highly political, like Mtutuzeli Matshoba's short stories about migrant workers in hostels and prisoners serving out their sentences as farm laborers. Although newspapers have been heavily censored at times, these days the government largely ignores fiction, perhaps figuring that it doesn't have a mass audience. Black writers still have a rougher time than white ones, however, and some of their publishers have been hit by bombings or other harassment. A group of talented black short story writers and poets appear in *Staffrider* magazine, which takes its name from the word for someone who clings precariously to the outside of the packed electric commuter trains that run from Johannesburg to Soweto.

Even in Afrikaans, there is an eruption of alternative culture. A bold new opposition weekly, *Vrye Weekblad,* has gotten some of the same official threats and harassment dealt out to other democratically minded newspapers. It broke several of the major stories in the police death squad scandal. The name of a music group, Die Gereformeerde Blues Band, mocks the conservative Dutch Reformed Church; one of its songs is about black townships so bleak it is as if "we've landed on the wrong side of the moon." A new Afrikaans novel by Andre Letoit plays with his people's central myth: the hero turns an armored car into a time machine, and calls in the modern South African Defense Force to fight the Zulus at Blood River.

Some Afrikaans writers, like Breyten Breytenbach and André

Brink, are well known to American readers. A lesser-known but intriguing one is Karel Schoeman, only one of whose books has been translated into English. This dreamlike novel, *Promised Land,* is set in the future, an account of an exiled Afrikaner's return to South Africa. His family's farm has been mysteriously destroyed. His poverty-striken countrymen are scratching out a living with no electricity and little food. They talk fearfully but cryptically of the police. Many seem to have met early deaths, in unspoken ways. Only gradually do you realize that they are living in a white homeland in a black state, under almost exactly the same conditions—certainly no worse—as rural Africans today. It is a subtle tour de force.

All this intellectual richness is surprising. For black South Africans, the country is, by any usual definition of the term, a police state: the government locks people up whenever it wants; the black townships are in effect under martial law. Americans tend to assume that the first assault of any totalitarian government will be against free speech. There are plenty of such assaults here, but it is still remarkable how much free speech exists. While in the last thirty years the entire apparatus of state repression has become far more sophisticated, there is now an opposition culture that did not exist three decades ago. It is as if the avant-garde Weimar Germany of Brecht and Grosz and Weill had been superimposed on the Nazi, concentration camp Germany of the 1930s.

Culture alone is, of course, no substitute for political and economic power. Perhaps cynics high in the government think: *Let the liberals have their precious free speech if they want it; words alone will never bring us down.* And partly they are correct. But culture and politics cannot be so easily separated, for freedom in one awakens hope for freedom in the other.

South Africa's opposition newspapers and magazines have mushroomed in recent years, for desktop publishing has made possible low-budget newspapers in poor, black communities. Both at the local and national level, opposition periodicals have been sporadically closed at the government's whim; their reporters have been jailed; their offices have been fire-bombed. But they draw eager readers nonetheless.

Nationally, the two most important such papers are *The New Nation* and *The Weekly Mail*. The government has already forcibly shut down each for short periods, and that could happen again. The weekly *The New Nation* is edited, written, and read almost entirely by blacks. Its original editor, Zwelake Sisulu, son of Walter and Albertina Sisulu, was detained for two years, much of it in solitary. Published with Macintosh computers from spartan Johannesburg offices donated by the Catholic Church, the paper is a lively compendium of investigative reporting and political news.

Each week it wraps its news pages around an educational supplement of self-help material in English, history, and math for survivors of South Africa's underfinanced black schools. Even this text carries a strong political message. "How Mandela Was Arrested" is the topic of the passage to be studied for reading comprehension one week. At the end are questions to answer and definitions of new vocabulary words for the week: "treason," "incitement."

Like *The New Nation*, *The Weekly Mail* strongly supports the politics of the ANC, but it reaches a somewhat smaller, mostly white audience. Packed with political news, commentary, and criticism of the arts, the *Mail* has published some remarkable investigative coups: a first-person series on life as an apprentice black miner; a report on conditions in the Soweto schools, for which a black *Mail* reporter posed as a student; and an exposé of the country's convict labor program. To do the last story, *Mail* reporters said they were white businessmen in need of workers, and rented several prisoners for a day's labor, at about 55 cents each. Despite the censorship minefield in which it must exist, the *Mail* is one of the best political newspapers in the world.

Most of all, I like the *Mail*'s sense of humor, and the way it always pushes to the very limit of what is legally allowed. While I am in Johannesburg, Nelson Mandela is still behind bars and his picture therefore cannot be published. The government, trying to soothe world opinion, moves Mandela from his prison cell to a warder's house and announces that he will not be returned to an ordinary prison. "If that is true," says *The Weekly Mail*, "he is no longer, legally speaking, a prisoner—and photographs of him may be lawfully printed." It runs five Mandela photos in one issue, under the headline: AT LAST: A FACE NOT SEEN FOR 25 YEARS. In a few hours, the issue sells out on every newsstand in Johannesburg. The next week, the government is forced to announce that Mandela, despite his new villa, *is* still a prisoner.

When several black political detainees dramatically escape from prison and take asylum in the U.S. Consulate, the *Mail* publishes an escaper's guide to embassies, rating them with stars, in the style of hotel guidebooks, and adding comments:

The U.S. Embassy: "If you can convince them you do not want a green card, you're in."

The British: "A trouser press is a must."

The French: "There's no other place for the gourmet guerrilla."

Music and the theater seem freest of all. I see a wonderful one-man revue that skewers one official target after another. While the audience drifts into their seats, actor Peter-Dirk Uys stands on one side of the stage, in sunglasses. As the crowd grows, he whispers into a police-style walkie-talkie with more and more alarm. Then, in succession, he plays a South African woman singer returning from "her triumphal tour of Uruguay and Taiwan" (two of South Africa's diminishing number of friends); a heavy-accented German TV producer directing a race riot (officials have charged that it is the presence of foreign TV crews that makes blacks demonstrate); a woman in a TV commercial: "My husband is a prison warden and Omo is the *only* detergent that will take the blood out of his uniform"; and a salesman of riot control gear, offering "vicious Alsatians in three sizes: medium large, large, and bloody large," and "rubber bullets programmed for full frontal impact no matter where you fire them from, so they can't say we shot the buggers in the back." When the show is over, he goes offstage, but then his voice comes over the loudspeaker with an Afrikaans accent: "You've got five minutes to disperse in an orderly fashion."

The audience for this particular show was largely white, but there is also a vigorous black theater movement in South Africa, much of it centered in the labor unions. One union play deals with sexual harassment—a big problem for urban black women, made worse in factories where they work for white male supervisors.

Another tells of a woman from the countryside going to Durban to look for her husband, a migrant worker who has abandoned her for a city girlfriend. In *Gallows for Mr. Scariot Mpimpi,* an obsequious black foreman is told by a white factory owner (played by a black actor in whiteface) that if there were only "a hundred of your kind, South Africa would indeed be able to defeat her enemies!" The owner tells the foreman to lay off workers, and he begins "firing" members of the audience, until he is finally fired himself.

Most of these plays have no fixed scripts, just a sequence of events the actors have agreed on. They are "workshopped" into being by the workers themselves, after hours, in a union office or deserted warehouse. Props are simple, rehearsal time scarce, and often the audience demands a replay with a different ending. Sometimes it is hard to tell where the play ends and the real world begins. Striking workers at the Sarmcol plant near Pietermaritzburg put together a play, *The Long March,* about their long struggle for union recognition. Since the factory involved is British-owned, the play included a scene of Margaret Thatcher. The cast performed mostly in Zulu for worker audiences in Natal, and in English in Johannesburg, Cape Town, and elsewhere. In the midst of these performances, Inkatha vigilantes murdered several unionists, including Simon Ngubane, one of the actors and the leading force behind the play. Another actor took his place, and the play was updated to include his murder. At the end of each performance, the actors came forward and introduced themselves to the audience: "Bongani Mchunu, still on strike. . . . Isaiah Mzimande, still on strike. . . . Clement Mnguni, still on strike. . . ."

One stage on which some of these plays are performed is an unusual one—the aisles of the crowded evening commuter trains hurtling from Johannesburg to Soweto and other black townships. After the latest uprisings began in 1984, trains became a favorite site for political meetings and later for plays as well: they are almost impossible for the police to raid. *Emzabalazweni,* this moving stage or meeting room is called, "a place of struggle." Actors sometimes recruit passengers to play parts.

Johannesburg's former produce market has been redeveloped into a non-profit complex of large and small theaters, a coffee shop, a bookstore, and a gallery. In the courtyard outside is a sculptural protest against capital punishment: six nooses hanging from a metal coatrack. One evening at the Market Theater I go to a concert of two all-black musical ensembles, Bayete and Sakhile. They sing in a mixture of English and Zulu. Some songs are those of migrant workers; one goes, in translation, "With high hopes we are heading to the city of gold, carrying our sticks and our shields." The instruments range from traditional drums to electric guitars, and the music is a lively, sophisticated combination of traditional rhythms, American jazz, a touch of break dancing, and mime—miners digging, police putting on handcuffs, guns shooting, feet marching, and a chugging steam train taking migrants back home. Occasionally the male singers sing in falsetto voices (you can hear the same thing in recordings by *a cappella* groups like Ladysmith Black Mambazo), a style of song born in migrant worker hostels, where there are no women to sing the high parts.

The audience is perhaps 60 percent black, 40 percent white. The whites clap; the black women ululate. At the end of the concert, the entire audience rises and sings the liberation anthem, "Nkosi Sikelel' iAfrika," swaying slowly from side to side. On the bodies swaying in front of me are several black babies asleep on their mothers' backs; the back of a young white woman's jeans jacket bears a slogan supporting draft refusers: NO! DON'T GO. Everyone leaves exhilarated by the music. "It's one of those moments," says a friend I've come with, "when you can look around and think, 'What's the problem?' "

Full liberation for South Africa is a long way off, but in its cultural life, you can glimpse the embryo of a new society already alive within the stubborn shell of the old.

# A Carpet-Bombing

While I wait to see the country mark the December 16th holiday, there is one more side trip I want to take, a visit to a battlefield. Not a battlefield of the Great Trek this time, but one of the present. The road to it leads west from Johannesburg, unrolling through a particularly fertile area of South Africa known as the Maize Triangle. Beside the highway are nurseries growing sod for the spacious backyards of Johannesburg's white suburbs; INSTANT LAWN, says one sign. Going the opposite way on this road, an occasional car or *bakkie* carries a white farmer and his wife and children. Some of these bear the red, white, and black three-legged swastika of the AWB and are hauling small trailers of camping gear; they are heading for the right-wing trekkers' camp near Pretoria, where the faithful are now flocking in preparation for the Day of the Vow. The wide *veld* the road cuts through is bordered at the horizon with rocky ridges. Except for being studded here and there with eucalyptus trees, the landscape feels like the plains of Colorado or Wyoming. This is land the Voortrekkers began taking 150 years ago, and today, because it is fertile, the seizures continue. Residential apartheid may be crumbling in certain neighborhoods of Johannesburg, but out here on the open plains, under the harsh light of the summer sun, it is still a-building, with the pieces cemented into place year by year. This road leads to one of those pieces, Mogopa.

In South African parlance, Mogopa is a "black spot." This means that black residents must move from a district tagged for white ownership. There are also, government planners will quickly tell you, "white spots" in the black homelands, and these people have had to move, too. The entire process is called "consolidation." Consolidation is even-handed, officials say: each race can thrive best by itself, each must make some sacrifices, each will be happier on its own land . . .

Since 1948, some 3.5 million South Africans have been forced to move against their will.

More than 99 percent were black.

Some five thousand of them were moved from Mogopa.

The village of Mogopa was an extraordinarily prosperous one by the standards of black South Africa, or of anywhere on the continent. Its several hundred families had had title to their home for more than seventy years. They also communally owned several thousand acres of fields and pasture, on which they grazed their cattle and grew maize, beans, and other vegetables. They grew enough crops both to feed themselves and to sell the surplus, a rare event in South Africa's generally overcrowded black farmland. With that money, plus wages earned by some of the men who went off to work in Johannesburg or on nearby white farms, the people of Mogopa bought cars, trucks, even tractors. With no government subsidy whatever, the people of the village collected money and built an elementary school, a high school, and a clinic. During World War II, villagers collected an amount equal to $1,700 and donated it to the government for the war effort. They sank boreholes, bought water pumps, and built a reservoir. They supported several black-owned shops, including the Swartkop General Dealers Store, that sold everything from feather dusters to shoes to bicycle bells. And the people of Mogopa were proud, perhaps above all, that they had worked hard enough to build themselves something extremely unusual for the black South African countryside: sturdy houses of cut stone.

For almost all of this century, Mogopa lived in peace, a self-sufficient island in an economy built on exploitation. Then the pace of "removals" increased dramatically, as bureaucrats trucked millions of protesting Africans away from their homes and resettled them in the rural slums of the homelands. Mogopa, surrounded by many miles of white-owned farmland, was designated a black spot, scheduled to be rubbed off the map. As the 1980s began, the Mogopa people sent delegations to Pretoria and filed legal briefs, asking to be allowed to stay where they were.

All was in vain. For, like most rural areas in the Transvaal province, the surrounding countryside had become a stronghold of the ultra-right—indeed, the farms of Eugene Terre Blanche and his brother are just down the road. Fearful of losing white votes, the government did not want to appear to be appeasing blacks. Officials came and painted numbers on the stone houses of Mogopa. In June 1983, when most Mogopa residents still refused to move, government bulldozers showed up and bulldozed three churches. They removed the engines from the water pumps. They bulldozed some homes. They destroyed the medical clinic. They bulldozed into rubble the cut-stone schools, paid for by the villagers themselves.

The bulldozers were from the Department of Cooperation and Development.

The state hoped these actions would force the remaining people of Mogopa to move. It offered them new land at a place called Pachsdraai, more than a hundred miles away. But the land was not their ancestral land and it had little water. More ominously, the new land was scheduled to become part of the "independent" homeland of Bophuthatswana, which was the last place anyone from Mogopa wanted to be, since then they would lose what fragmentary rights they still possessed as South African citizens. Furthermore, the only available housing in Pachsdraai was tin shacks. Most people still refused to move. The women were particularly militant, cleaning up some of the damage at Mogopa and refusing to accept removal notices from the police.

To add to the pressure, the government stopped the bus service between Mogopa and the nearby town of Ventersdorp, where some Mogopa people shopped or worked. They ceased paying old-age pensions. And they left a bulldozer parked next to the ruins of the school.

Six months after the partial demolition and after the other pressures began, the Mogopa villagers still had hope. Lawyers were making appeals; the case was attracting attention in South Africa and abroad; and the Deputy Minister of Foreign Affairs assured the press that Mogopa people would not be turned out of their homes. Another minister, one of the most skilled burnishers of Pretoria's reform image, Pieter Koornhof (who has since become South African Ambassador to the United States), declared that the day of forced removals was over. From here on, Koornhof said, it would only be "voluntary removals." It was unclear what they might be.

And so the villagers began to rebuild. They bought a new water pump and repaired the streets. People left their jobs and volunteered full time to rebuild the school. Within a month it was finished. The rest of the story is said best in a report from TRAC, the Transvaal Rural Action Committee, a group which, despite being bombed out of its office at Khotso House, continues to offer help and legal advice to threatened communities like Mogopa:

In the early hours of February 14, 1984, Mogopa was surrounded by armed police. At 4 a.m. the people were informed through loud hailers that they must load their possessions into trucks and go to Pachsdraai. . . . [A]ll the leaders . . . were handcuffed and put into police vans. Their families refused to pack their possessions—government labourers did so. Women were carried into the lorries and buses. People tried to run away and children were loaded with the furniture and dispatched to Pachsdraai. All of this happened in the presence of armed policemen who had dogs at their disposal. People caught standing together outside their houses were beaten with batons. . . .

No outsiders were allowed in. The press, diplomats, priests, lawyers and members of The Black Sash, were turned back at the entrance to Mogopa. Those who managed to sneak in through back ways were caught and charged. The police initially said Mogopa was an "Operational Area" but subsequently corrected this; they said that since it was black land, no whites were allowed to enter—excepting the police of

course, and the white farmers who had free access in and out
to buy the people's livestock at a tenth of its value.

After that traumatic night, bulldozers leveled what remained of
Mogopa. The authorities told villagers that if they returned to the
ruins of their homes, they would be guilty of trespassing. Most
refused to live at Pachsdraai and settled elsewhere, some at a place
called Bethanie where a sympathetic chief from their ethnic group,
the Bakwena, offered them a small amount of land. Litigation
continues. But since the desolate Pachsdraai was the spot to which
the Mogopa people were officially "removed," there is no guar-
antee that people who go somewhere else will receive even partial
compensation, either for their land at Mogopa or for the more
than seventy years' worth of communal improvements they and
earlier generations have paid for.

A winding dirt road turns off the highway. At the end of the road
lie the smashed ruins of the village's four hundred stone houses.
Dotted around the outskirts of the rubble, and sometimes within
it, are something else I did not expect: large heaps of dirt, higher
than a person's head. These, I learn from the TRAC fieldworker
with whom I've traveled here today, are the leavings of white
prospectors; since Mogopa was bulldozed, they have begun digging for diamonds. The stone rubble lies in the orderly rows of
the village grid of streets, as if after a carpet-bombing; next to
these ruins are the prospectors' piles of dirt, like giant anthills. If
I could pick one place to which to bring the smooth-talking cabinet
ministers who are on TV here every night with their talk of progress and sharing and a place in the sun for all South Africans, it
would be this spot. Here, its history etched in the very material
of the earth, stone and dirt, South Africa has been caught naked.
     At one end of the long tract of stone ruins, several black men
are putting up a shack. Their materials are simple: rough sheets
of corrugated metal, thin tree trunks for the corner posts and roof
supports, wire to bind the wood and metal together, and rocks to
put on the roof to keep it from blowing away. With a crowbar,
one man is digging a hole for a corner post.
     These men are mostly in their fifties and sixties. They are from

here, from Mogopa. After several years of petitions and appeals, they have gotten permission to return here temporarily, to clean and repair the community's graveyard, the only part of town that did not get pulverized by the bulldozers. Since they are officially allowed to visit, they have also been given official temporary housing: some portable, prefabricated huts and toilets which government trucks have deposited several hundred feet away. But they refuse to stay in government-supplied houses on land where they once built their own. So they are building again, even though the scrap metal shacks are small and crude and the wind whistles through the cracks.

Tending the graveyard is both why and not why the men are here. The care of graves is enormously important in southern African culture. But at the same time this group of men has no intention of being here only temporarily. What was five men at the start has now grown to seven. They are in constant touch with their families and friends in the communities to which Mogopa residents were dispersed. They hope, they say, to have one or two more people join them each week, slowly building an expanding settlement, squatting on the sites of their former homes. After all, despite the fury with which this "black spot" was removed, no whites have settled here. And the diamond hunters so far don't seem to have found much—at least nobody is digging today. After all the embarrassing attention from around the world attracted by the original eviction from Mogopa, would the government dare evict them *again?* They hope not, and so they plan to gradually reoccupy the site.

Joseph Kgatitsoe, the leader of the men encamped here and a member of Mogopa's fifteen-person village committee, takes me for a walk. He was born here sixty years ago. He is a somber, thoughtful man, with a bearded face scarred by acne, and a hand with a finger missing—lost in an industrial accident, in a printing plant in Johannesburg. He is sick with a chest cold today, and moves slowly. He wears a wool hat and a tan jumpsuit.

As we walk between the smashed heaps of stones, he says he can recall who lived in each house. He points out some ruins of the stone walls of *kraals,* for holding cattle. I feel I am in Dresden or Hiroshima: as we walk along what was once Mogopa's main street, I can see the distinct, regular, crisscross pattern of side streets, some with trees still on them. But not one stone building is still standing.

Kgatitsoe points to one pile of rubble that was his own house.

And these were good houses, he adds, in a voice threaded with deep sadness, "some of stone, some of bricks, and so on. Some were very expensive stone. In the old years, the happy time, we used to plow. There was no hunger. We stayed in peace. There was no trouble. We used to have cattle. Everyone had his own cattle."

He talks about the churches—"there was AME, Wesleyan, Roman, Lutheran"—and the schools. He points out a larger heap of rubble that was the primary school. He went to school there; it was where he learned English. Next to this is the broken brickwork of the new school, the one that was built in those brief months of false hope after the first school was destroyed, only to be smashed in its turn.

The graveyard is on a hillside just beyond the end of the town. Kgatitsoe and the others have cleaned and neatened it. He explains how the engraved headstones can sometimes cost the equivalent of several thousand dollars, and so a family may save their money for years, and then have a big ceremony at the unveiling of the tombstone. At moments of sadness or crisis, you come and talk to your ancestors here. During the years of their diaspora, the people from Mogopa have returned to bury their dead here. The newest graves, the ones awaiting proper headstones, lie beneath low, coffin-sized piles of rocks, gathered from the stony ground that surrounds us. Most piles have favorite objects of the dead person atop them: a vase, a teapot, or, for a child, a toy.

I ask Kgatitsoe whether he and the others have been harassed since their return here several months ago.

"The second day when we were here there was a car of police coming in to where we stay, and they want to know, who are we? Where we come from? Why did we build shelters here? How long are we going to take? And so on. That was the only troubles we have had. Until there was one day big helicopter. Then the next day people of Pretoria come and beg us please don't build more houses." One of the diamond prospectors, Kgatitsoe adds, had been trying to charge him and his comrades the equivalent of $12 a month for taking water from a well—the same well their ancestors dug.

Is he optimistic about more Mogopa people joining them here?

"Yes. I think so. People are afraid but we hope that they will come. Yes."

And will the village someday be rebuilt?

"It will be quite a long time. We've got no more money."

Was it a happy village?

"Too much happy."

Kgatitsoe falls silent. Dust blows in the wind. We turn and walk slowly back toward the cluster of metal shacks. The starkness of the surroundings—the bare, rocky ground, the bright sun, the piles of stone ruins, the weary faces of the men, their talk of a community crushed and scattered—gives the scene a biblical quality. Like Job or Abraham, it seems, these men are living out some harsh fable. But they are trapped in the middle of it, and no reward has followed their afflictions.

In the hour or so Kgatitsoe and I have been walking around, the men have almost finished erecting the hut they were starting when we set off. Kgatitsoe shows me the inside of his own hut, where he has been living for several months now, as pilgrim, squatter, grave tender, and, he hopes, as part of a reoccupation force. The contents of the hut are: a metal bedframe, a thin foam mattress, a few dishes, the springs and shell of an old sofa. The floor is dirt; there is no window.

A photographer taking pictures for *The Weekly Mail* is here with the TRAC worker and me, and the Mogopa men invite us to stay for tea. The metal huts are clustered around a cooking shack with a fire. A kettle is on. A white goat provides the milk—and eventually, perhaps, will furnish these men some meat. The men are tending a few potted plants in tin cans. These turn out to be cuttings from the fruit trees of Mogopa, which will be sent back to villagers still living in exile—figs, mulberries, apricots, Duke of York peaches. When it is time for us to return to Johannesburg, Kgatitsoe insists we take a small plastic bag of apricots. It is both a gift and an affirmation: despite the ruins and the uncertain future, this is his home, these are his trees.

# The Mirror

The only book not about South Africa that I have brought along on my trip is one I had started before leaving home—Theodora Kroeber's biography of Ishi, the last California Indian to live in the wilderness. One night in Johannesburg, just before going to sleep, I read about an attack on Ishi's diminishing band of Yahi Indians in 1865, led by a white settler named Hiram Good. "The terrified Indians leapt into Mill Creek, but the rapid current was a sorry protection. They became targets there for Good's guns, and Mill Creek ran red with the blood of its people." Struck by the resemblance to Blood River, I wonder if the book is not about South Africa after all—or, more to the point, whether the history of South Africa is not about us.

White Americans like to look down their noses at South Africa, as a benighted society far different from our own. The country is a universally agreed-upon villain, which few Americans mention without pursed lips and a disapproving shake of the head. But is its history as different from ours as we would like to think? The Boers of the Great Trek knew that a similar migration by covered wagon was under way in the United States at the same time, and knew that American democracy of the day was, like their own, for white males only. On their way to Natal in 1837, 170 Voortrekkers under the command of Piet Uys signed one of the Trek's many manifestos, declaring, "We purpose to establish our settle-ment on the same principles of liberty as those adopted by the United States of America."

In dozens of academic monographs and college courses, South African racial injustice is compared to relations between American whites and blacks. But the closer analogy really is to relations between whites and American Indians. For it was the Indians who were in North America when Europeans arrived, and it was the Indians who were killed or subjugated by the Europeans in the name of Christianity, civilization, and progress. The great differ-ence between how the United States and South Africa evolved is rooted mainly in relative numbers: in southern Africa, the indig-enous inhabitants always vastly outnumbered those from Europe; in North America, it was soon the other way around. If it had not been, would American whites have ever dared allow Indians such rights as the vote?

Even as it was, the patterns of conquest were strikingly similar in both places, down to the very language. Just as South Africans today use the word "removal" to describe the fate of uprooted communities like Mogopa, so too did the U.S. Congress when it passed the Indian Removal Act of 1830. Just as South African homelands are filled with hundreds of thousands of people, brought in by truck, often with no ancestral tie to the land in-volved, so the Cherokee Reservation in Oklahoma is unconnected to the much larger area the Cherokees once occupied in and around North Carolina. How different was that "removal" from forcing the citizens of Mogopa to move to barren Pachsdraai? The Cherokees had a much longer journey, and they had to make it on foot. Of the fifteen thousand Cherokees herded across the country by U.S. Cavalrymen, an estimated four thousand died en route.

There are similarities, also, in the two countries' self-comforting white myths. The way Afrikaners justify their history at first seems bizarre and unique: forgetting the hundreds of thousands of Af-ricans they killed and instead remembering only the martyrs— Piet Retief's party and the victims of the Great Murder. Yet the conquerors of the American West and their descendants have also worked hard to see themselves as victims. In all the Indian Wars of the nineteenth century, in which hundreds of thousands of Indians died at the hands of white conquerors, what is the single encounter most white Americans could name? Custer's Last Stand. And in the Mexican-American War, in which we won half of Mexico's entire territory, what is the one battle we remember? The Alamo.

Besides canonizing martyrs, the American pioneers, like the Boers, found other ways to justify what they were doing. Both groups turned to the belief that the conquest was foreordained, part of the natural order of things. Our version of this was less religious than that of the Afrikaners, but similar in spirit. What the Vow did for the Boers of the Great Trek the idea of "manifest destiny" achieved in the United States. The phrase itself was coined only a few years after Andries Pretorius, hot in pursuit of Dingane's armies, led the Voortrekkers of his revenge expedition in reciting the Vow.

The resistance of the conquered peoples had many points of resemblance, too. They fought with what weapons they had, until at last gunpowder did them in. And then they turned, as the South African historian and anthropologist Monica Wilson has pointed out, to remarkably similar kinds of millennial prophecies. The South African prophets like Makana and Nongquause who preached of blood red suns, food springing from the earth, and the repelling of the invaders, were echoed by the "ghost dance" cults that spread in the late 1800s among the Indians of the American West, from Nevada to South Dakota. As the Indians, like the Xhosa and the Zulu, saw their land taken over and their villages destroyed, prophets arose who promised the restoration of Indian land and food supplies, and the return of ancient heroes from beyond the grave.

What about the United States and South Africa today? Not only do the two countries share histories more similar than white Americans like to admit, but the ties between them are far more extensive than you would think, if you judged by all the condemnations of apartheid coming from the White House or the State Department over the years.

Foremost, of course, are the economic links, even though their growth is now curbed by sanctions laws. As the 1990s began, the United States still had $1.6 billion worth of direct investments in South Africa, and American banks had $2.4 billion in outstanding loans to the country. Despite the supposed pullout from South Africa of many U.S. companies, more than 120 remained. And licensing, franchising, and sales arrangements mean that South Africans are still drinking Coke, eating Kentucky Fried Chicken, accepting American Express cards, and consuming every other American product you can think of.

Less noticed, however, is a series of other links between the two countries, links through which the U.S. government has, behind the scenes, helped shore up South Africa at key moments. One such tie has been loans. Almost every time South Africa has had a major upheaval, enough to strain the economy and cause strong pressure for change, the United States comes through with a loan. It happened after the Sharpeville shootings in 1960: the country was in turmoil; investors lost confidence; the government suspended the hated pass laws. Then U.S. banks made crucial loans that allowed the whole apartheid apparatus to remain in place. It happened after the 1976 Soweto uprisings, when South Africa faced its worst economic crisis in many years. This time it turned to the U.S.-dominated International Monetary Fund (IMF), which then loaned South Africa—the wealthiest country on the continent—$464 million, or more than it loaned the rest of Africa combined. The Carter administration, despite its human rights talk, strongly backed the deal. The same thing happened one more time in 1982. South Africa had been shaken by student revolts, and also faced the costs of suppressing township rebels and fighting an increasingly expensive war in Namibia and Angola. It turned to the IMF again, this time for more than double the last request, $1.1 billion. Many other countries resisted; without American approval, there would not be enough support in the IMF's weighted voting system for the loan to go through. The United States voted for the loan and South Africa got the money.

Another area where American help has been crucial is high technology. The same kind of computer components that set off a major security flap when discovered on their way to the USSR in 1983 had been routinely shipped to South Africa with no U.S.

government agency objecting. The most important single contribution U.S. technology has made to apartheid has been the engineering of South Africa's coal-to-oil conversion plants. At the height of construction, three hundred Americans from the Fluor Corporation of Irvine, California, mostly engineers, were directing nearly twenty thousand South African workers. These are the crucial refineries that allow South Africa to turn its huge coal supply into gasoline and diesel oil—and thereby protect itself against the international oil embargo. When I was in South Africa in 1980, the plants were not all operating yet, and you could feel the pinch: gas stations shut down from noon Saturday until Monday morning. (I thought I was done for one Sunday night when a gang of young toughs surrounded a car I was driving in Soweto—but it turned out that what they wanted was to siphon some gas out of the tank.) Today, thanks to Fluor, there is no more gasoline rationing in South Africa.

On the night Ronald Reagan was elected President in 1980, whites in Pretoria sent up fireworks from all-night parties. They expected still stronger ties to the United States, and they got them. We still do not know the full extent of some of these links. It appears for example, that South Africa was one of the many channels of support for Reagan's beloved *contras* in Nicaragua. South Africa has also been a transshipment point for some of the U.S. arms going to Angolan rebel Jonas Savimbi, whom both countries have supported. The United States supplied electronic equipment that helped South Africa eavesdrop on ANC radio transmissions. And, since South Africa has no satellites, the United States gave the South African Directorate of Military Intelligence information American communications satellites picked up about the ANC.

A dissident former officer of the U.S. National Security Agency, which does our electronic eavesdropping, described to reporter Seymour Hersh a meeting in England in the mid-eighties between U.S., British, and South African intelligence officers, at which the three countries arranged what kinds of intelligence they would trade. The South Africans particularly wanted information on the movements of ANC leader Oliver Tambo and certain members of his staff, and any intercepted diplomatic and intelligence messages from Angola, Mozambique, Zambia, and Botswana.

Along the way in all these exchanges, there has been plenty of personal camaraderie. In the late 1960s, the U.S. Ambassador to South Africa, John Hurd, went pheasant-shooting with top South African government leaders on Robben Island. On the island, aware of these shooting parties, were Nelson Mandela and the other top ANC leaders, locked up during the harshest period of their imprisonment, one that saw strip searches, hunger strikes, and exhausting work in the island's lime quarries. South African Defense Minister Magnus Malan is a graduate of the U.S. Army Command and General Staff College at Fort Leavenworth, Kansas, an opportunity the United States sometimes gives to officers from "friendly" countries. In the 1970s, according to Gordon Winter, William Rourke Jordan, whom Winter identifies as head of CIA operations in South Africa and a key planner of South Africa's 1975 invasion of Angola, spent his Sundays driving a tractor at the Transvaal farm of South African intelligence chief General H. J. van den Bergh. Van den Bergh himself, who spent part of World War II in prison as a Nazi sympathizer, was a frequent visitor to Washington when George Bush was CIA director. One press report describes him as a "close friend" of Bush.

It is impossible to know exactly how close this friendship was, but South African officials have gone out of their way to cultivate such ties over the years, and often there is a pay-off. The biggest one of all came in 1962, although journalists did not stumble onto it until nearly a quarter of a century later. In January of that year, Nelson Mandela secretly left South Africa, arranged military help overseas for the ANC's new guerrilla warfare operation, then returned home to organize this underground network. He traveled around the country clandestinely, until in August he was seized at a roadblock near Pietermaritzburg, disguised as a white man's chauffeur. The person who tipped off the police was a CIA officer at the U.S. Consulate in Durban, whom Mandela was on his way to meet. Mandela had evidently believed that America's denunciations of apartheid at the United Nations and elsewhere counted for more than its ties to a long-time economic partner that was staunchly anti-Communist. Few people in the liberation movement have made the same mistake since.

□

It is impossible to stay long in South Africa without being struck by the countless ways, large and small, it is like home. In the white neighborhoods there are video stores, kids on skateboards, health food juice bars. Compact discs, saunas, and car phones are all in fashion. When you charge something on your Visa card, they run it through one of those little gadgets that calls the same central computer, wherever it is, that gives the O.K. when you shop in Boston or Seattle. You get your rock concert tickets at Computicket, and a helicopter cruises over the Johannesburg freeways at rush hour to give traffic reports on the radio. The white people running this country, benefiting from its wildly unequal distribution of wealth, are for the most part not Boer farmers flogging their laborers. Rather, they are, a white American comes to feel, *people like us.*

How much, then, are we like them? For in the end what is important about South Africa is not the ways in which it is unique. Those are safe for the outside world to condemn. The real lesson of South Africa, what it displays with such laboratory clarity, is that it brings together in one place what are usually oceans apart: the First World and the Third. A politically aware person growing up in Europe or America today knows, in a vague, distant way, that our standard of living partly rests in some manner on the work of people in Asia, Africa, Latin America. But we do not become outraged that the sugar in this morning's cereal was picked by cane cutters in the Philippines earning 30 cents an hour, or that the cloth in a new shirt was made by a mill in Sri Lanka whose workers are paid even less. We are scarcely aware of these things because we do not see them directly. But in South Africa, Third World and First are everywhere only a few minutes' walk apart: shantytown shack and suburban swimming pool, township coal stove and *nouvelle cuisine* restaurant. South Africa is the world economic order compressed into one country, the empire with no clothes on. In the slogan you can find on brochures at your travel agent's, the South African Tourism Board says more than it knows: "Discover Our World in One Country."

The reflected image that South Africa holds up to the United

States is not an exact duplicate. Parts of the image are greatly distorted and magnified. But still it reflects something back, not only about our relation to the Third World, but about how we are developing into two separate societies at home. Is the social and economic distance from Soweto to one of Johannesburg's leafy white suburbs that much greater than the distance from Harlem to New Canaan, or Watts to Beverly Hills? On the day I am writing this chapter, *The New York Times* has a story about new van services that take American blacks from inner cities where the unemployment level is 50 or 60 percent (as high as some South African townships) to the suburbs. The story profiles blacks in Chicago who are now grateful to get transportation, for $2 a day, to "good jobs" in the suburbs at $5.85 an hour. How can one raise three or four children on $5.85 an hour? And yet this story of the new transport services is supposed to be, given the downward slide of American inner cities, a hopeful one.

"Looking into South Africa," writes Breyten Breytenbach, "is like looking into the mirror at midnight. . . . A horrible face, but one's own."

# *Midnight*

DECEMBER 16, 1838:

By the early hours of the morning, the soldiers of both Andries Pretorius's commando troop and of Dingane's army knew that this would be the day of their battle. It was Dingane's last chance to turn back the Boers who so wanted his land.

The confident, well-organized Pretorius, with his force of 468 men and 64 ox wagons, had ridden across Natal, bound for Dingane's headquarters. His Voortrekkers had skirmished with some Zulu scouts, and so he knew that Dingane's armies were near. Pretorius had stopped for the night at what seemed an especially good defensive position. The expedition's religious leader, Sarel Cilliers, was as ready as ever to see the hand of God: "I cannot omit to bring to the notice of all how the Lord in His holy providence had appointed a place for us, in which He had determined the fight should occur."

The place was on a wide plain, where a river named the Ncome, "the pleasant one," so called for its clear water and green banks, broadened into a long, deep hippopotamus pool. The pool was deeper, the Trekkers had found, than the long handle of one of their ox whips, so no invader would be able to wade across. At one end of the pool, the river met a steep-sided ravine. At this intersection where, Cilliers said, "the camp, by God's mercy, was protected on two sides," the Trekkers had set up their fortified *laager* of encircled ox wagons. Hotheads among the Boers wanted to pursue the Zulus and charge them on horseback, but Pretorius knew better.

"Do not let us go to them," he said. "Let them come to us."

After repeating the Vow, praying, and singing hymns and psalms, the Trekkers had set up lanterns with thick candles, hanging from whip handles just outside the circle of wagons. The light was dim, but it was the only way they could see any intruders; there was no moon. It had rained heavily a few days before, filling the river and turning it into a protective barrier. But luckily for the Boers, there was no rain now. This would have rendered their gunpowder useless.

The *laager* was arranged in the methodical way the Boers had now perfected over the past three years of trekking and fighting. For its time, the *laager* of the Great Trek was a remarkably efficient mobile fortress. The wagons were chained together, so no attackers could pull them apart and breach the circle. Oxhides lashed over the wheels provided places where defenders could crouch for protection against hurled spears. Thornbushes stuffed underneath the wagons were the natural equivalent of barbed wire. Portable fencing called "fighting gates" between the wagons made a further barrier against anyone trying to penetrate the encampment, but allowed the Boers a space from which to fire their muskets.

For days, as the Voortrekkers had drawn closer to Umgungundhlovu, the Zulu forces had been watching their approach. The Zulu army was under Dingane's top commander, Ndlela—the leader of the troops who had so effectively ambushed the Vlug Commando and sent it fleeing. During the night, Ndlela's soldiers took up positions around the Boers. Mist covered the camp. To the Zulus, it is said, the dim circle of lanterns seen through the mist gave the Trekker camp the ominous look of a place inhabited by spirits.

After surrounding the Boers, Ndlela made a crucial and ultimately disastrous error: he failed to order his men to attack under cover of fog and darkness. On this moonless night, the Trekkers would then have only been able to aim their weapons by lantern light. Instead, he waited to make the classic Zulu charge by daylight, when the sight of the massed warriors in full costume was designed to strike terror into the heart of any enemy.

Once in the hours before dawn, the mist cleared for a moment, and Boer sentries could see the signal fires of the Zulu armies on nearby hilltops. As dawn approached, the Trekkers heard what many first thought was the sound of distant rain. It was thousands of *assegais,* beating on oxhide shields. At first light, the mist began to clear again. At last the Boers were able to see facing them the main force of Dingane's army, an estimated ten to fifteen thousand men, sitting silently in full regalia: ruffles of oxhide on their ankles, arms and legs decorated with oxtail tufts. Men of the different regiments were distinguished by differently colored oxhide shields and feathered headdresses. One Trekker described the awe he and his comrades felt: "All of Zululand sat there."

"Sunday, the 16th, was a day as if ordained for us," writes Pretorius's secretary, J. G. Bantjes, who kept a journal during the expedition.

> The sky was open. The weather clear and bright. Scarcely was the dawn of day perceptible, when the guards, who were still on their posts and could scarcely see, perceived that the Zulus were approaching. . . . Their approach, although frightful on account of the great number, yet presented a beautiful appearance. They approached in regiments, each captain with his men following him . . . until they had all surrounded us. I could not count them, but it is said that a Kafir prisoner had given the number of thirty six regiments. . . .

The first attack came around 5:00 a.m., and the battle raged through most of the morning. The Zulu tactics and weapons had proven invincible against all rival black peoples: terrifying war cries, and then the disciplined, carefully maneuvered charge, in "ox-head" formation, with *assegais* used for stabbing at close range. The terror the Zulus counted on to make their enemies flee depended on their forming themselves into a human wall that hurled itself at the opposing force. But this very mass made the most inviting possible target for the Trekkers' muskets—and even more so for their three cannon. The cannon, including one affectionately named Old Grietjie, were loaded up with whatever was handy: grapeshot, stones, broken pot legs. Their fire carved swath after swath through the Zulus.

The attackers were so densely packed together that the Boers shooting their muskets from the "fighting gates" between the wagons barely had to aim. A Trekker named D. P. Bezuidenhout recalled later:

> At the back of each wagon there were little heaps of gunpowder and bullets; and when the battle was fought, and the Kafirs in thousands were no further than ten paces from us, we had scarcely time to throw a handful of powder into the gun and then slip a bullet down the barrel without a moment even to drive it home with the ramrod. Of that fight nothing remains in my memory except shouting and tumult and lamentation, and a sea of black faces; and dense smoke that rose straight as a plumb-line upwards from the ground.

By 8:00 a.m., a thousand Zulus were dead. The piles of their bodies formed an additional obstacle to new regiments coming up to attack. These new, doomed waves of attackers also had to charge through the ranks of wounded men staggering away from the battle. Still they came, whistling and shouting, while the dense clouds of black powder smoke hung overhead.

Several times, when the attacks slackened, Pretorius ordered one wagon shoved aside. Riding out of this gate, squadrons of men on horseback charged at clusters of Zulus. One group was led by the pious Sarel Cilliers:

> I called for volunteers to clear the ravine, and we went with eighty men. The ravine was broad, and the Kafirs were huddled together, so that they could not use their arms to hurl their assegais . . . a severe fire was opened on them. More than 400 fell . . . the word of our Lord was fulfilled: "By one way shall your enemies come, but by the blessing of the Lord they shall fly before your face."

By mid-morning the Zulus pulled back out of musket range. Andries Pretorius was worried on two counts. One was that his ammunition was getting low. His other fear was that the Zulus might surround his camp at a distance, and besiege it. He wanted to provoke a final attack, which would deplete the Zulus so badly they would retreat. And so he sent his brother, Bart Pretorius, who was fluent in Zulu, to ride outside the *laager* and taunt Dingane's soldiers in their own language.

At last the Zulus' final reserve force, the three thousand men of Ndlela's elite White Shield and Black Shield regiments, fell upon the camp again. This was the last of four great charges the Zulu forces made that day. To participate must have taken suicidal courage, for the ground was covered with the dead and the air filled with the cries of the dying. We can only guess at what the Zulu soldiers felt, for they left no written accounts. It was one of those moments when an entire army must have had the sickening realization that it had prepared for the wrong war. Like the World War I troops ordered to charge into machine-gun fire, the attacking Zulus found a world that had changed. All their bravery and all their carefully practiced tactics were now irrelevant. They attacked nonetheless.

Again they were struck down in hundreds by musket and cannon fire. As their remnants milled in confusion, Pretorius again ordered the gate opened, and he led some two hundred men out of the *laager* in a wild horseback charge against the fleeing Zulu regiments. Firing muskets from their saddles, the Trekkers chased the Zulus for miles across the plains. When the Boers ran out of bullets, they fired pebbles, and when they ran out of gunpowder, they rode the Zulus down, trampling them beneath the horses' hooves. Pretorius himself got off his horse to attack one Zulu warrior hand to hand. Before anyone could come to his aid, he was speared in the hand—one of only three Trekkers to be wounded that day.

Another group of Zulus, trapped between the river and the charging Trekkers on horseback, desperately took refuge in the deep hippopotamus pool. "When they saw that there would be no escape," said Cilliers, "... they jumped into the water and were among the rushes at the river's edge. I believe that all were killed, that not one escaped. I was witness to the fact that the water looked like a pool of blood: whence came the name of Blood River."

DECEMBER 16, 1988:
The Day of the Vow begins with explosions. In the early morning darkness, three bombs go off near Cape Town: At Paarl, site of a monument to the Afrikaans language, a bomb damages the Magistrate's Court. At Parow and Goodwood, the blasts hit entrances to each town's City Hall, which, in each case, sits on a street called Voortrekker Road. The bombs shatter windows and set off shop burglar alarms. There are no injuries. Police and soldiers stand guard at the sites all day. So, the ANC underground, *Umkhonto we Sizwe,* the Spear of the Nation, is marking the holiday too. To Africans, this date has always been known not as the Day of the Vow, but as Heroes' Day.

Although none of the newspapers mentions it, Goodwood's City Hall was probably chosen as a target to protest something now happening a few blocks away. A freeway crosses Voortrekker Road in Goodwood, and next to the crossing is a cemetery. The state plans to build a new off-ramp at this interchange, and in order to make room for it is planning to dig up and move 3,619 bodies in the cemetery. Naturally (otherwise the move would never be considered) most of the bodies are black. Just a week ago the government published advertisements with lists of all the dead:

> ... a large number of graves in the Maitland Cemetery are
> ... affected by the proposed layout requiring the reverent
> exhumation of the deceased remains buried in such graves
> and their reinterment in an area ... specially set aside for
> such purpose. Existing memorials will be suitably re-erected
> there and a Garden of Remembrance established for the re-
> burial of the remains of those who at present do not have any
> memorials ... the nearest adult relatives of any of these de-
> ceased persons are being sought. ... The broad community
> of the travelling public stand to benefit significantly from the
> proposed improvements to this intersection. ...

There is, however, not enough room to rebury all the bodies in this cemetery, and some will have to be cremated to fit. Even in death, South Africa's removals continue.

At dawn on this 150th anniversary, I am on the freeway from Johannesburg to Pretoria. As the sun rises over the *veld* in the northeast, country-and-western songs on the radio mingle with patriotic tunes about "Die Vaderland." In Pretoria, I stop for gas. When I pay, some change is left over and I hand it to the black attendant. Instinctively, he makes the quick, habitual gesture of black South African waiters and porters accepting a tip: two hands cupped beneath mine, a habit born of centuries of receiving coins from whites who do not want to touch black skin. *"Dankie, baas,"* he says.

Some twenty miles east of Pretoria, I swing off the freeway and follow a long, rutted road to Donkerhoek Farm, scene of a Boer War battle and the final stopping place of this year's right-wing trek. Several thousand people have been camping here all week, most of them AWB supporters. Hundreds of tents, camper trucks, and charcoal grills are spread out over rough, muddy ground. Crude group showers for men and women—a hose tied to a metal frame, canvas around the sides for privacy—give the site the look of an army camp. There seems almost a quality of self-flagellation about the inhabitants of this tent city, as if by camping in the mud for a week they can recapture the feelings of endurance and hardship, danger and sacrifice, at the heart of classic Afrikaner nationalism. At dawn each morning this week, a "daybreak commando" has roamed into the surrounding countryside on horseback, in imitation of Voortrekker patrols.

It is only 6:30 a.m., but already the reenactment of the Battle of Blood River is under way, as the battle itself was at this hour. The surroundings emphasize the grim seriousness of the occasion, for this is no pageant watched from padded theater seats. Respectfully hushed, some three thousand white men, women, and children are sitting or standing, on boulders or on the rocky ground, on the sides of a treeless ravine. Against the sky, along the rims of the ravine, are dozens of crossed whip handles ten or twelve feet long, with lanterns on the end. They have been burning all night, as the Voortrekkers' were, and are still alight now, in the dawn.

At one end of the ravine are a dozen ox wagons, fastened tightly together. Echoing through the ravine are Zulu war cries—a distant, haunting ululation. However, no black people are within miles of here right now. The war cries are on tape, coming over a public address system.

"The Zulus were asked to come today," an Afrikaner newspaperman friend whispers to me as we watch the proceedings, "but they demanded a rematch. . . ." He translates the goings-on in a low voice, not wanting to be heard speaking English among these Afrikaner fundamentalists. With reason—later today, not far from where we are standing, two English-speaking white reporters from *The Weekly Mail* will be severely beaten by Eugene Terre Blanche's bodyguards, one suffering a damaged kidney and the other a cracked rib.

Now, over the loudspeakers come prayers and psalms—the words of the Voortrekkers in Pretorius's *laager,* praying before the Zulu attack. The crowd listens, hushed. Many women wear white bonnets and the long traditional *sisrokke*—chintz Voortrekker dresses; little blond girls wear bows in their hair; little boys wear *riempieskoene,* leather-thong shoes with ankle straps. Some men wear the old costumes, too, but many more are in the short-sleeved khaki uniform of the AWB, with the red, white, and black swastika-like patch on their sleeves.

Again there are whistles and war cries, and then a voice saying: "They're surrounding us!"

The chants over the loudspeakers now turn into full-throated shrieks, and the sound of *assegais* rattling against shields. The Voortrekkers respond with Bible verses. A voice commands: "Hold fire! . . . Hold fire!" Below us, men on horseback with broad-brimmed hats canter back and forth along the line of ox wagons. Then at last a voice calls: "Now!"

Gunfire rings out, not from the loudspeakers this time, but from blank charges in old-fashioned *voorlaaiers,* muzzle-loading muskets, fired by men and boys sighting out between the ox wagons. Smoke fills the air. The crowd on the stony hillside cheers. A voice on the loudspeaker calls out: "They're fleeing!" Men begin firing much noisier charges from one or two small cannon, also pointing out between the wagons. Tethered horses rear at the sound of cannon fire. The crowd laughs raucously when a roar and puff of smoke engulf a startled television crew who didn't realize they were standing in front of a cannon's muzzle. With their camera and microphone, they must be either foreigners or from the government TV, either of which makes them enemies of the ultra-rightists here.

"Look, they're falling back!" Voices on the loudspeaker are discussing strategy. "We'll send out our best horsemen!"

More war cries, cannon and musket fire, smoke. The smell of gunpowder covers the ravine's sides. Then several men move aside a wagon in the center of the line, and through the gap a dozen or so horsemen gallop out, to enthusiastic roars from the crowd. They charge along a road and disappear from sight behind a nearby hill. Then, after a long enough interval to slaughter fleeing Zulus has passed, they gallop back, through the gap in the ox wagons, to more applause.

Again there are war whoops and battle sounds. Afrikaans voices say: "The fight is not over! Their crack regiment is still in reserve! They're attacking!" A larger group of people on horseback, fifteen or twenty this time, including a few boys and girls, gallops out between the wagons, then around behind the hill and out of sight, pauses and then gallops back again. The crowd cheers lustily, and the ravine's sides erupt with the waving of flags. They are all flags of the AWB and of the old Boer republics; not a single South African flag is among them: it contains a Union Jack in the middle, symbolizing the union with the hated English speakers.

Finally over the loudspeakers come birdsongs: the battle is over. There are more prayers; then the audience sitting on the boulders stands and the men remove their hats. Everyone sings a psalm, and then, in unison, recites the Vow, which they all know by heart: "Here we stand before the holy God of heaven and earth to make Him a vow: that if He will protect us and deliver our enemies into our hands, we will observe the day and date each year as a day of thanks. . . ."

The crowd picks its way among the rocks, heading to the campsites for breakfast before returning to the ravine for a scheduled morning rally. By this point my Afrikaner friend has had to leave, and I stay on for a while, on my own. Soon I begin to feel uneasy about being recognized as a foreigner among all these grim people in their Nazi-like uniforms. It is definitely time to go. As I drive out the dirt road leading from the farm, an immense single file of cars and farmers' *bakkies* is slowly coming in. It extends some three miles, out to the gate of the farm, down the road to the freeway, along the exit ramp, and for a mile or more along the freeway itself. Some license plates are from as far away as Namibia. Thousands of Afrikaners there, appalled at the thought of living under a black government, are strong AWB supporters.

The cars in this long line are often older ones, carrying a husband and wife in the front seat and three or four blond children in the back. The people have the look of a crowd in Appalachia, flocking to a revival meeting. Many hands extend out car and truck windows, waving AWB and Boer republic flags. A man in an incoming car leans out a window, shakes his fist, and curses at me angrily in Afrikaans—apparently because I'm leaving early, before the speechmaking.

There will be a lot of that in this rocky ravine today, and that's what these thousands of carloads of people are coming for. The real crowd-pleaser is to be Eugene Terre Blanche, surrounded by bodyguards carrying pistols or hunting rifles: "We share our power with no one. The AWB knows no fear. We will die defending our cause. Our goverment is creating a new poor white class, and we must rise as a nation out of this. We will be ready physically and militarily just as we were at Blood River."

From Donkerhoek I drive half an hour to the rival Blood River celebration, the government's. It is taking place at the Voortrekker Monument. As I arrive, it seems as if all the symbols of white South Africa's past and present military might are in sight on this clear, warm, blue-skied morning. Here is the final resting place of "Old Grietjie," Andries Pretorius's cannon. Large statues of Pretorius and Piet Retief look out from the base of the monument. Beyond a nearby hill is the big military base of Voortrekker Heights, where many white draftees are trained on their way to army units fighting the rebellion. Just over another rise is the Atomic Research Centre at Pelindaba, where South African and Israeli physicists did some of the work on their atomic bomb.

This is the hilltop monument's big day in the year: at noon the ray of sunlight will strike the sacred stone inside. Around this huge, square monolith, the ambience is as formal and efficient as at Donkerhoek it was homespun. Dozens of police and soldiers with walkie-talkies guard checkpoints and direct traffic. VIPs with permits have a special, close-in parking lot. Near the base of the monument, the rows of large olive drab tents I saw the soldiers putting up the other day now house everything from a first-aid station to piles of Bibles.

The ceremony takes place in an amphitheater on the hillside that slopes down from the monumènt. To the music of a military orchestra, cabinet ministers and other dignitaries take their seats on a wide stage. They wear dark suits and their wives elaborate hats; they sit in red plush chairs under a canopy that shields them from the sun. A khaki-clad general steps out of a Mercedes and joins them. Finally, some fifty cavalrymen, carrying lances fluttering with blue and gold pennants, escort the silver limousine of the State President to the base of the stage. Out steps P. W. Botha and his wife, accompanied by a naval aide in a white uniform with gold braid and a chestful of medals.

The crowd in the amphitheater is much sparser than National Party organizers had hoped for; embarrassingly large patches of seats are empty. Press estimates will put this crowd at the monument at less than ten thousand, but the audience for Eugene Terre Blanche at several times that. It's no wonder the far right wins today's contest of numbers; if this morning's battle reenactment is any guide, they can put on a better show. As the government inches uneasily toward a future of compromise, negotiations, and reform, it is the right wing that offers Afrikaners the emotional appeal, holding high the clear, bright, familiar flame of Afrikaner martyrdom.

This government ceremony, by contrast, is three hours long and Germanically ponderous, as solemn as those nightly prayer and psalm sessions on the Great Trek itself must have been. Teenage

Voortrekker scouts march about, salute, and raise flags. The crowd applauds politely, but with no passion. Speakers deliver greetings from various organizations. The Administrator of each of South Africa's four provinces drones on about how Voortrekker virtues are practiced in his domain. The endless ceremony is an orgy of pomp, as if enough clicked heels, raised flags, salutes, and speeches could somehow fend off that inevitable day of reckoning for just a while longer.

By late morning, this cloudless day becomes ferociously hot. Men in the audience take off their suit jackets and mop their brows. Dark sweat patches appear in the armpits of shirts and dresses. Roving medical teams minister to people who've fainted from the sun. My head feels as if it's in an oven. The only shade in the amphitheater is under what looks like the press tent, an army-green enclosure set up on some lower rungs of seats, directly in front of the speaker's stage. I head for it.

At the entrance, a security guard who, surprisingly, is black, looks at my reporter's notebook and nods. I step inside. It is such a relief to be out of the furnacelike sun that it takes me a moment to realize that this is not the press tent. It is, instead, the production booth—the electronic heart of this spectacle. The people inside, seated at a long table, are so concentrated on what they are doing that they don't notice an interloper. One man operates an enormous, rock concert–sized console controlling the loudspeaker system. A young woman with earphones is watching a TV monitor: the South African Broadcasting Corporation is showing this whole event live. Two men next to her are talking into walkie-talkies, all in Afrikaans except for words like "breaker" and "over." They bark out orders about when soldiers and Voortrekker scouts are to start marching and when bands are to parade past, even switching to English to tell the orchestra conductor to speed up his tempo. Looking over their shoulders, I see they are working from a big, single-spaced script many pages thick, with exact times in the margin. Everything has to be scheduled right to the minute: the ceremony must come to its climax on the very dot of noon, when the sun's rays inside the monument will strike the stone.

The side of the tent facing the stage is open, and so, from the luxury of shade, I watch the spectacle continue. Beefy plainclothes-men with sunglasses and binoculars constantly scan the crowd. Uniformed police and soldiers in red or green berets patrol at its edges. This all-white crowd is far more elegantly dressed than the farm families at Donkerhoek; many men wear neckties and the women churchgoing clothes. One man even wears a New York Yankees cap—this is the upward-bound cosmopolitan part of Af-rikanerdom, not afraid to admit having traveled overseas.

The orchestra plays a fanfare, and soldiers take up honor guard positions. At last, in the climax of its months-long journey, the red and green ox wagon pulls up in front of the stage. The crowd applauds. One of the black grooms is leading the oxen. Another is guiding blind Pierre van Zyl by the elbow. I feel happy to see him. As he stiffly marches beside the wagon, van Zyl looks awk-ward and quite out of his rough-hewn character as he sports full, formal nineteenth-century costume: a black top hat and maroon tailcoat. I can imagine him grumbling about having to get into this damned-fool getup today.

At the appearance of the wagon, an official in the production tent is so excited that he turns to me and begins talking enthu-siastically in Afrikaans. I am at once unmasked as an *Engelstalige,* an English speaker, and a foreigner to boot. They ask me to leave the tent.

I watch the rest of the ceremony from back in the broiling sun. President Botha is presented with a scroll that has traveled in the wagon all the way from Cape Town. More flags are raised. Four Impala fighter jets—made in South Africa—pass by in diamond formation, with a deafening roar, a few hundred feet overhead. Four helicopters in camouflage colors, each trailing a huge South African flag, thunder past in another direction. Finally P. W. Botha gives his speech, in slow, emphatic tones.

It is a familiar message: We're Not Racists—But Nobody's Going to Push Us Around. He tells the audience that South Africa must proceed on the basis of "healthy intergroup relations" and the "principle of good neighborliness between all communities of the population." Then comes the But. "However, we must also not abandon that which is our own or allow it to be taken away."

A children's choir sings. Ministers ask blessings. Botha and his wife, Elize, sign a ceremonial Bible. Finally a cheer goes up from a crowd inside the monument itself, as, exactly on schedule, the sun's rays strike the stone. Trumpets blow a fanfare. Banners unfurl from the monument's four corners. Hundreds of doves are released from its roof. P. W. and Elize climb into a waiting helicopter and whirl off into the sky.

# *Journey's End*

DECEMBER 17, 1838:

On the day after their momentous victory, the Voortrekkers counted the Zulu dead. They came to more than three thousand. Some of Dingane's warriors lay where they had fallen outside the *laager* of wagons; some had drowned in the river; some had walked or crawled a few hundred yards across the plains before dying of their wounds.

For southern Africa, Blood River was the pivotal battle of the nineteenth century. Its importance was symbolic: the battle did not break the Zulus as a military force, but it established beyond any doubt that, without fighting from a stone fort, a relatively small number of fighters with gunpowder could defeat an immensely larger number with spears. Word of the battle spread widely, and from what it proved flowed the next half century's events: the continuation of the Great Trek, the British conquest of Rhodesia, the expansion of the Portuguese colonists inland from their coastal trading ports, and the brutal Belgian seizure of the Congo. At the time of Blood River, most Africans had never seen a white face. Less than fifty years later, the pinstriped representatives of the great powers of Europe were sitting down at a Berlin conference table to draw colonial boundaries on the map, dividing almost the entire continent among themselves.

On this first day after the Blood River battle, the pious Sarel Cilliers later remembered, "the Kafirs lay on the ground like pumpkins on a rich soil that had borne a large crop." In the days and months that followed, the Boers chased Dingane and his armies out of the region and took those parts of Natal they wanted. When a party of Voortrekkers returned to Blood River a year later, they found the ground literally white with bones.

DECEMBER 17, 1988:
My last day in South Africa. Tonight I will begin twenty-four hours in planes and airports; tomorrow I will be at the other end of the world.

Although long accounts of yesterday's ceremonies fill this morning's newspapers, South Africa is already forgetting the Day of the Vow. Today, a Saturday, is the start of the main holiday season in this land where Christmas vacation comes in midsummer. White eyes are on a big horse race today, and on the Natal beaches, which will be overflowing with tanning bodies for the next two weeks. This morning, on the highways out of white Johannesburg, many cars have wind-surfing boards strapped to their roofs.

In Soweto today there is a Tea Party.

Some of the opposition groups began using this expression a few years ago after seeing the government ban many political meetings. They hoped police would not break up less formal gatherings under another name. Today's Tea Party is jointly organized by white professionals and a Soweto community group. It is a gathering of recently released political detainees, and of families of detainees still in jail. A meal will be served, and people can talk about their problems in small discussion groups. Those who need further help can meet here, or be referred to, lawyers, doctors, social workers, and psychotherapists.

This event is in the White City area, deep in Soweto, and one of the most militant districts of the vast township. Even today, when they have been crushed elsewhere, it still has functioning street committees, whose members patrol streets against burglars. In 1986, it was the scene of the "White City War," where police

killed thirty Africans in battles over a rent strike. This week the
township has been tense; three days ago two policemen and a
White City resident died in an accidental shootout with army
troops. Both police and soldiers thought they were shooting at
ANC guerrillas.

Ominously, at the entrance of the church-connected Ipelegeng
Community Center are several yellow police armored cars and a
dozen or more soldiers with rifles. But inside, the Tea Party is
under way nonetheless, spread out across two adjoining meeting
rooms. There are perhaps 150 black ex-detainees or family members here, divided into four group discussions in the African languages. A social worker or counselor, black or white, is at the
center of each. People talk in low voices, sitting on folding metal
chairs that are pulled together in four tight clusters.

The authorities have not banned today's Tea Party. They are
simply attending it.

Around the edges of each discussion group, and throughout the
two large rooms in which they take place, are strolling both black
and white riot police in blue uniforms, caps, and boots, plainclothes
cops with pistols on their hips, and khaki-clad soldiers with rifles
or submachine guns slung from their shoulders. More soldiers are
outside, and I can see only their black berets and the tips of their
rifle barrels as they patrol past the windows. Altogether there seem
to be about forty soldiers, forty uniformed riot police, and perhaps
twenty white plainclothesmen from the Special Branch, the security police. The plainclothesmen have the hardest faces.

Some police take chairs at the edges of group discussions, and
lean forward to overhear. Intimidated and uncomfortable, people
lower their voices still further. And so the two rooms are remarkably quiet, echoing with a thin layer of whisper overlaid by
the creaking of the soldiers' and policemen's leather boots on the
linoleum floor.

The soldiers—young white draftees who would probably rather
be elsewhere—are expressionless and silent. But the white riot
police and plainclothesmen make their presence felt. They say
nothing to the Soweto people attending the meeting, but talk in
Afrikaans into their walkie-talkies in low voices. When one of the
former detainees fumbles for a light, a policeman casually tosses

him a cigarette lighter. When an anxious-looking black woman appears uncertain which group to join, another policeman, with mock graciousness, makes a little bow and gestures toward a vacant chair.

A two-man police video crew is also attending the Tea Party. Three of the four discussion groups, however, are in corners where there isn't enough light for the camera. So they train it on the fourth group, which rapidly shrinks to a hardy half-dozen people.

The groups continue talking, an act of will. On a veranda outside, several young white women provide child care, energetically leading young black kids in songs and games, clapping their hands and singing. But beneath their cheerful voices, there is a foreboding in the air. This is the third time in several weeks that masses of police have turned out for a Tea Party in the Johannesburg area; just last week, someone tells me, the police took mug shots of everybody attending one in Alexandra.

Standing against the walls are a dozen or so white people who seem to be neither volunteers nor police, and I ask who they are. They are foreign diplomats, it turns out, who often come to events like this, as a way of making symbolic anti-apartheid gestures that don't carry the price tag of economic sanctions. "If the cops didn't see all those embassy license plates outside," a volunteer tells me, "they'd have tear-gassed the lot of us by now."

I am relieved by their presence, but have mixed feelings. What does this Frenchman think about France's building South Africa a nuclear power station? How do these two Germans feel about their country's role as South Africa's largest trading partner, and the supplier of ships and technology to its navy? Would this pleasant young man I chat with from the American Embassy tip off the police if he knew a wanted man's whereabouts, as another American official once did, allowing police to capture Nelson Mandela?

I talk for a few minutes to David Webster, one of the Tea Party's organizers. A forty-four-year-old anthropology professor, he is one of the best-liked of Johannesburg's white anti-apartheid activists. He has worked for several years with victims of detention. A short, unassuming man in a suit and tie with a round, smiling face, he looks remarkably relaxed considering the circumstances. Webster's main worry at the moment, he says, is that people will be intimidated by all these armed men and will leave before the food is cooked. In the community center's kitchen, black and white volunteers are busy preparing a meal.

The discussion groups break up. The 150 people form a line before some tables where volunteers will be dishing out chicken, rice, beans, and coleslaw. The line is silent; police and soldiers stroll up and down it. Webster is still uneasy: the food isn't quite ready yet.

But gradually the people waiting for food realize that diplomats are here—and that therefore the cops will not be bashing heads today. And then something amazing happens. Like spontaneous combustion, everyone starts to sing. And dance. With unbelievable, pent-up fervor. They sing while waiting in line for food, and they sing once they start eating, balancing a plate of chicken in one hand and shooting a fist into the air with the other. Laughing women dance with babies on their backs; men do the rhythmic shuffle of the *toyi-toyi,* and then a wilder step, raising a knee up to chest level and bringing the foot down on the floor with a tremendous, exuberant slap. The policemen and soldiers still walk up and down frowning and muttering into their walkie-talkies, but the songs have overwhelmed the noise of their boots. People translate phrases for me:

"We will follow our leaders!"

"Sisulu! He will release us from repression!"

"Tambo! He will release us from repression!"

"Mandela! He will release us from repression!"

"Come, guerrilla, bring your AK-47!"

People cluster in small groups, still eating, heads bobbing to the songs. The women ululate. The teenagers mimic the sound of hand grenades. They shout, right index fingers pointing in the air:

"Viva ANC Viva!"

*"Amandla! Ngawethu!"*

"Viva UDF Viva!"

"Mandela long live!"

"ANC long live!"

Above the uproar, I talk with three men in their twenties from the now-banned Soweto Youth Congress. All three have recently been, as they say, "inside." They describe the problems that have brought them here today for counseling: stomach troubles after months of prison food, money, finding jobs, trouble sleeping, repossession (if you're buying a car or dishwasher on credit and you are detained, it is taken away). "And fear," one says. "Whenever the police are coming around, you think they are coming to arrest you."

Another tells me that like many ex-detainees, he has trouble concentrating when he reads or studies. "And after this party, you will see, some of us will be detained again."

His eyes nervously scan the faces of the policemen patrolling around us. Among those in plainclothes, he says, he sees several who interrogated him in prison.

Finally the singing and dancing die down and everyone is summoned to the Tea Party's close, in one of the meeting rooms. Several speakers take their place on a stage. Soldiers and riot police station themselves around the walls. Sophie Masite, a detainee support worker, holds up crossed index fingers, the sign for silence. The audience quiets down. Masite talks to the crowd in Zulu. Rev. Paul Verryn, the white Methodist minister who lives in Soweto and is the target of many death threats, is introduced to lead a prayer. A few people don't want to pray, but voices quiet them: "Comrades! Ssshhh!" Verryn prays "for those who will be detained in the next day, the next week, and the next year."

As the speakers are talking, the white plainclothesmen, with pistols on their hips and mostly wearing blue jeans, walk into the room and form a phalanx between the stage and the crowd, crossing their arms and staring at the audience. One cop glances sideways at the notes I am taking. I quickly put them away. Why is it so much more chilling to see a holster on the hip of a man not in uniform? Even in a country like South Africa where we should know better, a uniform still confers some faint aura of legitimacy. The pistol on the plainclothed hip is the look of the gangster, of the death squad.

David Webster speaks last, briefly but eloquently. He thanks people for coming, then talks about the need to look to the future of South Africa and not to the past. He ends by saying, *"Even these people"*—he draws out the words and sweeps his hand at the plainclothesmen in front of him—"will have a place in a non-racial, democratic South Africa."

Finally the crowd rises and sings "Nkosi Sikelel' iAfrika":

> *Nkosi sikelel' iAfrika,*
> *Maliphakamis'we 'pondolwayo . . .*
> *Iswa imithandazo yethu*
> *Nkosi sikelela, nkosi sikelela.*

> God bless Africa,
> Let our nation rise . . .
> Hear our call
> God bless us, God bless us.

I have heard this song sung dozens of times across southern Africa, from thirty years ago in colonial Rhodesia, whose freedom anthem it was also, to funerals, churches, and meetings in South African cities today. But never has it seemed so powerful, so vibrant, so able to reach to the pit of your stomach and make you shiver, so rich with multiple harmonies and with the soaring treble of the women's voices as it does today, sung here, within this ring of armed police and soldiers.

As the ocean of sound fills the room, I look into the heart of the darkness: the faces of the plainclothesmen. Is this the one who tossed the tear-gas bomb into Emelda Nkosi's cell? Is this the one who fastened electrodes to Gladys Shezi's breasts? Is this the one who beat the boy, Sipho? Is that one among those who tried to kill the Watson brothers? Some of the plainclothesmen smirk, and whisper to each other. Several narrow their eyes bitterly. But one man looks genuinely disturbed, as if he is feeling some conflict or pain. I recall the episode Frantz Fanon writes about, where a torturer and his victim accidentally meet in an Algerian mental hospital, both driven mad by the same act. Is this man before me capable of such feelings?

Finally my eye settles on the side of one of these men standing right in front of me. I find it is this image that I take away, and remember on the long plane ride home, my last snapshot of South

Africa. On this plainclothesman's hip, his holstered revolver sits next to the Calvin Klein patch on his jeans.

In the months that followed this gathering, David Webster continued his work with former detainees. He had already been the object of official harassment, and two Tea Parties he organized were broken up by police. At one, witnesses heard a Captain van Haystings of the security police say to Webster, "You will not have any more Tea Parties."

On a holiday morning in May 1989, some four and a half months after the Tea Party I attended in Soweto, Webster and his fiancée, Margaret Friedman, were in front of their Johannesburg home, unloading some plants they had just bought at a nursery in preparation for a day of gardening. From a passing car, a white man fired a shotgun. Webster received the blast full in the chest, and died on the spot.

# Epilogue: Old Bricks, New Building

A story made the rounds while I was in South Africa in 1988 researching this book: Nelson Mandela, Soviet leader Mikhail Gorbachev, and the American President-elect George H. W. Bush are all talking to God. Bush asks how long it will take for his country to solve its problems. "Not in your administration," God says, "but in the next one." Gorbachev asks the same question. "Not in your lifetime, but in the lifetime of your children," says God. But when Mandela asks how long it will take for South Africa, God shakes His head and replies, "Not in my lifetime."

In the South Africa I saw that grim year, virtually no one expected major political change any time soon. Despite the strikes, the consumer boycotts, the rebellions in the black townships, the government had firm military control. It had the strongest, most efficient army in Africa. It had the atomic bomb. Behind the elaborate dreamworld façade of black homelands, State President P. W. Botha was committed to white supremacy. It appeared likely that Mandela and the generation of African National Congress leaders jailed with him would never wield political power.

Ever since the mid-twentieth century, South African history had unfolded in waves of severe repression followed by great popular uprisings. The South Africa I had seen in 1988 was clearly in the trough of one of its harshest crackdowns ever. It was likely that another wave of uprisings would follow, and it did.

A nationwide hunger strike by more than six hundred political detainees helped trigger the new upheavals. The strike started at Diepkloof Prison in Johannesburg in early 1989 and spread rapidly to jails throughout the country. Fearing more sanctions from abroad if people began dying in prison, a reportedly divided cabinet let almost all the hunger strikers out of jail.

Emboldened by this victory, hundreds of thousands of other South Africans took to the streets for the biggest demonstrations in many years. The foreign press covered the marches in cities like Cape Town and Johannesburg, but thousands of protesters also turned out in remote small towns and rural areas that had seldom seen this kind of activism. Ten thousand people marched in Stutterheim, ten thousand in Fort Beaufort, thirty thousand in Acornhoek. An astonishing fifty thousand marched in the remote QwaQwa homeland, a desolate, mountainous spot crowded with "removed" people, close to where Piet Retief crossed the Drakensberg.

Thousands of swimmers and picnickers of all colors occupied previously all-white ocean beaches. Despite cursing, flag-waving AWB counterdemonstrators, black and white swimmers dove into a whites-only pool in Johannesburg. More than fifty sick black people showed up—and were accepted—for treatment at the white Johannesburg General Hospital, which had long had hundreds of empty beds while Soweto's hospital was notoriously overcrowded. In Rustenberg, in the conservative Transvaal farming country, blacks moved onto the town's whites-only soccer and rugby fields and started playing. Black miners began using locker rooms and cafeterias reserved for their white supervisors. In several cities, crowds of African schoolchildren marched on half-empty white schools, demanding that they be opened to all races. Dozens of banned or restricted people and groups announced that they were "unbanning" themselves. Twenty former detainees, forbidden to speak in public, addressed a large meeting in Cape Town.

Such a wave of renewed defiance to apartheid was perhaps inevitable, but something else happened that could not have been predicted: P. W. Botha had a stroke and was forced to retire from politics. In mid-1989 he was replaced as State President by a younger and more pragmatic man, F. W. de Klerk.

De Klerk had risen through National Party ranks as something of a hard-liner. But once confirmed in office by an election, he showed clearly that he knew that white supremacy in the country's politics could not last forever. He and other realists in his cabinet also knew that if they were to negotiate a peaceful settlement to the existing turmoil, they had a time window of five years in which to do so. It would be five years before they would have to call another election, and five years might be all the time that any white government would have to negotiate with ANC leaders like Mandela, already in his seventies. The next generation of black leaders would be more uncompromising, having come of age politically not in the civil disobedience campaigns of the 1940s and '50s but in the street fighting and guerrilla warfare of later decades.

Historians looking back at the closing years of the twentieth century will see some striking similarities between F. W. de Klerk and Mikhail Gorbachev. Both inherited control of authoritarian, economically sluggish, multiethnic nations ridden with unrest. Both were reformers who threw overboard considerable ideological baggage but who had risen to power as the most loyal of party *apparatchiks.* Both wanted not revolutionary change but an end to long and costly semi-isolation from the economies of the United States and Western Europe. Some of South Africa's economic problems, like drought and a fall in gold prices, de Klerk and his cabinet were powerless to control. But if the rest of the world were to lift sanctions, the country stood to receive a powerful shot in the arm. It urgently needed new overseas bank loans, which had been mostly frozen for five years. A drop-off in investment from abroad, the international oil embargo, and other such pressures were costing South Africa an estimated five to eight billion dollars each year.

And so de Klerk acted forcefully, going further and faster than anyone expected. With a string of decisive moves, he recaptured the initiative, and the newspaper headlines, from the new revolts that had racked the country since early 1989. He released the top African National Congress leaders from prison. He legalized the ANC and the South African Communist Party. He removed restrictions from the United Democratic Front and dozens of other organizations, and from hundreds of individual activists. He greatly eased press censorship, and South African state television gingerly began interviewing black leaders it had ignored or vilified as terrorists only a few months before. When de Klerk finally released Nelson Mandela from more than twenty-seven years of imprisonment, supporters of the liberation movement experienced a euphoria never known before.

It turned out that during his last half decade in prison, Mandela had been informally talking with various high government officials, exploring paths to resolving the country's long strife. This did a great deal to lay the groundwork for what happened subsequently. But the big steps forward were not possible until the stubborn P. W. Botha left the political scene. By that point, four factors, long in the making, seemed to point a way towards a possible political settlement.

One was that internal black resistance to the regime from civic groups and the powerful trade unions was clearly not going to go away. The wave of new upheavals underlined this. Anti-apartheid pressure from overseas—economic boycotts and embargoes, the shutting out of South Africa from international sports, and much more—was only going to grow worse. The National Party government knew it could contain the resistance militarily, and that South Africa's cornucopia of natural resources meant it could withstand any economic pressure from abroad, but the cost of doing both would be high.

Second, it was abundantly clear that the resistance would never achieve a military victory. For some thirty years, the ANC had waged sporadic guerrilla warfare against the regime, infiltrating men into the country in an attempt to blow up police stations, electric pylons, power plants, and the like. They succeeded in setting off many such bombs, some of which claimed victims, including innocent civilians. But on the whole, despite much he-

roic rhetoric about the "armed struggle," the ANC's guerrilla of-
fensive was an embarrassing failure. Except in the northern border region, guerrillas never posed much of a threat. For whites,
life went on in that eerily normal Sunny South Africa of spear
fishing, beauty contests, and golf championships. Only 2 percent
of South Africa is forested, so guerrillas had no cover to shelter
them, like those who had hidden in the rugged tropical forests of
Cuba or Vietnam. The rest of the country, including almost all of
its border, is open plains, which the South African military pa-
trolled with helicopters and armored cars—most of them homemade by the Southern Hemisphere's leading military-industrial
complex—capturing would-be guerrillas by the hundreds. Those
who managed to reach the cities often were betrayed by informers or their own carelessness about security, or were seized at
police roadblocks. Skillful *agents provocateurs* drove many young
black would-be guerrillas into police traps when they thought
they were going on a raid or being smuggled out of the country
for military training. Furthermore, almost all successful guerrilla
armies have sanctuaries nearby. But bombing raids by the apartheid government forced all nearby countries to deny bases to the
ANC. When the organization finally suspended its guerrilla war,
the nearest ANC military camps to South Africa were in Tanzania and Uganda, half a continent away. We will never know the
statistics, but it is likely that for every ANC guerrilla who managed to plant a bomb somewhere, several dozen were killed or
imprisoned before they could do so, usually being tortured for
information first.

Third, by the late 1980s, something else was clear: the Soviet
Union was unraveling. In 1989 its long hold over Eastern Europe vanished along with the Berlin Wall; by 1991 the country
itself would dissolve into fifteen separate ones. With the Soviet
economy in trouble and turning towards capitalism, Soviet support for the ANC was drying up and it was obvious the Kremlin
had no interest in subsidizing a new socialist revolution at the
other end of the world. South Africa would never be a Cuba.

Fourth, and particularly crucial, South Africa's corporate leaders had been signaling for some time that they wanted a settle-

ment. They were not afraid of the Soviets (with whom they had long cooperated profitably in keeping tight control of the world diamond market); and they were exasperated with South Africa's political isolation, with its stagnant economic growth, and with the purposefully abysmal black school system that was turning out people unprepared to become either the middle-class consumers or the skilled workers big business needed. The most dramatic statement of business desire for political change had been an airplane flight. On September 13, 1985, an Anglo-American Corporation private jet took off from Johannesburg. It carried a half dozen of South Africa's top corporate leaders, including Anglo's chairman, Gavin Relly, to Lusaka, Zambia. There they spent a full day talking with the exiled leadership of the ANC. This was the first time that the country's business elite and its major liberation movement had openly sat down across a table from each other, to be photographed for all the world to see. (One thing the world saw was that the ANC officials wore the usual diplomatic attire of suits and ties, while the white business chieftains, uncertain of how to dress when meeting representatives of a liberation movement, were in shirtsleeves.) Although P. W. Botha rebuffed it at the time, the country's major CEOs were sending a clear message to their government: "It's time to make a deal."

What shape should the deal take? From the beginning of serious talks in 1991, this combination of factors pointed almost inevitably to what we could call a Grand Bargain. Simply put, the Grand Bargain's terms were fated to be: blacks get the vote, whites keep the money.

Everyone had to be allowed to vote. The boycotts and embargoes from abroad, and the rebellions and rent strikes in the townships, were not going to stop otherwise. At the same time, South Africa's powerful army, its police, and its corporate establishment had to agree to the deal. And they were never going to accept anything that cost them the wealth that white South Africa possessed: the grand homes, the servants, the farms that had been in one family since the Great Trek, factories, gold mines, and much more. These, then, were the constraints on the Grand

Bargain: all the people of South Africa would have to have basic democratic rights. But there could be no radical redistribution of wealth.

For some two years there were intensive negotiations over the exact shape of the Grand Bargain. The talks stalled several times as problems threatened to derail the process: resistance from Chief Buthelezi and Inkatha; resistance from the white right; embarrassing revelations about how de Klerk's government was continuing to fund Inkatha death squads; a Polish immigrant's assassination of Chris Hani, who had been seen by many as a possible successor to Mandela. But in the end, in late 1993, the Grand Bargain was made and signed. It was agreed that the following April, for the first time in its long and tormented history, South Africa would have a fully democratic election. Many on the ANC side felt they had given away too much, and had abandoned the promise in the organization's 1955 Freedom Charter that someday South Africa's land would belong to those who till it, factories to those who work in them, and the great riches under the soil to all. But at the end of the day, significantly more just and egalitarian versions of the Grand Bargain, so easy to imagine, would have been impossible to negotiate.

While South Africa negotiated its settlement, Bosnia and much of the rest of the former Yugoslavia went up in flames. Civil war continued to rack Sri Lanka and half a dozen other countries. Hundreds of thousands of Indian and Pakistani troops continued to face each other in the half-century-long conflict over Kashmir. The fighting continued between Israel and the Palestinians. Whatever its limitations, the Grand Bargain brought to an end what had seemed one of the twentieth century's deepest and most intractable conflicts. There has been nothing fully comparable in any other part of the world.

March 1994:

As you approach any South African city from the air, the colors become blue, green, and red. The blue is the thousands of swimming pools in the white suburbs. The green is the lawns in which they are set. The red is the red earth of southern Africa, bared to the sky in the tight crisscross of unpaved streets in the black townships and shantytowns. In the shantytowns there is no blue, nor even green: you can't keep a lawn watered when several dozen families share a single faucet; trees and bushes don't last when you need every branch for firewood.

On my Boeing 737 descending into Port Elizabeth, every seat is full. All but three of the passengers are white. If any of them are perturbed by the thought of losing their political monopoly in the elections a few weeks from now, they are not showing it. Two businessmen in the seats just behind me are cheerfully making plans for how many unit managers they need per terminal control area, whatever that may be. Whatever business their work is part of, they know the new government will not force them to share it more equally among the country's people.

That is the depressing side of the Grand Bargain. But, as I begin several weeks in the country covering the first democratic elections as a newspaper correspondent, there is another side, and it takes my breath away. The last time I was in Port Elizabeth, five and a half years ago, it was a war zone. Hundreds of local activists were behind bars; towering khaki-colored armored personnel carriers roared through the city's black townships; almost weekly, vigilantes torched or vandalized the offices of black community groups and labor unions; plainclothes security police were scattered through the audience of the Human Rights Festival I attended (pp. 33–35). Today, this is a city at peace. Every lamppost in the downtown is hung with an ANC campaign poster: JOBS PEACE FREEDOM. The very day I arrive, eighteen organizations, from the local Chamber of Commerce to the Communist Party, sign an agreement that officially starts dismantling decades of apartheid in Port Elizabeth, beginning the vast job of making sure the entire city, and not just the white areas, fairly shares every type of municipal service, from library books to street-cleaning crews to garbage trucks. In the city council's meeting room, I attend the evening signing ceremony, which is cochaired by representatives of the National Party and the ANC. To laughter from all, one speaker addresses his remarks to "Mr. Chair and Comrade Chair." Afterwards, I go to a party of local activists where burning candles are in the ANC colors: black, green, and gold. People are giddy beyond the copious quantities they drink; none can quite believe this is all happening.

The next week I follow Nelson Mandela on the campaign trail for a day. He and the other ANC parliamentary candidates campaigning with him do not talk about great visions of social justice and transferring wealth to the people; they know the terms of the Grand Bargain all too well. He speaks in a sober voice about very concrete matters: making schoolbooks free for those who can't afford them; bringing electricity, clinics, hospitals, running water to those who don't have them; paving those red-dirt township streets; starting to build new houses with flush toilets for the seven million people in squatter camps. But, he warns the crowd, "these things cannot be achieved overnight. You must be patient." The message is down-to-earth, restrained, and Mandela's speaking style is somber, almost wooden. But when a smile lights up his face, his very presence is electric. In Pretoria, thousands of labor unionists have traveled by bus for hours to hear him. As his motorcade speeds out of the city, cars on side streets are held up by traffic police, both black and white. The white ones are expressionless behind aviator sunglasses; the black ones grin and salute. At a diamond mine to the east of the city, some miners have been sleeping on a small hillside all night, to be sure of having a place from which they can see him when he speaks. As his motorcade arrives, several hundred of them, in orange jumpsuits and orange safety helmets fluttering with small ANC flags, race exuberantly alongside his car, escorting it into the mine grounds.

Visitors from the rest of the world mainly came to South Africa, it sometimes seemed, to shake their heads disapprovingly over apartheid. But during these heady weeks leading up to the election, they are here to celebrate. At one point I attend a campaign rally in an outdoor stadium. Before it begins, four people come walking slowly onto the stadium's soccer field. They shake hands with the organizers, then with the journalists. They stroll through the crowd, greeting people, pausing to chat. They are wearing blue baseball caps, blue armbands, and blue vests; they are four of more than a thousand official election observers from the United Nations. These observers have fanned out across the country, attending campaign events large and small, mediating disputes when asked. Why, in this land riven by conflict for so long, is it so profoundly moving to see these four people in blue: two men, two women, black, white, brown? Their presence is a statement: the world is watching. And at last South Africa is not a pariah, but an inspiration.

I go up and ask the four where they are from. One woman is from India, one from Nigeria. One man is from Switzerland. And the fourth? "I am from Bosnia," he says. "I can do nothing there. I can here."

The world kept watching as long rows of people of all colors patiently waited in line at voting booths. And, as the returns came in, giving the ANC nearly two thirds of the seats in Parliament and Mandela the presidency, there was, surely, never before an election so widely celebrated in so many countries. In May of 1994, Mandela was inaugurated; his coalition-government Deputy Presidents were F. W. de Klerk, whose government had once held him in prison, and Thabo Mbeki, the son of his longtime fellow prisoner Govan Mbeki (p. 35). Heads of state came from throughout the world for the occasion.

During the five years of his presidency, Mandela did not involve himself much in the day-to-day affairs of government. But he made a series of public, stunningly effective gestures that reached out to former opponents and brilliantly took the wind out of the sails of potential resistance from white right-wingers. He went to call, for instance, on Percy Yutar, the retired prosecutor who had argued the case that sent him to jail for life. He descended in his presidential helicopter to have tea with the ninety-four-year-old widow of Prime Minister Hendrik Verwoerd, the major architect of the apartheid system. When South Africa's rugby team—rugby is traditionally an Afrikaner pastime—won the sport's World Cup before a huge, overwhelmingly Afrikaner crowd, Mandela walked onto the field wearing the team captain's jersey to present the trophy. The astonished crowd went wild.

Reconciliation was, of course, not just a spiritual matter, but one of practical politics. The ANC well knew that white flight would ruin the economy, as had happened when hundreds of thousands of Portuguese left Angola and Mozambique when they became independent in 1975. Every skilled white person who emigrates from South Africa, it is estimated, can mean the loss of up to five, mostly black, jobs, whether those of house servants, assistants in a dentist's office, or employees of a small business. But at the same time the desire on the part of newly empowered black South Africans to have a genuinely nonracial society ran far deeper than that. Nonracialism was always a cornerstone of ANC politics, and these gestures of openheartedness and forgiveness from Mandela, coming from a man who had spent more than one third of his life in prison, could not help but move all but the hardest white supremacist heart.

There were other symbolic gestures as well, some reaching back into the past. The old monument to the Trekkers at the Blood River battle site, a *laager* of linked metal ox wagons, is still there. But a new monument to the dead Zulus has now gone up beside it. The Day of the Vow is now officially renamed the Day of Reconciliation. Surprisingly, the people I saw commemorate the day with their reenactment of the Battle of Blood River, on December 16, 1988, Eugene Terre Blanche and his AWB, withered into insignificance faster than anyone expected. Terre Blanche got caught up in a series of sex scandals, then later spent several years in prison for attempted murder, and now claims to have found Jesus. He still appears on December 16 to rail against the marginalization of the Afrikaner people, but the much-shrunken AWB is so desperate for new members that part of its Web site is in English.

One feature of the first years of a democratic South Africa that caught the world's attention was the Truth and Reconciliation Commission. Headed by Archbishop Desmond Tutu, the commission spent more than a year holding hearings around the country. It was an unusual, imaginative attempt to come to terms with the nation's long legacy of political violence and repression without clogging the courts with thousands of cases.

The basic idea was that victims of state violence, or their survivors, could tell their stories in public at last, and that the perpetrators, if they fully confessed their crimes and apologized, would be granted amnesty from prosecution.

In practice, it worked imperfectly. There were victims aplenty to testify in horrifying detail, but the former policemen and jailors willing to come forward were fewer and low-ranking. They were foot soldiers, not commanders. Almost no high officials confessed to anything; efforts in the courts to prosecute several prominent ones, such as the former defense minister, General Magnus Malan, failed. And yet for all the flaws of the process, the TRC went further than any such body has gone anywhere else. There have been similar commissions in other countries, but none looked so soon and so deeply into the heritage of tyranny. Highlights of the hearings appeared weekly on prime-time television, and so the entire South African public was able to watch mothers talk about young sons who had vanished, former prisoners describe the tortures they had undergone, and, perhaps most riveting of all, former security policemen who were seeking amnesty explaining their actions. Few who saw it will ever forget the hearing where a beefy Captain Jeffrey Benzien, now clad in an unpolicemanly three-piece suit, sat astride one of his former victims, who had challenged him to demonstrate what he did, and showed how he had repeatedly placed a wet bag over the man's head to bring him to a point of near suffocation. Can there ever be full reconciliation between such victims and such perpetrators? Probably not. But even if they failed at reconciliation, the Truth and Reconciliation Commission hearings indelibly put the truth on the public record, and there it will remain.

What outsiders always assumed would be most difficult—people of different races living, working, and going to school together in relative peace—has been the easiest thing to achieve in post-apartheid South Africa. Other problems, particularly economic ones, have been far more thorny.

To begin with, when the election of 1994 brought to power a new regime, the machinery of government it took over was not a smoothly functioning apparatus that was now merely transferred into the hands of a democratically chosen Parliament. It was, first of all, a crazy quilt of ten pseudo-state homelands, plus vast bureaucracies that were duplicating one another's work. There were, for example, nineteen education departments: one each for whites, Africans, Coloureds, and Indians; one for each of four provinces; one for the national government; and one for each of the homelands. And the schools for Africans were deliberately designed to educate them only for farm work and menial and service jobs. It will take a generation or more just to train enough teachers to turn these into decent schools.

None of these bureaucracies could be easily remodeled or disassembled, because part of the Grand Bargain agreement was a sunset clause that guaranteed civil servants tenure—or an expensive buyout. These civil servants were mostly either black collaborators with the homeland system or conservative Afrikaners; both were dismayed by the thought of working for a Mandela administration. Nowhere was this more true than in the police, which for years had spent most of its energy on suppressing the liberation movement. Beating or torturing an activist into confessing to something he did—or didn't do—is relatively easy for those with no scruples; good police work, even under the best of circumstances, is hard. During the unrest of the 1970s and '80s, the South African police had concentrated on the first and ignored the second, and ordinary crime soared. In the chaos of unrest and transition, international narcotics syndicates established a stubborn foothold in the country. Crime rates have come down somewhat since 1994, but you are still twelve times more likely to be murdered in South Africa than in the United States. Violence against women is particularly horrendous; rape statistics are among the world's worst for a country not at war. And danger from any kind of crime is far more serious in the vast, underpatrolled black townships and shantytowns; the national police force Mandela's government took over had 75 percent of its stations protecting white residential or commercial districts.

Furthermore, the government that the ANC and its coalition partners inherited was close to bankruptcy. Years of international boycotts and embargoes had taken their toll; there were few foreign-exchange reserves; large government debts to foreign commercial banks from the apartheid years remained to be paid; and, knowing their mini-regimes were doomed, homeland leaders had spent their last months in office running up extravagant new debts, all of which were inherited by the new regime. This meant that when, say, the government wanted to do something about the more than 25 percent of schools for Africans with no electricity or running water, there was little money with which to do it.

Other deep economic problems remain. Combined with the relatively low gold price, which lasted through the 1990s and beyond, was the fact that the remaining gold and other minerals under South Africa's soil are deeper and more expensive to get at. As the cost of mining rose and the gold price fell, mines closed. Automation cost still more miners their jobs. One large complex of gold mines around the city of Welkom had 122,000 employees in 1992 and only 17,000 a decade later. Nationwide, the number of gold miners fell from nearly half a million in 1980 to 175,000 a quarter century later. For every miner laid off, of course, half a dozen or more family or extended family members are likely to lose their chief source of income.

Such changes have meant, even with faster growth and more foreign investment than in the late apartheid years, that as I write this in 2007, the national unemployment rate, depending on how you measure it, is more than 40 percent—and higher still for Africans, especially for women and the rural poor. The glaring racial inequities, which largely mean those between people with a decent education and people without, remain: in 2002, the rate for African unemployment stood at more than eight times that for whites. The veteran South African journalist Allister Sparks, whose book *Beyond the Miracle: Inside the New South Africa* is an excellent survey of the first decade under democracy, cites an old saying: the only thing worse than being exploited is not to be exploited at all.

Such changes for the worse undo many changes for the better. For example, the government proudly claims that in the first decade after 1994, more than nine million people who didn't have it before gained access to water, and that the percentage of homes with electricity more than doubled. It's fine to have these things, but only as long as someone in the house has a job to pay for them. In these same years, at least ten million South Africans have at one time or another suffered water or electricity cutoffs for nonpayment.

The ending of the country's partial isolation from the world economy has been a mixed blessing. When South Africa came in from the cold internationally, in the early 1990s, it was just when rapid globalization was putting immense pressure on the nations of the world's south. The "Washington Consensus" mindset of the World Bank, the International Monetary Fund, the World Trade Organization, and most foreign-aid donors held sway. Consequently there would be little in the way of loans, investment, or aid to any country that tried to mount a massive jobs-creating public works program, that tried to protect infant industries with tariff barriers, or that wasn't relentlessly privatizing everything possible. Like most of the world, South Africa is now part of an economy where companies everywhere compete globally against one another to bid up the salaries of the top executives they want, and similarly compete to outsource manufacturing and other work to wherever the wages are lowest.

As a result, South Africa, like the United States, has seen a rapidly widening gap between the earnings of corporate CEOs and top managers on the one hand and a company's lowest-paid workers on the other. In South Africa, of course, those CEOs are overwhelmingly white and those at the bottom entirely black. And those black South Africans even employed by a corporation with a CEO are the lucky ones; the many millions who have no jobs, or who eke out a living as street peddlers or the like, are worse off.

South Africa's is not the only government that came to power with revolutionary hopes and then found it hard to buck the Washington Consensus. The Brazilian regime of the former radical trade unionist Luiz Inácio "Lula" da Silva was another. Wary of making the modest stream of job-creating investment flowing into the country dry up again, South Africa's new government, during its first decade in power, chose not to do any New Deal–style public works job creation. The Grand Bargain blocked it from any real redistribution of wealth—or farmland, more than 80 percent of which remains in white hands. Instead, the government has pushed a program called Black Economic Empowerment. This is a combination of formal regulations and informal pressure for affirmative-action hiring, preferential granting of government contracts to black-owned businesses, privatization of state assets into black hands, and pressure on corporations to add black directors, executives, and shareholders.

White South Africans will tell you endless stories of competent people not hired for jobs because they are white, and incompetent ones promoted to head universities, newspapers, or corporate or government departments because they are black. No doubt some of this is true. But whatever the affirmative-action hiring going on now, in scale it pales in comparison with the vast, institutionalized, decades-long pro-white affirmative action of the old regime. And without some kind of pressure like this, the change in distribution of jobs in South Africa's workforce would be glacially slow. A less savory aspect of Black Economic Empowerment is that through corporations' haste to claim some black ownership, a small number of black businessmen—a dismaying proportion of them top ANC officials who left the government—have gotten rapidly and spectacularly rich. Little of that wealth has trickled down to benefit anyone else. Economists measure inequality in the distribution of income by something called the Gini coefficient. In the ten years starting in 1991, the Gini coefficient of *every* racial group in South Africa worsened significantly, and that for Africans slightly more so than the national average. Despite a growing number of black faces at the top, what was long one of the world's most unequal societies to begin with is slowly getting more so.

The ANC increased its share of the vote in the two national elections since 1994. By a dozen years later, it controlled the governments of every one of the country's provinces and all but one of the major cities as well. Given its long struggle for full human rights for all, that the ANC should draw this kind of allegiance is no surprise. But to have one party so totally dominate the politics of a country indefinitely is seldom healthy. As Mathews Phosa (himself a former high ANC official) writes in his poem "The Price of Freedom":

> Now we, too, ride in official limousines
> And humbly get yes-master, yes-sir, yes-minister,
>      yes-everything
> The no-people of the struggle have learned
> yes-habits swiftly and without explanation.*

The ANC's huge majority does not mean there is a lack of political debate in South Africa; rather, it means that the debate that matters is the one that takes place inside the party, largely behind closed doors. And there the main conflict is between the dominant group in the ANC, around President Thabo Mbeki, who favor Black Economic Empowerment, privatization, and pro-business politics as the key to growth, and dissidents on the left, mostly members of the Communist Party or the Congress of South African Trade Unions, who want greater social spending and public works programs and as much redistribution of wealth by taxation and other means as the Grand Bargain will allow. You can hear this debate in South Africa's press and among its lively culture of NGOs and civic organizations, but not in Parliament.

The very design of Parliament itself is a serious problem, little noticed outside the country. Like most democratic countries, South Africa has proportional representation—which can be an excellent system, making for a far wider spectrum of opinion in a national legislature than in the American Congress, for instance. But, unlike almost all other countries with proportional representation, South Africa has no parliamentary constituencies. A

---

* As translated by William Mervin Gumede in *Thabo Mbeki and the Battle for the Soul of the ANC* (Cape Town, 2005), p. 291—another book that is a good guide to the post-1994 years.

voter casts a vote only for a political party's entire slate of candidates; a member of Parliament does not answer to the voters of a particular town or city or district. So MPs owe their seats solely to the party bureaucracy and not to any body of voters they encounter regularly, whose concerns, suggestions, and complaints they have to respond to. The system concentrates vast power in the hands of a tight circle of the ANC leadership—which also selects the provincial premiers. Structurally, it is profoundly undemocratic. It is no wonder that, in the election of 2004, some four million fewer South Africans bothered to vote than had done so ten years earlier.

The ANC as a political party has also become less democratic: party congresses now happen only every five years. And a sign of how beholden to big business the party has become is that it now gathers more funds in corporate contributions than it does in membership dues. It has come a long way—too far, many feel—from its roots.

The ANC that took power in 1994 was, in its internal culture, curiously disparate. On the one hand, the great bulk of its local activists, and some of its leadership, were people who had been in South Africa during the 1970s and '80s, members of trade unions or of the civic organizations in the African townships which banded together into the United Democratic Front. These groups were often disorganized and chaotic, hampered by repeated raids and arrests, but at best they practiced an authentic grassroots democracy. I once heard the head of COSATU, the black trade union federation, address a large convention of union members. "Comrades," he said, "if your local union officers and shop stewards aren't doing a good job for you, throw them out! Elect new ones! It's up to you." Most American union leaders would never say something so bold.

By contrast, the ANC in exile was trying to mount a guerrilla war. It ran military training camps; it was constantly, though not always successfully, on guard against infiltrators; military discipline prevailed. Certain ANC cadre, including Thabo Mbeki during his twenty-eight years out of the country, even needed permission to marry. The political culture known, then, by the thousands of ANC members who returned to South Africa from exile in the early 1990s was one of tight party discipline, where loyalty mattered above all and where there was little tolerance for those who said "no, minister" instead of "yes, minister."

In the contest for key cabinet positions and the like after 1994, it was the network of returning exiles—burnished with the somewhat spurious glory of having been in the guerrilla camps—and their supporters who got most of the spoils. The more independent-minded of the UDF and trade union activists got mostly provincial ministries or were eventually forced out of politics. The culture of tightly centralized party control has prevailed. Paradoxically, the former guerrillas exercising this control have done so on behalf of neoliberal, unreservedly pro-business economic policies that show every sign of continuing.

At this writing, many trade unionists, radicals, and veteran activists from the 1980s are increasingly angry that this approach has failed to address the country's widening disparities of wealth and the cruel 40 percent unemployment rate. It is possible that the ANC might in the future split along this fault line, which could in the end make for a more vibrant political democracy. If not, there is a risk that South Africa may someday look like Mexico under the long rule of the Institutional Revolutionary Party, or PRI: a country democratic in name and form, with considerable civil liberties, but dominated by a single party that came to power with revolutionary credentials and then ossified into a corrupt network of officials dedicated, more than anything else, to perpetuating themselves and their chosen successors in power.

For the five years of his presidency, Nelson Mandela was quick to tell everyone that the person who really ran the country on a daily basis was Deputy President Thabo Mbeki. In 1999, the urbane, pipe-smoking Mbeki replaced Mandela as President, and in 2004 was elected to a second five-year term. A man of considerable intellect, charm, and managerial skill, he nonetheless epitomizes the tight-discipline insider mentality of the ANC cadre who spent years in exile. His secretive and thin-skinned personality makes a painful contrast to the generosity of spirit of his larger-than-life predecessor. Maintaining iron control over party machinery, Mbeki is quick to accuse white critics of racism; his black critics within the ANC often find themselves forced out of government and sometimes publicly accused of plotting against the party.

By 2007, South Africa had more than five million people with AIDS or HIV, the largest number of any nation in Africa. AIDS has spread with deadly speed in South Africa, in part because the large number of migrant workers separated from their families much of the year guarantees a booming trade in prostitution. Mbeki's most catastrophic flaw has been his bizarre, fatal skepticism that HIV causes AIDS. He embraced a small coterie of oddball scientists and nonscientists, some of them also believers in UFOs and astrology, who see alarm over AIDS as a conspiracy perpetrated by the drug companies. Even leaders of immense moral stature like Mandela and Bishop Tutu have been publicly excoriated by Mbeki's underlings when they forthrightly criticized Mbeki's beliefs about AIDS. Under pressure from an energetic lobby of AIDS victims, the Treatment Action Campaign, supported by unions, churches, and civic groups—encouraging testimony that civil society in the country is still alive and well— Mbeki's government has been forced against its will to begin dispensing the necessary anti-retroviral drugs. But this has come far too slowly and too late. The country's death rate from AIDS has already soared past six hundred a day, which means that the disease claims, every year, many times more victims than all the uprisings against apartheid combined. The epidemic had causes far beyond Mbeki's control, but his stubborn and perverse attitude towards AIDS disastrously slowed the response. History will not judge him kindly.

March 2006:

My first trip back to South Africa in a dozen years. At one level, I almost don't recognize the country. The row of passport-stamping booths at the Johannesburg airport was always staffed only by Afrikaner men, whose faces seemed to me hostile, looking long and hard at my passport as if they suspected that my

tourist visa disguised a possible journalist, which it did. Now
the array of officials is a rainbow of colors—black, white, brown,
and both men and women. The same is true almost everywhere I
go: the people behind the counter in any kind of store, the children in a schoolyard, the reporters and editors in the city room
of the newspaper where I have come to teach some writing workshops. For someone whose memory of South Africa dates mainly
from the 1980s and earlier, the difference is astounding.

The look of so much else, however, is the same. The vast shantytowns of corrugated metal shacks, with rows of pillbox-like
concrete privies behind them, by the tens of thousands, sprawl-
ing across the flatlands of Cape Town. The high walls around virtually every house in the white areas of Johannesburg, including
districts where the houses were never walled off before. Sometimes there is a security guard's booth and a railway-crossing-
style gate blocking the entrance to a street, something one didn't
see before. And where previously a white homeowner was content
with a row of spikes or some barbed wire along the tops of those
walls, now, it seems, the fashion is for multiple strands of electri-
fied wire. Almost every suburban apartment building has a similar wall, and a guard who opens a gate for you. The difference is
that there is now a sprinkling of black government officials and
business executives living in such places; not even the fanciest
suburb is exclusively white anymore. But everything I see during
a short visit, from the beggars on the streets to the traffic jams of
sleek new cars that clog Johannesburg's leafy northern reaches at
rush hour, makes clear that the country's vast disparity of wealth
remains. As time goes on and these privileged classes gain ever
larger numbers of blacks, this disparity between top and bottom
will be more and more one of class than race. But if the gap remains so wide, how much progress is that?

Among a host of such worries, the bloom is off now. Nowhere do I find the exhilaration of 1994, the proud sense that
this country was pioneering something unmatched anywhere on
earth. Instead, a dozen years into the new South Africa there is
a widespread feeling that now the place is just another middle-
sized country, an unusually beautiful and complicated one, per-

haps, but facing problems all too common the world over: AIDS, poverty, crime, burgeoning corruption scandals, unwanted immigrants flooding across the border, and senselessly high military spending. Presiding over the latter, incidentally, is Defense Minister Mosiuoa Patrick Lekota, whom I saw last in the prisoners' dock at the Delmas trial (pp. 182–185) in 1988.

And yet, unexpectedly, there are still moments that can bring a lump to the throat, and the confidence that, whatever the disappointments, those who fought the old regime did not suffer or die in vain.

Consider, for example, a new building on a hilltop on the north side of downtown Johannesburg, a light, airy structure of wood, brick, and glass. South Africa today has the world's most progressive constitution, explicitly prohibiting discrimination by race, religion, gender, age, or sexual preference, and providing iron-clad guarantees of reproductive rights, free speech, the right to join a trade union, and much more. In the new South Africa, the death penalty, torture, and corporal punishment have all been officially abolished. This building houses the Constitutional Court, which has the final authority to interpret that constitution, and has on occasion overruled President and Parliament to do so.

My guide around the building this autumn day is missing an eye and his right arm, and his face is pitted with scars from shrapnel wounds—all the result of a bomb planted in his car by agents of the old regime when he was living in exile in Mozambique in 1988, the same year I was following the Great Trek commemorations here. Albie Sachs, a longtime member of the ANC, is also a survivor of several spells in prison, including many months of solitary confinement. Today he is a justice of the Constitutional Court.

Second only to human rights among Sachs's passions is modern art. He has led a drive to fill the corridors and galleries of the court with the liveliest collection of contemporary South African painting and sculpture to be found anywhere. Instead of being a monument to solemnity and authority, as courthouses usually are, this one is an almost boisterous celebration of the human body and spirit, in color. There is no marble. The building is filled with tapestries, beadwork, bright forms in oil paint, sculpture in wood and stone, and even the outlines of South Africa's provinces in neon. Some of the art looks back on the sacrifices that allow this celebration. Most moving to me is a series of black stone panels, perhaps four feet high and three feet wide. Each of them is filled with thousands of crosshatchings, the way people keep count of something: four vertical strokes with a diagonal slash through them, repeated endlessly. On the edge of each panel, etched in very small type—you have to be very close to read it—is a man's name and a number, usually in the range of nine to ten thousand. The number is the sum of days spent in prison. There is a panel for Mandela and one for each of the other longest-serving political prisoners. One of them visited recently, says Sachs, and came upon the panel with his name. "He was quite overcome."

Every possible space in this building is open. Instead of closed corridors, walkways are suspended in air. Where there has to be a wall, it is glass. Where there has to be a door, it is often open metal grillwork. The sun floods down from skylights. A stunning chamber of wood and glass houses the largest human rights library in the Southern Hemisphere. And in the heart of the building is the courtroom itself. Not square, as courtrooms usually are, but oval. Although the judges sit behind a raised bench, the seats for the spectators slope sharply upwards like an amphitheater, so that some of them look down on the judges, unlike almost any other courtroom in the world. In the sweeping arc of wall behind the bench, there is a long, curving window, only around eighteen inches high. It looks out on an outdoor plaza at ground level, so that all you can see, from inside the courtroom, are the shoes and socks of people passing by. "Why?" Sachs asks rhetorically. "Because when that's all you can see, you cannot tell if someone is old or young, man or woman, black or white. Justice is impartial."

The wall above and below this window is red brick. The brick came from a large, notorious prison, known as Number Four, which functioned on this spot for ninety years. Mohandas Gandhi was a prisoner in it. Nelson Mandela was a prisoner in it.

Tens of thousands of others—political prisoners, ordinary criminals, and black South Africans who for decades ran afoul of the hated laws requiring them to carry passes—were prisoners in it. Parts of the old prison complex have been left intact, as a museum. Parts have been rebuilt. The old women's jail now is the home of the new Commission on Gender Equality, whose chair, Joyce Piliso-Seroke, was herself a political prisoner here after the Soweto uprising of 1976. Another part of the complex houses the staff of the Public Protector, an ombudsman's office established under the new constitution. One forbidding stone wall of the old prison has been left standing; it lines one side of a long set of steps rising gradually to the courthouse door. On the other side, facing it, triumphantly higher than the prison wall, is the wall of the court building itself—all glass, the art treasures visible behind it. The old prison's bricks are used throughout the new building. Four of the old stairwells have been left standing, poking up through the new construction. "They will have glass boxes on top," says Sachs. "These will be lit up at night. Like beacons."

South Africa will need many beacons to light its way out of its problems in the years ahead, and the path will not be easy. Legal rights do not necessarily translate into the good jobs, schools, homes, land, and everything else so unfairly shared in this world of ours—and seldom more unfairly than in South Africa. But, like a building, such rights are a frame within which much can happen that could not happen before. Of all the countries in Eastern Europe, Africa, and Latin America that passed into some form of political democracy in the closing years of the twentieth century, none, compared with South Africa, did so after so long and so intense a struggle by its own citizens. Millions of South Africans feel that they fought for the rights that are embodied in this building, and it is that heritage that offers the most hope that they can slowly succeed in constructing a new and more just society out of the very bricks of the old.

*January 2007*

BIBLIOGRAPHY
AND ACKNOWLEDGMENTS

INDEX

# Bibliography
# and Acknowledgments

Partly because one of its major languages is English, South Africa may be the most analyzed and documented tyranny of all time. If apartheid could be destroyed by words alone, it would have drowned under a flood of books, articles, and doctoral theses many years ago. The books I've listed in the following paragraphs are by no means all the important works on South Africa, nor are they all that I consulted in the preparation of this book. These sources are only those which I relied on most, and which therefore might be of most interest to someone wanting to read further on the themes I have dealt with. Almost all the books below have been published in either the United States, England, or South Africa, and sometimes in all three countries. When a book has an American edition, I have so indicated; otherwise I have given the original location and date of publication.

On the history of the Voortrekkers in Natal up to the Battle of Blood River, and the battle itself, most surviving primary sources are collected or excerpted in the first volume of *The Annals of Natal,* edited by John Bird (Pietermaritzburg, 1888), or in *The Natal Papers,* edited by John Chase (Cape Town, 1968). Both are compilations of diaries, letters, government reports, treaties, and other documents of the time. *The Great Trek,* by Oliver Ransford (London, 1972), is the best single secondary source, although like most books on this era it generally sticks to the Trekkers' point of view. I drew some additional information from Eric Walker's *The Great Trek* (London, 1934), Manfred Nathan's *The Voor-*

*trekkers of South Africa* (London, 1937), C. Venter's *The Great Trek* (Cape Town, 1985), and the monographs of the Natal Provincial Museum Service. The best short account of the Great Trek is in *Heaven's Command: An Imperial Progress* (New York, 1973), the first volume of James Morris's history of the British Empire. *The Washing of the Spears: A History of the Rise of the Zulu Nation under Shaka and Its Fall in the Zulu War of 1879,* by Donald R. Morris (New York, 1965), is a military history of the Zulus that includes their battles with the Voortrekkers.

There are many histories of the Afrikaners; a particularly well written one is *The White Tribe of Africa: South Africa in Perspective,* by David Harrison (Berkeley, 1981), an offshoot of a BBC series on the subject. A provocative analysis of that history, from which I drew much, both in ideas and quotations, is Leonard Thompson's *The Political Mythology of Apartheid* (New Haven, 1985). Thompson is also, with Monica Wilson, one of the editors of *The Oxford History of South Africa,* an important landmark in the rewriting of South African history in our time; parts of the first volume, *South Africa to 1870* (New York, 1969), touch on the Trek period.

The lack of documentary sources means there is no comprehensive history of these times from the Zulus' point of view. However, *The White Man Cometh,* by Louis du Buisson (Johannesburg, 1987), makes a good start; du Buisson shows how much Donald R. Morris and other conventional historians of the Zulus depend on early, unreliable accounts by white traders. *Indaba, My Children,* by Vusamazulu Credo Mutwa (Johannesburg, 1964), fills in another part of the story: the oral epics and legends that were a major part of Zulu culture. The author's great-grandfather was King Dingane's High Witchdoctor and was present at the killing of Piet Retief's party. *The Black People and Whence They Came: A Zulu View,* by Magema M. Fuze (Durban, 1922), is of interest as the first known book by an African in Natal. *Apartheid: The Story of a Dispossessed People,* by Motsoko Pheko (London, 1984), tells the story of the white conquest of South Africa from the black consciousness perspective.

Works ranging into parts of South African history before or after the Trek period that I found of particular interest included Edward Roux's *Time Longer Than Rope* (London, 1948), Marianne Cornevin's *Apartheid: Power and Historical Falsification* (Paris, 1980), and especially Peter Dreyer's *Martyrs and Fanatics: South Africa and Human Destiny* (New York, 1980), a quirky, impassioned, and eloquent book of essays that made me aware of a number of things, including the quotation from which the title of this book is drawn. *Robben Island: Out of Sight, Out of Mind,* by Simon de Villiers (Cape Town, 1971), includes the torturer/executioner's pay scale reproduced on pages 150–151. The various quotations from Anthony Trollope are from his *South Africa* (London, 1878). The essays of Charles van Onselen, whom I have cited several times in the text, are collected in his two-volume *Studies in the Social and Economic History of the Witwatersrand, 1886–1914* (New York, 1982). Despite the heavy-sounding title, these pieces are a pleasure to read, as is, even more so, his *The Small Matter of a Horse: The Life of "Nongoloza" Mathebula, 1867–1948* (Johannesburg, 1984). Allister Sparks's wide-ranging *The Mind of South Africa* (New York, 1990) was published too late for me to draw on it, just as this book was going to the typesetter; it is an eloquent addition to the small shelf of essential books on South African history.

Astonishingly, given the usual politics of its publisher, the work of the new generation of radical historians is embodied most comprehensively in the mammoth *Reader's Digest Illustrated History of South Africa: The Real Story* (Pleasantville, N.Y., 1989). This book is encyclopedic in scope, lively, readable, lavishly strewn with maps, old prints and photographs, and basically from the point of view of the dispossessed. I know of no equivalent for the history of the United States.

Some of these works on South African history spell certain proper names differently from the way I have done in this book. Both Afrikaans and the languages of black Africans were spoken tongues long before, in a consistent fashion, they became written ones, and so the same word is often found spelled in many different ways. Although today's town named after him is Louis Trichardt, the Great Trek leader who first arrived there spelled his name Tregardt. He was christened, however, as Louis Tregard; and some of his descendants have called themselves Trigardt or Triegaardt. Similar variations occur in many Zulu or Xhosa words. When faced with such choices, I have usually opted for the most modern or most common form of a word and made all instances of its use conform, including those in quotations.

In describing contemporary South Africa, any reporter learns from the eyes of others who've already been there. My own perceptions have been particularly sharpened by two English journalists, Anthony Sampson, whose most recent book about South Africa is *Black and Gold: Tycoons, Revolutionaries and Apartheid* (New York, 1987), and James, later Jan, Morris, who has written about the country in *South African Winter* (London, 1962) and elsewhere; and by three Americans, Joseph Lelyveld, *Move Your Shadow: South Africa, Black and White* (New York, 1985), James North, *Freedom Rising* (New York, 1985), and William Finnegan, *Crossing the Line: A Year in the Land of Apartheid* (New York, 1986) and *Dateline: Soweto* (New York, 1988).

In writing about mining and the South African economy, I drew, among other sources, on *South Africa, Inc.: The Oppenheimer Empire,* by David Pallister, Sarah Stewart, and Ian Lepper (New Haven, 1988), *Gold and Workers,* by Luli Callinicos (Johannesburg, 1981), *King Solomon's Mines Revisited: Western Interests and the Burdened History of Southern Africa,* by William Minter (New York, 1986), *Capitalism and Apartheid: South Africa, 1910–84,* by Merle Lipton (Totowa, N.J., 1985), *The Political Economy of U.S. Policy Toward South Africa,* by Kevin Danaher (Boulder, Colo., 1985), *Another Blanket,* by the Agency for Industrial Mission (Johannesburg, 1976), and on various issues of *Leadership* magazine, the voice of South Africa's business elite.

There is a voluminous literature on sanctions and divestment, of which the best books are *The Sanctions Handbook,* by Joseph Hanlon and Roger Ormond (Harmondsworth, Middlesex, 1987), *Sanctions Against Apartheid,* edited by Mark Orkin (Cape Town, 1989), and *South Africa: The Sanctions Report* (London, 1989), the book version of the report on the subject prepared for the Commonwealth Committee of Foreign Ministers on Southern Africa.

*Gatsha Buthelezi: Chief with a Double Agenda,* by Mzala (Atlantic Highlands, N.J., 1988), is the best of several books on the subject. See also "The Chief," by Michael Massing, in *The New York Review of Books,* February 12, 1987. Steve Biko's writings appear in several anthologies, including *I Write What I Like,* edited by Aelred Stubbs, C.R. (London, 1978). My description of labor union theater comes mostly from *Organize & Act: The Natal Workers Theater Movement, 1983–87,* by Astrid von Kotze (Durban, 1988).

*Lives of Courage: Women for a New South Africa* by Diana Russell (New York, 1989) is a good introduction to the double burden South African black women must live under, as is *Call Me Woman* (San Francisco, 1985), the autobiography of the writer Ellen Kuzwayo.

For penetrating analysis of many aspects of South Africa's political and economic scene, there are few better sources than the excellent *South African Review,* a series of anthologies published at irregular intervals by Ravan Press in Johannesburg. Martin Murray's *South Africa: Time of Agony, Time of Destiny—the Upsurge of Popular Protest* (New York, 1987) is a thorough survey of resistance politics through the middle 1980s; Tom Lodge's *Black Politics in South Africa Since 1945* (Johannesburg, 1983) focuses mainly on the preceding decades. Two books on the military confrontation between the South African Defense Force and the African National Congress are *Apartheid's Rebels: Inside South Africa's Hidden War,* by Stephen M. Davis (New Haven, 1982), and *South Africa at War: White Power and the Crisis in Southern Africa,* by Richard Leonard (Westport, Conn., 1983). *Society at War: The Militarization of South Africa,* edited by Jacklyn Cock and Laurie Nathan (New York, 1989) is more recent and ranges into many areas, from war toys to state-supported black vigilantes. *Beggar Your Neighbors: Apartheid Power in Southern Africa,* by Joseph Hanlon (Bloomington, Ind., 1986), and *Frontline Southern Africa: Destructive Engagement,* edited by Phyllis Johnson and David Martin (New York, 1988), both document the toll of South Africa's little-reported military and economic war on other states in the region. The *Race Relations Survey* published annually by the South African Institute of Race Relations in Johannesburg is an essential reference work. The various articles, pamphlets, and newspaper columns by the Institute's Steven Friedman are also always worth reading. *Uprooting Poverty: The South African Challenge,* by Mamphela Ramphele and Francis Wilson (New York, 1989), is a searing, authoritative account of the country's maldistribution of wealth—with some suggestions for overcoming it.

South Africa's better-known white writers of fiction, especially the great Nadine Gordimer, are widely read abroad. Black writers tend to be far less known. The best anthology I have found is *Hungry Flames and Other Black South African Short Stories,* edited with an introduction by Mbulelo Vizikhungo Mzamane (Harlow, Essex, 1986). A number of other works are worth reading, among them *Fools and Other Stories,* by Njabulo Ndebele (New York, 1986), and *Call Me Not a Man* (Johannesburg, 1979), by Mtutuzeli Matshoba, a gritty, vivid picture of the underside of township life.

Magazines and newspapers covering South Africa are as plentiful as the books. I have relied especially on *The Weekly Mail* of Johannesburg and on *Facts and Reports: International Press Cuttings on Southern Africa,* published in Amsterdam. The latter is the best of the several digests of press clippings about the region, because it reprints material from the British and French press as well as the South African. Both it and the *Mail* are available in many American libraries. In major U.S. and British publications, the best coverage of South Africa over the years has often been that of *The Economist* in London.

The TV show "South Africa Now" is on the air in many cities in the United States and in a number of other countries as well; it consistently shows parts of the South Africa story the rest of the American news media miss, as do the documentary films of Lindy Wilson and other South African filmmakers. A number of good documentaries about South Africa are available on both film and videotape from California Newsreel, 149 Ninth Street, San Francisco, California 94103.

□

Dozens of people helped me in many ways to research and write this book. I owe most to my wife, Arlie, who encouraged me in low moments, rejoiced with me in high ones, gave me several thoughtful readings of the manuscript, willingly endured my absences, first in South Africa and then for long hours at my desk, and somehow managed to do much of this while putting the finishing touches on a remarkable book of her own.

In South Africa itself, I am first of all grateful to those people who let me interview them, most of whose names appear in the text. For those in the liberation movement, talking to a foreign reporter can be a risky business: in 1988 a death squad murdered Sicelo Dhlomo immediately after he appeared on a CBS documentary. Nonetheless, most people I interviewed were willing to talk for the record. And some of them, as well as a number of friends new and old, also generously went out of their way to give me a meal, a bed for the night, an introduction to the next person down the line, good advice on how to make sense of what I was seeing, or simply the pleasure of being with kindred souls while a long way from home. And so I am grateful to Neville Alexander; Aninka Claasens; Max, Audrey, and Neil Coleman; Nadine Gordimer; Peter and Joan Kerchhoff; Lungile and Refi Makapela; Ruth Rice; Rory Riordan; Refiloe Serote; Andries van Heerden; Paul Verryn; Johannes Wessels; Tim Wilson; and, above all, to Francis and Lindy Wilson, who helped open doors for me all over the country. There are one or two others I had best not name, but they know who they are, and I thank them. I salute all these good people—and look forward to seeing them again in the democratic South Africa they are working for.

In the United States, many people helped as well. The library staff at the University of California at Berkeley always amazed me by how readily they could find some dusty, leatherbound book published in Pietermaritzburg or Cape Town a century ago. For other help, I am also grateful to George Labalme, Jr., Brian Sellers-Petersen, Jonathan Cohen, and to my literary agent, Georges Borchardt. Nan Graham of Viking Penguin has been, both on this book and the last, the kind of editor every writer dreams of. Hunter Pearson braved many varieties of South African accents and mumbles to transcribe some of my taped interviews, then dug up information in the library, and finally took on the daunting job of trying to verify every fact, statistic, or quotation in all the historical parts of the manuscript and in most of Part I. The job of similarly fact-checking the entire remainder of the manuscript was done by Jeremy Bernstein, who fortuitously appeared on the scene at just the right moment, equipped with a great fund of knowledge about his native South Africa.

Finally, my gratitude goes to those friends, in South Africa, Britain, and the United States, who read part or all of the manuscript. Their comments, which were often voluminous, helped me find hundreds of places where there were either outright mistakes or simply writing that was windy and foggy. For these readings, I owe much to Ayi Kwei Armah, Harriet Barlow, Georges Borchardt, Bill Finnegan, Louis Freedberg, Joseph Hanlon, Saul Johnson, Violaine Junod, Peter de Lissovoy, Susan Moon, Ruth Russell, Brian Sellers-Petersen, Denise Shannon, Allen Wheelis, and Francis Wilson. Jeffrey Klein and Orville Schell not only each read two successive drafts of the manuscript, but over the years have provided more help than they know in other ways as well. Almost all these readers were wise enough to give me, with the reasons behind it, the advice that every writer needs: "You're not finished yet." Now that I finally am, I thank them all.

# Index

## ABOUT THE AUTHOR

Adam Hochschild was born in New York City in 1942. His first book, *Half the Way Home: A Memoir of Father and Son,* was published in 1986. Michiko Kakutani of the *New York Times* called it "an extraordinarily moving portrait of the complexities and confusions of familial love . . . firmly grounded in the specifics of a particular time and place, conjuring them up with Proustian detail and affection." It was followed by *The Mirror at Midnight: A South African Journey* and *The Unquiet Ghost: Russians Remember Stalin.* His collection, *Finding the Trapdoor: Essays, Portraits, Travels,* won the PEN/Spielvogel-Diamonstein Award for the Art of the Essay. *King Leopold's Ghost: A Story of Greed, Terror, and Heroism in Colonial Africa* was a National Book Critics Circle Award finalist. *Bury the Chains: Prophets and Rebels in the Fight to Free an Empire's Slaves* was a finalist for the National Book Award. It received the Los Angeles Times Book Prize, the Lionel Gelber Prize, and the PEN USA Literary Award. His books have been translated into twelve languages.

Besides his books, Hochschild has also written for *The New Yorker, Harper's Magazine,* the *New York Review of Books, Granta,* the *New York Times Magazine,* and many other newspapers and magazines. His articles have won prizes from the Overseas Press Club, the Society of Professional Journalists, and the Society of American Travel Writers. A cofounder of *Mother Jones* magazine, he has also been a commentator on National Public Radio's *All Things Considered.* He teaches writing at the Graduate School of Journalism at the University of California at Berkeley and has been a Fulbright lecturer in India. He lives in San Francisco with his wife, the sociologist and author Arlie Russell Hochschild. They have two sons and one grandchild.

## BURY THE CHAINS: Prophets and Rebels in the Fight to Free an Empire's Slaves

*FINALIST FOR THE NATIONAL BOOK AWARD*

A taut, thrilling account of the first grass-roots human rights campaign, which began in London in 1787 and in time freed hundreds of thousands of slaves around the world. **ISBN 978-0-618-61907-8**

## HALF THE WAY HOME: A Memoir of Father and Son

"An extraordinarily moving portrait of the complexities and confusions of familial love." — Michiko Kakutani, *New York Times*

In this deeply honest memoir of Hochschild's relationship with his disapproving father, the author reflects on his childhood on his family's Adirondack estate, his cultural heritage, and his experiences with the upheavals of the sixties. **ISBN 978-0-618-43920-1**

## KING LEOPOLD'S GHOST: A Story of Greed, Terror, and Heroism in Colonial Africa

"An enthralling story, full of fascinating characters, intense drama, high adventure, deceitful manipulations, courageous truth-telling, and splendid moral fervor." — *Christian Science Monitor*

Beginning in the 1880s, King Leopold II of Belgium carried out a brutal plundering of the territory surrounding the Congo River. *King Leopold's Ghost* is the harrowing account of a megalomaniac of monstrous proportions and those who bravely fought him. **ISBN 978-0-618-00190-3**

## THE UNQUIET GHOST: Russians Remember Stalin
*with a new preface*

"An important contribution to our awareness of the former Soviet Union's harrowing past and unsettling present . . . illuminating." — *Los Angeles Times*

In 1991, Hochschild spent nearly six months in Russia talking to gulag survivors, retired concentration camp guards, and countless others who were confronting their memories of Stalin's quarter-century reign of terror.

**ISBN 978-0-618-25747-8**